FAST TRACK TO
WASTE-FREE
MANUFACTURING

FAST TRACK TO WASTE-FREE MANUFACTURING

Straight Talk from a
Plant Manager

JOHN W. DAVIS

Productivity Press • New York

Most Productivity Press books are available at quantity discounts when purchased in bulk. For more information contact our Customer Service Department (800-394-6868). Address all other inquiries to:

Productivity Press
444 Park Avenue South, Suite 604
New York, NY 10016
United States of America
Telephone: 212-686-5900
Fax: 212-686-5411
E-mail: info@productivityinc.com

Cover design by Shad Lindo
Text design by Susan Swanson
Page composition by William H. Brunson, Typography Services
Art creation by Smith & Fredrick Graphics
Printed by Sheridan Books in the United States of America

Library of Congress Cataloging-in-Publication Data

Davis, John W.
    Fast track to waste-free manufacturing : straight talk from a plant manager / John W. Davis.
        p.   cm.
    Includes bibliographical references and index.
    ISBN 1-56327-212-1 (hardcover)
    1. Waste minimization.   2. Manufacturing processes—Waste minimization—Case Studies.   I. Title.
    TS169.D38   1999
    658.5'6–dc21

99–17090
CIP

05 04 03   10 9 8 7 6 5 4

To all the wonderful coworkers I came to know

and learn from during my years in manufacturing,

and with special thanks to those who worked tirelessly

to help me make the principles, concepts, and

techniques outlined in this work a reality.

Contents

Publisher's Message

OVER THE LAST DECADE AND A HALF, many U.S. manufacturers have learned how to use the various tools, concepts, and techniques of JIT (lean) manufacturing with some obvious improvements in their facilities. Yet, although they've been learning how to apply kanban, poka-yoke, SMED, takt time, one-piece flow, and kaizen, they are unable to sustain a truly waste-free enterprise. In fact many factories, once they are left to their own devices to implement lean manufacturing, lose their way and abandon their efforts or implement half-measures that fall short of tapping into the true benefits of lean manufacturing.

In *Fast Track to Waste-Free Manufacturing: Straight Talk from a Plant Manager*, John Davis takes the position that over the last decade and a half U.S. manufacturers have been working with JIT concepts that have been *almost totally inadequate for their particular needs*. Why? According to Mr. Davis, for many batch manufacturers these tools move far too slowly to change the most important element in their factory: *the existing system of production*. He believes part of the problem of why lean manufacturing is taking so long to take hold in the United States has been the piecemeal fashion in which manufacturers have adopted the tools and methods. Mr. Davis says, "What has occurred, as more and more companies are trying to adapt JIT in their plants, is that they realize it is far more complicated to implement than ever anticipated. This is because the process has both a physical and physiological makeup. The root problem is that JIT consultants and managers often miss the point that implementing kaizen or JIT has little long-term and sustaining value without a plan to totally change the existing system of production." According to Mr. Davis, what's been missing is a philosophy of waste-free manufacturing that can totally incorporate the process on a plantwide basis. Waste-free manufacturing (WFM) is such a philosophy (or system of production) because it establishes a foundation and builds steps so a factory can *rapidly* deploy waste-free manufacturing *and* change its system of production.

For Mr. Davis, getting on the fast track to waste-free manufacturing is paramount because most U.S. manufacturers do not have the luxury of taking a methodical approach to becoming lean (waste-free). If they do, many of them will simply not survive. As John Davis says: "What

U.S. manufacturers must realize is that what took Toyota forty years to accomplish in developing the Toyota Production System (TPS) may never be achieved in U.S. industry, or for that matter, elsewhere in the world. There is just not enough time to emulate what they've accomplished. What is needed is a new systematic, rapid approach that can take these lean principles and universally apply them so plants can get on a fast track to becoming globally competitive." WFM is that new approach—because every step in this new methodology is geared to rapid deployment.

Many of you will recognize that the tools and techniques used in WFM derive from TPS, but there are three unique aspects to WFM. First, Mr. Davis believes it is the responsibility of plant managers to refocus and commit themselves to leading a factory from conventional manufacturing to waste-free manufacturing. They must become effective leaders. To help plant managers lead change Mr. Davis has developed a plant manager's manifesto, which includes advice on overcoming the mental and physical barriers to change and valuable tips on how to effectively communicate change to the work force, how to deal with the six common paradigms in the technical and professional ranks that can bog down implementation, and how to establish the production worker as the center of value-added production. He gives advice on dealing with other issues often skirted by authors (and consultants), such as how to partner and include the union in the change effort, and how to retain and utilize your displaced production workers once you begin implementing the new process. Mr. Davis also provides an ongoing case example of a factory moving from conventional to waste-free manufacturing. You'll sit in on production meetings and view first-hand the obstacles a plant manager must overcome to be successful.

The second unique aspect of Mr. Davis's system is that he's created and linked four new drivers—workplace organization, uninterrupted flow, error-free process, and insignificant changeover. These drivers will show you which steps to take first, what areas to focus on, what tools and techniques to use, and what obstacles you will confront as you move from one driver to the next in becoming waste-free. WFM provides you with a 10-step road map to implementation and key measurements to support the drivers, and it replaces 5S with a new staircased system called 6C. Mr. Davis also discusses the importance of getting equipment and facilities to point of use, uncovering hidden waste, setting and staffing your promotion office, and installing a product-oriented cell organization. Several checklists help you stay on the fast track, including a 7-point checklist to assess where your operation stands in becoming waste-free, a 15-point checklist to determine if you are still operating the old obsolete mass manufacturing principles, and an 8-point checklist of owner-operator responsibilities. And to help the change leader stay focused and committed, Mr. Davis provides revolutionary pointers at the end of each chapter and a continuous improvement pyramid that links the six major stages of concentration required to reach continuous improvement in your factory.

Finally, Mr. Davis's methodology is unique in that it can *rapidly* transform any batch manufacturer to a globally competitive one in as little as 12 to 18 months. By going against the conventional JIT wisdom that says you must incrementally implement change to become a world class manufacturer, Mr. Davis, by rapidly deploying the JIT process, was able to expand upon JIT techniques and tools, eliminate others, and uncover a series of new steps that substantially reduce implementation time. Although Mr. Davis uses the fundamental principles of JIT or lean manufacturing to help factories become waste-free, it is this focus on rapidly deploying the improvement process that enables them to change the plant's *entire system of production*. Rapid deployment was the key to creating WFM.

Fast Track to Waste-Free Manufacturing is a personal story as well as a methodology to change your system of production. It is told from Mr. Davis's successful experiences as a plant manager and consultant in helping conventional mass "batch" manufacturing facilities become waste-free and globally competitive. It is a story that will benefit anyone who is working in lean manufacturing. What is refreshing about this book is that Mr. Davis tells it like it is when dealing with the obstacles, frustrations, and challenges, and the sweet taste of success in transforming a factory. One of the fundamental planks of WFM is that it asks the plant manager, the person who is responsible for making the rubber hit the road, to be the true revolutionary leader in bringing U.S. manufacturers out of the deep dark dungeon of batch manufacturing. Mr. Davis has been that leader and when you hear him explaining his new production system, or providing tips on handling displaced workers, or ways of working with the union, or giving ideas on how to best use your industrial engineers, you will recognize in Mr. Davis someone who has been in the trenches, dedicated to working with production workers and management to take them beyond half-measures of implementing JIT to going whole hog to world class manufacturing.

For those readers coming from a batch manufacturing environment, WFM will be uncharted territory. For many of our loyal readers Mr. Davis, by offering this streamlined path to *changing your entire system of production*, will finally clarify many of the reasons why U.S. manufacturers have had trouble adapting JIT principles. It will also open new insights to help you on your never-ending journey of continuous improvement. As you will discover, Mr. Davis's waste-free manufacturing is a proven system that covers nearly every aspect of the lean manufacturing revolution, including the office. Here at Productivity we think waste-free manufacturing is a remarkable achievement and we are especially proud to add this book to our growing list of lean manufacturing products. Anyone interested in implementing lean manufacturing will learn much from this book. It supplies a vital need in helping those people on the front lines who are responsible for the hard, practical, day-to-day work of implementing effective change.

We wish to thank all those who participated in shaping this manuscript and bringing it to bound book: Gary Peurasaari for development editing; Susan Swanson, for text design, proofreading, and production management; Shad Lindo for cover design; Sheryl Rose for copyediting; William H. Brunson, Typography Services for page composition; and Smith & Fredrick Graphics for figure composition.

Steven Ott
President and Publisher

Acknowledgments

I AM VERY GRATEFUL to my good friend, Elizabeth Thomas, who worked as my secretary for a number of years and offered immeasurable help and support in the development of this work.

To United Technologies Corporation, for whom I worked for 24 years, I acknowledge with gratitude the opportunity provided me to lead a number of manufacturing operations within the corporation and later to travel the world, teaching and helping others put into practice the principles, concepts, and techniques of globally competitive manufacturing. Further, I would l like to acknowledge Lee Daily, the director of this special effort for United Technologies Corporation, for the confidence he placed in me and the others associated with this important initiative.

I would like to further thank all the wonderful people I came to know and highly respect during my years in industry. I am especially indebted to the following colleagues, who in their own way influenced me enormously: Barry O'Neal, Ed Cannon, Gary Rascoe, Roger Lewandowski, Rick Meisner, Jack Alexander, Bill Patterson, Dave Harris, Jim Wainright, Jack Walters, Bill Wilson, Rob Wagner, Thom Polera, Randy Dreher, Don Peterson, Walter Bolton, Jeff Bowles, Charlie Lingo, Tom Bruce, Sam Farney, John Fleming, Jack Bettis, Ronald Paul, and Omar Vanderbelt.

I am especially grateful to my wife, Kathy, and son, Scott, for the unerring encouragement they provided me as I put this work together over a number of years.

Last, but certainly not least, my sincere thanks to Productivity Press, who offered me the opportunity to publish this work, and great thanks to Gary Peurasaari for his excellent editing and enhancements to the manuscript, as well as to everyone at Productivity Press whose time, energy, and professionalism helped make this book a reality.

Preface

IN THE SPRING OF 1989, at the age of 51, I was asked to assume the position of plant manager at a manufacturing facility located in the Midwest. At the time I took the position, the plant was on the verge of becoming an unfortunate business statistic. Among other things, operating costs were completely out of control, union and management relationships were strained, to say the least, and customer satisfaction was at an all-time low. The factory itself was totally unkempt; huge quantities of work-in-process inventory were literally stacked to the ceiling, yet often parts needed to fill customer orders could not be found, and had to be filled through a hot list system of production. Production departments operated entirely independently and essentially had a warlike attitude toward one another. When problems surfaced the norm was to spend precious time and energy preparing excuses and pointing fingers. Professional functions within the salaried ranks had no specific ties to any common manufacturing mission, but rather focused on very narrow initiatives tied to making specific accomplishments in their particular areas—regardless if these in any way helped to address and satisfactorily resolve some of the plant's more pressing problems.

In general terms, the system of production was crisis based and driven by a mentality that called for *quantity* over *quality*. The end result was often one of two less than desirable scenarios: (1) parts and components that could not be immediately utilized, and (2) a serious shortage of parts or components required to meet specific customer demands.

Essentially it was a manufacturing facility that was in the business of *vast waste generation*. If a customer's needs were consistently met, it was probably more of an accident than anything else. Overall, it could best be described as a plant manager's worst nightmare, and there was absolutely no doubt in my mind that I was about to embark on the most serious challenge of my career.

Over the course of 24 months we changed every aspect of basic operating principles in the factory and, more importantly, we totally destroyed the old system of production and effectively deployed a new one. A work force that initially had little involvement in the operation became one that prided itself on having visitors and, when given the opportunity, on speaking about the considerable accomplishments that had been made.

Perhaps most surprising was that we accomplished this during a period when a significant downsizing effort was underway. Thus, employees did not end up supporting the changes because of stable employment. They did it because, due to the changes, their areas simply became a better place to work—more comfortable, more orderly, and more efficient. In addition, it ended up becoming a plant where they felt they were contributing real value in their work, and where they also felt they could actively participate in making the operation just a little better every day. It was a factory where what appeared to be quantum improvements were really made by taking small, collective, and extremely focused and sequential steps in the right direction—primarily through first recognizing and then clearly diverting energy *away* from generating wastes.

As a result of this unique experience a new method of implementing world class manufacturing evolved. Although most of the fundamental principles for improvement stemmed from and expanded upon just-in-time (JIT) or lean manufacturing, it was the principal objective of *rapid deployment* of the improvement process that changed the plant's system of production. Rapid deployment was the most interesting twist to applying JIT because it uncovered powerful new steps (and eliminated others) that grossly reduced implementation time, especially considering the magnitude of change. In fact, the improvements occurred over a period of time that many in the field of JIT would contend simply was not possible. However, as you will see, it is entirely possible, given two very important ingredients: the knowledge as to *how* and the *will* to make it happen.

After the turnaround, I was asked to apply this knowledge and experience to assist the corporation in developing a new manufacturing training initiative aimed at changing the way in which manufacturing, throughout the company, went about doing the basics of production. Eventually, I accepted a job designed to help carry forth this initiative and became a team leader for a group of internal consultants, selected from various business units within the corporation. We traveled the world teaching and demonstrating the considerable benefits of JIT designed to make substantial and rapid changes to the shop floor. Later we expanded the training to include even larger segments of the business, with particular emphasis on various functions that served to support manufacturing.

The results were often staggering, with accomplishments during these events approaching almost unparalleled levels. It was not unusual to see productivity improvements of 30 percent and more, the elimination of up to 90 percent of work-in-process inventories, and reductions in the space required to perform production work cut by as much as 50 percent. In addition, measurable quality indices almost immediately began to show some very substantial improvement trends. In both the plant management and consulting roles, I encountered almost every obstacle that could be tossed into the path of needed change. The power of this rapid process overcame most of them, because the quick results simply could not be ignored.

For those who have had some exposure to JIT or lean manufacturing, there is little in this book that is absolutely new. What you will learn is *why companies do not apply many of the JIT techniques or why they simply don't work.* What is new is an approach that makes lean manufacturing principles work. It provides a road map that can transform any conventional mass manufacturing to a lean one. I am convinced the fundamental problem with lean manufacturing is not ignorance of the tools and techniques, but inaction—most of which has been created through a lack of practical hands-on knowledge of which step to take first. As a result, the typical response to some of the most pressing issues in manufacturing has been to experiment with and demonstrate JIT in small, select areas within a factory—while business as usual goes on elsewhere.

This has helped to establish what I call the American Manufacturing Mayhem, for it has caused well-respected firms to overlook tremendous opportunities, blinded managers as to how fast change for the better can actually happen, created doubts and suspicions throughout the work force to "foreign" ideas, and established legitimate questions as to the real value of fully incorporating a lean manufacturing process. In short, matters are getting worse even though the tools and techniques exist to completely eliminate the problems. But what conventional mass manufacturers must clearly understand is that there is absolutely no way of avoiding this issue. They must totally change the way they manufacture goods and services.

It comes down to simple arithmetic. The U.S. manufacturing sector is shrinking and for many companies there is not a lot of time left before they disappear from the American landscape. This means U.S. industry needs to ramp up and use those qualities (e.g., ingenuity) in implementing world class manufacturing, not chip away at their problems. Some will say that rapidly changing a factory's entire system of production is nothing more than wishful thinking, that our very nemesis is this desire to "hit the home run." We are repeatedly warned that this type of thinking is totally unrealistic in a globally competitive environment. Many JIT consultants in the field have even attacked the core of America's past greatness, its winning spirit. Their standard advice is: "Work energetically at the change required, but don't expect to do in a few years what it took Japanese industry 40 years to accomplish." What is most depressing is that many manufacturing managers appear to believe this. Actually, not only is this bad advice, but nothing could be further from the truth.

What I have learned is that while there are many names for the lean manufacturing process, they all use the same basic principles, the same basic tools and techniques, and, unfortunately, the same basic slow, methodical approach. I wrote this book to share a means of rapidly and effectively implementing what I call *waste-free manufacturing*—and if I have one thing to offer the reader many experts in the field do not, it is first-hand experience in leading this type of change in a number of plants where the odds of making it happen were considered slim, at best.

Another reason I decided to write this book was to provide plant managers and others in leadership positions in manufacturing, with a step-by-step, plantwide approach to getting the change effort done. If one considers all the printed material that abounds on the subject of world class manufacturing, JIT, Toyota Production System (TPS), and lean manufacturing, what is seriously missing is a philosophy that provides specific directions on how to incorporate the process on a plantwide basis. As a result, manufacturing operations have learned, to a great extent, how to use the various lean tools, concepts, and techniques, but they have been largely left to their own devices in deciding how to go about deploying the process, which often has meant applying them in a piecemeal fashion. This is one of the reasons why lean manufacturing is taking so long to take hold in the United States.

Think of it like this: What if there were baseball coaches who spent time teaching youngsters just one of the various elements of baseball? In other words, teaching the youngsters nothing but how to steal a base, or how to bunt, or field a ball, or throw, or catch. What you would end up with, in all likelihood, would be a young person who was extremely adept in one or more of the basic skills associated with baseball, but who still would not understand what it takes to be a baseball player, and who certainly would not understand how all the elements fit together to make a baseball game.

As absurd as this may sound, this is exactly what is happening in modern industry's efforts to adopt world class manufacturing. Many plants are being taught how to apply kanban, poke-yoke, SMED, takt time, one-piece flow, kaizen—subjects we will cover in this book—but what often isn't recognized is that some of these concepts are not even elements of the process. Rather, they are tools of the trade (like a baseball bat, glove, or ball). Regardless, many plants are striking out with initiatives to make themselves a kanban-driven plant or an expert in quick setup and changeover. This is fine in itself, but it does nothing to change the existing system of production, which *is* the key element in implementing globally competitive manufacturing.

Many of today's JIT coaches, while highly competent when it comes to the tools, simply have no idea what the game is all about, or if they do, top management simply does not have the time to have it taught on the shop floor. The coaches become so focused on exceptional expertise in the tools of the trade, and top management in applying them, that they have no real workable concepts (or time) for dealing with *the overall process that is required to implement full, effective, and rapid change in manufacturing.* When these coaches are quizzed about such things as "How do you totally change a plant from a batch manufacturing approach to flow-production throughput?" or "How do you get the union to partner with you in needed change?" they most often skirt the question with a reply similar to this: "Well, of course, each plant obviously has to look at those things and figure out the best approach."

This "non" advice merely leaves the plant manager and others out on a limb as they try to determine the right thing to do—setting the stage for a trial and error approach. Already they have two strikes against them. More often than not, it establishes a process that can never fully get off the ground, eventually bringing the whole change effort to a screeching halt. Does any of this sound familiar?

What U.S. manufacturers must realize is that what took Toyota 40 years to accomplish in developing TPS may never be achieved in U.S. industry, or for that matter elsewhere in the world. There is just not enough time to emulate what they've accomplished. What is needed is a new systematic, *rapid* approach that takes these lean principles and universally applies them so factories can get on a fast track to becoming globally competitive. This is what waste-free manufacturing can do for you. If I have your attention at this point, then read on, for this book is about providing you with the tools and the approach. It is about the process of the whole game and about numerous issues relative to creating a globally competitive company.

Introduction

The Revolution Has Just Begun

THOUSANDS OF COMPANIES in the United States have been exposed to what has come to be termed world class manufacturing, and more recently lean manufacturing. This has been achieved through a practice referred to as kaizen or just-in-time manufacturing (JIT). Those who have some knowledge of kaizen and JIT understand they are not mutually exclusive processes and were, in fact, designed to complement each other.

Kaizen is a Japanese term which loosely translated means continuous improvement. The practice of kaizen involves accepting that absolutely no process is perfect, including those in the office areas. Kaizen enthusiasts contend there is always room for improvement, even though it may be very minor. But therein lies the power of the process—making small, continuous improvements that add up, over time, to a solid competitive advantage.

An oversimplified definition of JIT is an approach hinging on doing things in a manner that provides materials and components just when they are needed—but only after they have been called for, or pulled by the next operation performing work. JIT also entails one-piece flow and takt time which are integrated with a leveling method of production scheduling. (We will be discussing these concepts in more depth later.) These concepts are in stark contrast with conventional batch manufacturing where material is pushed onto each process.

Throughout the book I will be interchangeably using the terms JIT, Toyota Production System (TPS), lean manufacturing, world class manufacturing, and globally competitive manufacturing when referring to production systems. The production system I've developed is called *waste-free manufacturing.* To one degree or another all of these particular production systems are designed to achieve the lean production ideal. John Shook, one of the first people to bring TPS to the United States, and instrumental in launching NUMMI (New United Motors Manufacturing, Inc.), states in the book *Becoming Lean*:

> The concepts *mass production* and *lean production* do not refer to production systems. They reflect *ways of thinking* about production—the assumptions that underlie how people and institutions formulate solutions to the problems of organizing people, equipment, material, and capital to create and deliver products for customers. Mass and lean are paradigms that reflect and inform the thinking about production within particular cultures and eras. Production systems emerge from these paradigms. (p. 43)

In conventional mass manufacturing, parts and components are produced in very large quantities (batches), with sometimes months passing before they are fully consumed. As a result, scrap and rework become a way of life and, not so infrequently, parts sit for such long periods of time they can become obsolete. Thus, the manufacturer has not only paid for material it cannot pass on to the customer in terms of a finished product, but it also has invested labor and the added cost of disposing of what it now cannot use. Batch manufacturing is part of the mass production thinking—part of *waste-generating* production.

Because manufacturers around the world have been searching for ways to achieve and maintain a world class manufacturing status, many larger firms have hired consultants who work with both management and plant personnel in demonstrating and implementing JIT and kaizen. It would seem to be easy enough to do, given that the job was simply changing the basic techniques of production. But what has occurred, as more and more companies are trying to adopt JIT in their plants, is that they realize it is far more complicated to implement than ever anticipated. This is because the process has both a physical and a physiological makeup. In fact, the physiological aspects surrounding this type of change are often so dynamic that some managers, operators, and support functions have been unable to accept it.

I believe the root problem is that both the consultants and the plant managers often miss the point that implementing kaizen or JIT has little long-term or sustaining value without a plan to *totally change the existing system of production.* In fact, it can often be more damaging than beneficial. This has happened time and time again as companies have tried half-baked JIT efforts and come to the conclusion: "It just doesn't work for us." As a result, there have been growing doubts, by some, as to the value of the lean manufacturing process itself when really it is their way of thinking that is undermining their efforts to tap into the true benefits of lean manufacturing. Moving from batch processing to JIT or one-piece processing entails more than just a process—it entails a total change in the way we think about production systems.

Some of the nation's top experts and educators in the field of general business have taken the position that implementing JIT, TQM, and other lean manufacturing initiatives can be a sound strategy for using manufacturing to achieve a competitive advantage. However, there are those who have gone so far as to indicate that the "way" these programs are being implemented really isn't that important.

I take strong issue with the assumption that a problem does not exist in the "way (the programs) are implemented." While many businesses have started the JIT process and have begun to reduce lead times, downsize inventories, eliminate defects, and lower scrap and rework costs, most have not taken the process far enough, fast enough to truly sustain them. Thus, I believe the job of implementing JIT is far from complete on the average plant floor and in the average U.S. manufacturing firm. In fact they have barely tapped its potential, if one considers that there are very few true lean manufacturers in the United States. I also believe understanding the "how" of implementing is the most critical issue facing U.S. industry. Only in knowing the how will we truly find a way to make a total change to the existing system of production.

It is time to recognize that the task before us is not to produce "more with less" but rather to produce "less with less." This may seem to be a play on words, but there is a significant difference in the two philosophies, especially with regard to where emphasis and, subsequently, a long-term commitment is placed. In its ultimate form, lean manufacturing means producing only to direct customer orders, creating the need for less on-hand inventory. Additionally, it means producing to those orders in a flow that is as close as possible to one piece at a time. Doing this will create less work-in-process inventory, less scrap, and less rework. And when the problems that are inherent to conventional mass manufacturing then surface and you are forced to resolve them, you will end up with far less setup, less downtime, and fewer in-process quality defects. What factories eventually discover is that all this can be done with fewer operators and in less manufacturing space. Over time, this lean manufacturing approach establishes an operation that truly produces less with less, yet satisfies the customer as never before. As James Womack puts it in his book, *The Machine That Changed the World*:

> Lean production . . . is lean because it uses less of everything compared with mass production—half the human effort in the factory, half the manufacturing space, half the investment in tools, half the engineering hours to develop a new product in half the time. Also, it requires keeping far less than half the needed inventory on site, results in many fewer defects, and produces a greater and ever growing variety of products.

The challenge before U.S. industry is facing up to the need to totally change their system of production and accepting the fact that achieving this will entail more drastic changes than simply performing kaizen in a few select production processes on the shop floor. It means achieving a true change in thinking throughout the entire manufacturing arena. The irony of it all is that business firms that have invested huge sums of money experimenting with lean manufacturing are often as guilty as those that have never tried the process when it comes to *really* changing their thinking.

It is somewhat like the seasoned golfer who has developed a serious problem with his game. After continuously trying to diagnose the problem himself, he decides he needs help. He goes to a golf professional who suggests the problem is the golfer's grip (hand position and pressure on the club). The pro makes a hands-on demonstration of the change he feels is required and the golfer tries it with the professional looking on, offering pointers. The golfer hits a number of practice shots, some good, some not so good, but the pro insists he must practice with the new grip until it becomes comfortable. His advice is: "Don't slip back to your old grip." At the following Saturday outing, the golfer starts out with the change, but finds it extremely uncomfortable. Along the way he decides to go back to his old grip, and he immediately feels much better. Although his problem does resurface, he convinces himself it simply was not the right advice.

This is not unlike what happens with many, if not most, kaizen efforts taking place in modern industry. Consultants visit the plant and demonstrate the change required. Plant personnel practice the techniques by making changes to one or two small areas of the plant (usually over the course of a few days). The Monday following the event, the change starts to feel very uncomfortable and usually before the first day is over, things start to revert back to the old way of doing business, because it simply "feels much better."

When it became apparent that manufacturing in the United States had to change, the automotive and electronic industries began looking to their new competition for the answer. The same countries we opened our doors to as they struggled to rebuild their economies after World War II had now become our hope for repairing some of the damage inflicted on some of our most formidable manufacturers. This should have been a wake-up call for every manufacturing firm in the United States, but unfortunately it wasn't. It appears that what is seriously wrong with U.S. industry, in general, is that it must face impending disaster before it can bring itself to react to the need for total, revolutionary change.

U.S. industry must and can make the kind of revolutionary change required to keep the United States competitive on a global scale and we can do it faster than many can even imagine. Why? Because for the most part over the last decade and a half, *the way U.S. manufacturers have been working with traditional JIT concepts has been, in the end, almost totally inadequate for their needs.* What's been missing in particular is a fundamental philosophy of waste-free manufacturing that centers on establishing a proper foundation on which to build. Deploying JIT then becomes a matter of following a clear set of steps that build on each other until you achieve a production process that truly allows continuous improvement. Only then will the revolution begin for U.S. industry.

Waste-free manufacturing, by using a very different application of the standard principles and steps for creating a JIT environment,

begins this true revolution by zeroing in on the "how to" for implementing a rapid change from conventional mass (batch) manufacturing
to lean manufacturing. For example, unlike what most consultants in
the field suggest, the "how to" does not immediately move a factory
into one-piece flow, but instead first establishes a support structure so
one-piece flow can become a lasting reality. Otherwise the existing
batch system of production (which is there to support a completely different mode of operation) will force an almost immediate return to
business as usual.

What waste-free manufacturing offers instead are the principles,
tools, techniques, steps, and keys on how to deploy globally competitive
manufacturing in a relatively short period of time and manage the disciplines required to make a plant almost entirely waste free. In the
process you will change your thinking. Which is, after all, what a true
revolution is about.

1

Confronting the Deep Dark Dungeon

YOU ARE JUST OUT OF COLLEGE, tops in your class, interviewing for a job in manufacturing, and now you're on your way to visit the shop floor. The noise is the first thing you notice as you enter the plant—the relentless pounding of huge presses clanking away at huge sheets of rolled steel. You stop to observe one of them and note that it looks something like a character from *Star Wars*—a thing with huge mechanical jaws that slowly open, then slam shut on its prey, to cut and pierce and shape it into a new form before spewing it out, only to quickly grab another.

In the aisles, vehicles scurry along with an endless variety of materials hanging precariously from forks that extend from the lower carriage. You notice people working around machines and equipment. Some are almost shouting to be heard and occasionally their body language and facial expressions indicate frustration—if not downright anger.

Your guide leads you on to a zone where he stops to let you observe an operator changing over a die. The person at the machine is conducting the setup by himself, straining to loosen a series of bolts that tie the die to the bed of the machine. As you observe, the operator's rather awkward-looking crescent wrench slips off a locknut and before he can recover, his hand slams against the bolster plate. The man drops the wrench on the floor and grasps one hand with the other, bending over in obvious pain. Your guide walks over to him, placing a soothing hand on his shoulder. After a moment, the operator retrieves the wrench and begins again, but you can clearly see the skin has been peeled off the knuckles of his right hand. Your guide returns and explains what is already evident—the wrench slipped and the man had a minor accident. "He'll be fine," he assures you.

Next, you stop to observe a final assembly process, as your guide explains the product produced and the steps taken to assemble and test the units. On the line, you observe approximately 50 people at various work stations along each side of a moving transfer conveyor performing progressive assembly work. In the space of 10 minutes the line is down twice, and you witness a foreman hurrying from one operator to another trying to get things up and running.

At the back of the assembly line, a repair loop is completely filled with products needing rework, and workers are busy trying to complete the task and feed the products back onto the main assembly line. At the packing station, two operators are sitting idle, because the latter 30 feet of the transfer conveyor is completely empty. For the time being, at least, there are no finished products flowing off the assembly process.

As you move along to the next process, you see a person moving up the aisle toward you. He suddenly stops, glances down at his feet, and realizes he has inadvertently stepped into a small pool of oil that has dripped from a fitting in an overhead conveyor. He turns, steps to the edge of the aisle and wipes the bottom of his shoe against the edge of a parts container. While there, he drops the cigarette he is smoking on the floor and grinds it out, leaving a darkened footprint, before proceeding on his way. No one seems to notice or care. And as for you, you certainly are not impressed with this thing called *manufacturing*. In fact, later, after reflecting on the apparent chaos and confusion you observed throughout the operation, coupled with the obvious frustrations of the employees and what appeared to be a total disregard for safety and cleanliness, you are completely appalled and decide to seek a career elsewhere.

WORLD CLASS CULTURE SHOCK

Because of factories around our nation that resemble the one just noted, we have lost a global leadership role in manufacturing. This, along with steady increases in labor costs over the years, have resulted in operations being driven out of the United States to third-world countries. As a result, we have repeatedly seen once proud industrial plants in America age and close, throwing hundreds of thousands of people out of work and forcing them to take on less financially rewarding jobs and careers.

The root problem is that companies have not been quick to address "the hidden costs" which would effectively serve to offset most of the general labor increases and have been even quicker, as competitive pressures mount, to pull up stakes and move an operation to a more appealing labor base. But as the years go by, just as in the United States, labor rates will gradually increase in the new operation and those "hidden costs" (if not addressed) will still remain, thus setting up a never ending spiral.

Both management and labor share in the blame. Manufacturing management has, in general, failed to correctly utilize what is most often an extremely talented and experienced workforce and labor has most often balked at any kind of change to the status quo. Labor has been unwilling to give a little in order to preserve the jobs of many, and management has been unwilling (or unable) to grasp the opportunity associated with "the hidden costs" and to muster a concerted effort by the workforce to satisfactorily address and eliminate the wastes that are making them less than competitive.

Over the past few decades the American dream has indeed faded, and the likelihood exists that it could disappear entirely if we do not make a concerted effort to change some alarming trends in our manufacturing sector. Because the change I am referring to is radical, many production managers, supervisors, first-line support professionals, and shop employees have found themselves going through what might best be described as "world class culture shock." This is the result of first learning, then being asked to accept that almost everything going on in manufacturing today is ... wrong!

What they have been told is that the most fundamental procedures that have driven traditional batch manufacturing operations for decades are now essentially obsolete! Where in the past strong emphasis was placed on output—building more to maximize the utilization of each and every production process—today emphasis is placed on cutting lead times and concentrating on fulfilling direct customer orders, thus dictating less (but smarter) output and, consequently, much less overall waste.

Where in the past production workers were asked to basically "check their brains at the door," today they are being asked (if not expected) to contribute a wide variety of ideas for improvement. And these are only a few examples regarding the magnitude of change taking place in companies around the world. World class culture shock usually kicks into high gear when the work force begins to realize that even when they are willing to change the way they do business, their conventional system of mass production most likely will not allow it.

The production system in most factories can be likened to a vast ocean—for like the sea, it has a powerful inner force that is capable of creating unending waves of opposition, which can wash away any attempt at change like the waves washing the sand on the beach. Resolving this dilemma will not rest with further demonstrations of JIT, kaizen, employee empowerment, and the like. What must be done is to remove the cart from before the horse and understand that fundamental, effective, and lasting change cannot be achieved without first fully and completely changing the existing system of production.

Many in the field of lean manufacturing see the change required to be evolutionary in nature. I believe it is, but it must and can also be *revolutionary* on a practical hands-on level. Most plants can use a step-by-step method to move from a waste-embedded (traditional) batch mode of mass production to a largely waste-free status—*in as little as 12–18 months.* How can this be when so many companies struggle for years getting top management committed to a change effort, educating the work force, and then implementing it? By using waste-free manufacturing (WFM). WFM lays the groundwork to help leaders understand the kinds of things they will be forced to deal with and identify the kind of focus that is required to get down to the nitty gritty of changing the system of production. And it provides an implementation process that is doable, evolutionary, and revolutionary—a process that everyone will embrace. But first we must start with understanding the patient—the ailing factory.

CHANGING THE LIFESTYLE OF A FACTORY

Many manufacturing operations resist change until it becomes apparent that without it they may not survive. This is unfortunate because when a factory waits this long to face up to the fact that it is ill, competitively, it can be likened to a patient who has been rushed to the operating room with internal bleeding. If the patient is to fully recover, three things must be done—in very precise order:

1. Stop the bleeding.
2. Go through the healing/recovery process.
3. Decide what must change to avoid a recurrence.

The first step requires a skilled surgeon who doesn't have time to explain every move he or she makes. The surgeon must go about the business of surgery on the basis of acquired knowledge and skill. He or she doesn't ask others what to do, but tells them and expects them to follow every order, without question.

The second step deals with getting the patient well. The patient often undergoes considerable pain in making a full and absolute recovery, but generally accepts it as part of the healing process. Additionally, this is where other professionals take over for the surgeon and become the taskmasters. This is also the time when the patient receives an abbreviated education with regard to the illness, what brought it on, and what steps were taken to get back on the path to recovery.

The third step pertains to establishing a clear understanding as to how the patient's lifestyle must change to ensure no recurrence. It is then up to the patient to make a serious commitment to follow the doctor's orders, or stand the chance of having to go through the same painful experience again (assuming, of course, he or she doesn't die in the process).

There are some striking similarities between a manufacturing operation that has allowed itself to reach an unhealthy condition and a standard surgical procedure. The bottom line in both cases is that it is a matter of survival. Of course, if you change your plant's lifestyle before illness strikes you can avoid the very unpleasant experience of surgery. That's why you need some preventive medicine before you can confront the deep dark dungeon of mass manufacturing and become a world class manufacturer.

Where Are Our Manufacturing Leaders?

The term *world class manufacturing* was coined by Richard J. Schonberger. In his related books and seminars, Schonberger provides an outline that is in keeping with world class practices. Nonetheless, turning a manufacturing operation around from a seriously declining competitive position to world class is no small task. Change is complicated by the fact that people in manufacturing generally feel they have little control over their own destiny. They often see themselves as being slaves to the whims of others, and feel there is little they can do to make a real impact on customer perceptions—other than perhaps a negative one, should they produce and ship a shoddy product. Therefore, they are generally reluctant to extend themselves beyond what they are told to do, or what they know is clearly expected of them.

The truth is, manufacturing has been its own worst enemy. It has failed to take appropriate initiative in leading change for the better. It has allowed itself to be chained to the post of ill progress, without so much as a whimper. It has taken second best when it comes to talent and fundamental expertise, and it has shown little (if any) ingenuity in the entire process. It is responsible for creating the deep dark dungeon.

Our educational system has also been misguided as it continues to send hundreds of thousands of graduates into industry armed with inadequate skills. Additionally, professional organizations and institutions have not kept pace. Many have clung diligently to the past, doing little more than serving up modern computer applications to outdated, if not totally inadequate, manufacturing practices. Strong words? Perhaps, but we can decide to face the truth or continue to hide from it. If we choose the latter, we will continue the alarming decline in our industrial base.

The principal culprit for the shift that has aided and abetted the continuing decline in our manufacturing effectiveness is the lack of strong leadership at the manufacturing level and a general quest for self-esteem. This seemingly unrelenting quest has driven some of the best talent in the nation away from manufacturing, for manufacturing is generally perceived as being a slow track up the ladder of success. It is often visualized as the deep dark dungeon—a place for the second-best, a place that certainly does not offer the clean, spit-polished image that most young professionals associate with the rewards of a good education.

For those professionals who do venture into this dungeon, there is a tendency for apathy to quickly set in. They soon discover they are surrounded by leaders who have no interest in making the type of change that would seriously reengineer the standard way of doing business. Many of these leaders came up through the ranks. They are often hardened by the policies and practices they have worked under over the years. It's all they know or wish to know. They are busy with the business of mass manufacturing and have little time or patience for anyone or anything that does not allow the wheels to keep turning—producing parts and ultimately finished products.

They are far removed from the customer and have no idea who the customer really is, and they don't care. They are measured, disciplined, congratulated, rewarded, punished, chastised, complimented, and viewed as a success or failure based on how much volume they push through their areas of responsibility. The task is "meet the schedule" even when there is absolutely no connection between what they are doing and what the paying customer has ordered. Producing parts, components, and finished units become the measure, because this provides credited hours. The more produced, the more credit received.

Any suggestion for significant change in the way one goes about the business of manufacturing is usually taken as a personal threat by these "old-time" hardened leaders because they fear they will not, in all probability, play an ultimate role in it. They strive to perpetuate their breed where they can, bringing people into subordinate roles who think as they do. They know how to block change and they work at doing it, often quite effectively.

Now, before some readers form the opinion that I am, for some reason, against anything representing the establishment in modern manufacturing, this truly is not the case. I am simply convinced we must have a more serious commitment from leaders to make change than what we've seen over the past decade or so. Because thus far little has been done to address the real issues that are making us less than totally competitive. There are facts that should not be ignored, which clearly show that past successes can seriously blind any operation to the need for real change.

The Plant Manager As the Revolutionary—Being Committed and Focused
Joel Barker speaks about reliance on past successes in his extensive study of paradigms. He says: "Once a paradigm shift occurs, everything goes back to zero. Past successes mean absolutely nothing." I mention

this to reinforce the point that there has unquestionably been a serious paradigm shift in the worldwide manufacturing arena, and past successes will mean nothing when it comes to future survival in the field.

After more than 30 years in the manufacturing arena, I am convinced you cannot carry out true change without strong personal commitment and a great deal of focused involvement by senior plant managers. They must break down the business-as-usual mentality and be the leaders responsible for changing the lifestyle of the plant. They have an opportunity to be the true "revolutionaries"—the person between top management and the workers, the person responsible for changing the rules and implementing the standards as to how the rubber hits the road. Without plant managers' total effort and leadership, change just will not happen because the traditional mass manufacturing mentality in U.S. manufacturers and the forces of opposition—those living on past successes—are simply far too strong to overcome.

The Old-Fashioned Production Meeting

Joe Martin hurried toward the conference room that was a couple of doors down from his newly acquired office, carrying a ream of production reports that were waiting for him each morning, stacked neatly just in front of his office door. He was attending his third production meeting as the recently appointed plant manager and was a little tardy for the 8:00 A.M. start.

He entered the conference room, relieved that everyone had not yet arrived. He hated to be the last person to show up for a meeting. On the other hand, he felt a twinge of disappointment because it was 8:05 and only half the people needed to start the meeting were on hand. He took mental note of those who were there on time and after another 10 minutes of passing the time of day with them, the others finally arrived, carrying even larger reams of paper than he had brought. Joe politely listened to excuses—something about a computer being down and data not being received on time—and after another five minutes for everyone to get things appropriately arranged, the meeting was ready to start. It was 8:25.

Everyone took their places at the conference table. Although there was no specified seating arrangement, Ray, the materials manager, always took the first seat directly to Joe's left and Ken, the production manager, always assumed the one directly to Joe's right. This put them in a direct face-off: the person in charge of planning production on one side versus the person executing the production plan on the other. Not at all usual for the standard production meeting.

Just to Ray's left sat Dean, one of his direct reports who was in charge of covering performance to schedule at the meeting. Just to Ken's right were two key foremen, Jack and Terry. On both sides of the table were the rest of Joe's staff, most of whom were department managers.

Joe said very little during the first two meetings, asking only a couple of questions for clarification. However, he had not been particularly impressed with the format, and was already forming some ideas as to how he intended to structure things for the future. But for now, following precedence, he started the meeting by asking Dean to report on schedule performance. After carefully arranging the first view cell on the overhead projector, Dean proceeded:

"As you can see from this chart, we surpassed schedule on line Three, we were just short of schedule on Two, and had some problems on One. We missed schedule there by a hundred units."

Dean quickly pulled the chart off the screen and reached for the next overhead. Joe stopped him and asked that he put the last chart back up. After studying the three brightly colored lines for a moment (all headed in a steady downward direction), Joe asked, "What caused the problem?"

"Problem?"

"Yes, why did we miss schedule on lines One and Two?"

"I'm not sure," Dean said, turning to Ken. "Can you answer that?"

"Can I?" Ken replied, with some apparent frustration surfacing in his voice. "We were out of side plates on Two and didn't have enough people to finish the schedule on One."

"Out of side plates?" Joe responded, surprise in his voice. "We make side plates, don't we?"

"Didn't have the material," Ken answered, glancing at Ray. After a moment of silence, Joe decided to press the issue further. "There was a material shortage?" he asked.

Ray appeared perplexed by the news and it was evident he was thinking how to reply. Finally he spoke, addressing his question to Ken. "Why am I just now finding out that you were out of material?"

Ken was quick to reply. "It's not my job to chase down the materials department and tell them something they should already know. If you and your people would get out on the shop floor more often, you'd know we didn't have the material we needed."

"Gentlemen," Joe interrupted, trying not to let the meeting turn into a sparring match. "Let's settle down and see if we can get to the bottom of this."

(continued)

After hearing more on the subject, Joe asked Ken and Ray to collectively get back to him on the shortage and, most important, on what they planned to do to improve cross-functional communications on such matters in the future. With that he then asked Dean to continue.

"Overall for the month, we're behind schedule a little over five thousand units on line One and we're twenty units down, to be exact, on Two. The good news is that we're ahead of schedule on line Three. Let's see ..." Dean said, searching through his records, "the actual count is plus nine hundred and thirty units."

"Were the units we are ahead of schedule on shipped to the customer?" asked Joe.

"No," Ray interjected. "They are part of an order we've put out to the shop to build up some finished goods inventory. The customer wants us to carry a four-week supply."

"Why?"

Ray looked at Joe as if puzzled about the question. "Well, I guess the answer to that is they don't trust that we can always deliver their needs, so they want the inventory there just in case."

"I'll accept that for the moment, but let me ask another question," said Joe. "Were the units we missed on lines One and Two customer orders or units scheduled for inventory?"

"Some of both, but mostly customer orders," replied Ray.

"So we've built over 900 units that weren't immediately needed by our customers, while at the same time potentially disappointing customers who have given us firm orders," said Joe, calmly pointing out the obvious.

"That's about it, in a nutshell," said Ray.

"Well, I would like to examine this matter further, but we'll do that in another meeting. Let's proceed. Someone bring me up to date on the people issue on line One."

Ken was the spokesman again. "As I said before, the problem was we didn't have enough people. The reason is because at the present time we've got a lot of people on vacation since this is the last month they can get it before we turn over a new year, per our labor contract, and we've never been able to get the union to go along with us on a labor pool."

"Since we were ahead of schedule on line Three, why didn't we shut that process down and use the people to fill in as needed on line One?" asked Joe.

There were a couple of light chuckles before Ken responded, "Again, it goes back to contract. We can't transfer people from one line to the other without asking for volunteers, based on seniority."

"Okay, that's another one I'd like to learn more about. It appears we have some work force flexibility issues that need to be addressed. But for the moment, let's proceed. Max, could you report on how we are doing from a quality angle?" Max was the plant's quality assurance manager.

"Unfortunately, I don't exactly have good news either," Max stated. "I just found out before the meeting that everything we built on line One yesterday has to go on hold. Our audit indicates a part may be missing and that means we'll have to check every unit built to ensure no bad ones get to the field."

"You mean we didn't know the part was missing *before* we built all the units?"

"Believe it or not, it was a small screw that may have been overlooked. My people tell me it wasn't called out on the operator build instructions."

"What does all this mean?" Joe probed.

"It means we will have to inspect each and every unit and rework them if the screw is missing."

The conversation continued until a decision was reached to file a product hold report so customers would understand the problem was that the units could not be shipped until they had been inspected and reworked, as needed. Joe insisted the rework be done over the upcoming weekend, so the units could be shipped the following Monday. This started a whole new round of controversy.

Mary, the accounting manager, spoke up to remind everyone that overtime had not been built into the expense forecast for the month, which Joe found odd with the plant going into the new month almost 5,000 down on one product series.

"I don't see what difference it makes if we forecasted overtime or not," Joe said. "The facts are, we are behind on delivery to our customers and the proper thing to do is to get the units reworked as fast as possible. In the process, we can salvage as much goodwill as possible by letting our customers know we're working over the weekend in order to respond to their needs as fast as we can."

"I just thought I should point out that this is going to hit the bottom line in a negative fashion so you don't have any surprises when you start to get questions from the powers above," Mary explained.

Before Joe could respond to Mary, Ken intervened with a different subject. "I'll say one thing ... today is Thursday and if we're going to work this weekend, the contract clearly specifies that people must be given two days advance notice."

"What?" Joe retorted. "Two days? I've never heard of such a thing. What kind of contract do we have around here anyway?" Then, before anyone

(continued)

could respond, Joe continued, "Forget I said that. Ken, move forward with whatever needs to be done to get people notified and if push comes to shove, the worst thing that can happen is we end up paying people extra. I'm assuming that's a correct statement."

"That's correct," said Bob, the human resource manager.

Joe paused, leaning back in his chair and interlocking the fingers of both hands behind his head before letting a breath of air escape in frustration.

"What can you tell us about this, Bob? I find it hard to believe we have a contract that prohibits us from meeting customer requirements in an emergency situation."

"We can work, of course," Bob replied. "It's just that we will have to take volunteers rather than scheduling certain individuals for overtime."

"What if the volunteers don't have the skills required? Let's assume the people who want to work aren't familiar with the product." Joe glanced at Ken, who was looking at him as if he had finally said something reasonably intelligent.

"We don't have to take anyone who isn't qualified to do the work," Bob responded.

"And how is that decision made?"

"Well, Ken has the right to disqualify anyone who doesn't have the skill sets needed."

"How do you make that choice, Ken?" Joe asked. "Do you have something published that clearly indicates individual skills and qualifications?"

Ken chuckled lightly before answering. "You kidding? There's no good way to make a decision like that. We need the people who built the units. What we'll get is what we've always gotten, people who are willing to work overtime, but that's usually employees in lower classifications who are making less money than those with the skills we really need. We'll be holding their hands all the way, and it will take twice as long as it would otherwise. I'm not trying to be a wise guy. I'm just trying to point out the reality of the situation; but I'm encouraged you asked. I've been trying to make this point for years."

"I think you're overstating the problem," replied Bob.

"Yeah? Well, would you like to be here at 6:00 a.m. this coming Saturday and see for yourself?" challenged Ken.

"Maybe," Bob responded bravely.

"Enough . . . please," Joe intervened. He stopped long enough to glance at his watch before deciding to bring the meeting to a halt. It was 9:45.

What's Wrong with This Picture?

Joe Martin is a plant manager who finds himself in charge of a traditional manufacturing operation, one that is totally out of control and on the verge of becoming one of a growing number of factories that will find it cannot satisfactorily compete in today's fast-expanding, globally competitive environment. If we examine the evidence closely, we will see we have a factory:

- With substantial cost and quality problems.
- With customers that seriously doubt it can deliver as promised.
- With management and union relationships that are out of touch with world class manufacturing principles, concepts, and techniques.
- With an organizational approach that pits one function against another.

Without ever visiting this fictional factory and digging into the facts, there can be some strong assurance that:

- It is a batch (mass) manufacturing operation. One that believes in the departmentalization of production work (i.e., each department measured independently in terms of output, efficiency, cost, quality, and the like).
- It carries large volumes of both work-in-process and finished goods inventory.
- It generally operates on the basis of crisis management.
- It has very high downtime, scrap, and rework costs.
- It is not in tune with the beat required to focus extensively on customer orders, but rather builds to a schedule that will theoretically "take care of" requirements.
- It uses a system of production designed to cover for problems that can occur (rather than exposing problems, resolving them, and ensuring they do not recur).
- It is generally slow to respond to the introduction of new products and/or product design changes.
- It has a "fix it if it's broke" mentality.
- It has very long setup and changeover times throughout its manufacturing processes.
- It is extremely error prone.

As we can clearly see, Joe Martin undoubtedly has his work cut out. In the following chapters we'll visit him to see how he is solving these problems that were once considered normal manufacturing practice.

Revolutionary Pointers

- Manufacturing in the United States is currently going through a major transition, yet large numbers of manufacturers simply do not recognize what it's all about. Many still operate under outdated manufacturing practices and fail to see that the true enemy is not the competition, but rather their own system of production.

- Manufacturing has been its own worst enemy, chaining itself to old methods of the past and failing to take appropriate initiative in leading change for the better. It has taken second best when it comes to talent and fundamental expertise. This lack of leadership has been instrumental in shrinking our industrial base and creating the deep dark dungeon.

- Old-time hardened leaders usually take significant change as a personal threat because they fear they will not play an ultimate role in it. They strive to perpetuate their breed, bringing people into subordinate roles who think as they do, and block change every chance they get.

- World class manufacturing is a buzz word that has many faces, but what it represents for most industries is a way of establishing continuous improvement. Unfortunately, making enhancements and improvements to the wrong kind of production system provides no great competitive edge.

- Changing the system of production will not occur with the same demonstrations of JIT and kaizen, or in initiatives aimed at employee empowerment. To have fundamental and lasting change you must remove the cart from before the horse and fully and completely change your existing system of production.

- The practical step-by-step approach of WFM can move your waste-embedded batch manufacturing system to a largely waste-free status in as little as 12–18 months.

- The plant manager is the true revolutionary—the person between top management and workers, the person responsible for changing and implementing the rules. Without his or her commitment and focus, you don't have a prayer of moving from being a conventional mass manufacturer to a waste-free manufacturer.

2

The Plant Manager's Manifesto

WHAT IS IT THAT MAKES CHANGE, especially in a system of production, so difficult? Why do manufacturing managers, first-line supervisors, and operators (among others) tend to be reluctant to make change, even when it has become apparent that extensive problems exist in the current system of production? I believe there are two factors that serve to make significant change in manufacturing a very difficult task to accomplish. First are the mental barriers that employees typically place on such an initiative. They sometimes have an extremely difficult time allowing themselves to become "flexible workers." This is because the old system (batch production) does not typically call for flexibility, but rather for strict compliance to a set of operating rules requiring the worker to stay busy producing parts, components, and finished units—even if, at the time, there are no firm orders for the finished units in question. The second factor has to do with the depth of dedication required by all concerned to make change a true and lasting reality.

Making big change requires *work*—very often, very hard work! Making big change is also disruptive to the things people have become accustomed to and feel they should be busy doing. In addition, big change usually requires a big commitment in terms of the time and energy that typically must be applied. If all this leads you to believe I am somehow implying that people do not like change, especially *big* change, then I would say we are now *precisely* on the same wavelength.

THE NEED TO ENERGIZE FOR CHANGE

In today's manufacturing world, people generally hate change because it takes extra time and energy. And if the focus is on restructuring and downsizing, people are already physically and mentally stretched to their limits. Assuming there is something valid about this observation, what does it take to energize a work force into action? The answer is one or both of two things:

1. The clear recognition that without substantial change, employee jobs and their long-term future are in real jeopardy.
2. The clear understanding that something of value is in it for them.

Neither of the above is easy to accomplish, but the potential for an actual loss of jobs usually gets people's attention and their willingness to at least try something different. Certainly, convincing employees there is something of value in it for them is much more difficult. Therefore, the operation that is wise enough to address the need for change with its work force *before* it boils down to a loss of business and jobs unquestionably has the more difficult scenario to deal with. Let's examine why.

Assume there is a conventional batch manufacturing operation that is making good money and even growing its market share. The question becomes why, and the answer most often is that a competitor has not, as yet, come on the scene who utilizes a globally competitive manufacturing approach. If such operations could indeed come to believe that at some point others are going to enter their market and bring world class manufacturing practices into the arena, they probably could understand and see the need for doing what is necessary now to change beforehand. Right? Wrong!

As a young industrial engineer in the early '70s I worked for a sporting goods manufacturing firm, recognized at the time as the leader in its industry. I won't mention the name of the company, but there are those who will recognize it. One day I was in the design engineering department picking up some prints and I came upon the chief design engineer and one of his assistants examining a couple of bail fishing reels. Being inquisitive about what was going on, I entered the conversation and discovered they were examining a couple of "cheap Japanese reels" one of them had just picked up at the local sporting goods store.

I spent some time listening to them criticizing the reels. They had plastic rather than steel gears. The paint was terrible. No true fisherman in his right mind would buy one of those things. They had no brand name recognition—and the list went on. Quite honestly, I found myself believing what they were saying. I too, at the time, could not fathom how someone would even consider purchasing one of the reels. How wrong both they and I were.

To make a long story short, this was perhaps the initial invasion of the Japanese into a market essentially owned and controlled by U.S. industry. Over a relatively short span of five years, the Japanese bail reel invasion grew from infancy to full maturity and essentially put this particular U.S. manufacturing firm, as well as others, out of business.

What happened? The answer, as Joel Barker so aptly instructs, lies in the realization that a paradigm shift was in the making. The U.S. sporting goods industry was so ingrained with the thought that no one was going to purchase bail reels that didn't bear their name brand and that customers were not interested in "cheap" fishing reels, that they convinced themselves the Japanese would never get the idea off the ground. In fact what they were dealing with were reels that weren't cheap, but without question were less expensive. So inexpensive that the average American fisherman could purchase one, use it for a year or two, toss it and buy another, and still have change left over from what it would have cost to buy the U.S. brand. Not so amazingly, perhaps, was the fact that the early Japanese bail reels worked and held up exceptionally well.

Today, almost every bail reel on the market is a Japanese or foreign brand. And while the price of bail reels is still amazingly inexpensive, even compared to prices over two decades ago, the quality and performance of these reels have vastly improved—and their aggressive advances in this industry have never wavered since the early entrance with what many U.S. sporting goods manufacturers not so affectionately came to call "the cheap little toy reel."

Well, in this case, the cheap little toy became the catalyst for a paradigm shift that literally changed the entire market and drove some well-entrenched U.S. manufacturers completely out of the business. Could this have been avoided? Most definitely, but it would have required some foresight. Today, no manufacturer would take any new product from Japan that lightly, but what about the next "toy" that comes from one of the many developing nations in today's world? It is certainly something to think about.

Energizing for change is going to be key to U.S. industry in the decade to come. To do this, companies will have to put aside their old habitual paradigms and stop looking at even the slightest challenge as a major threat to their well-being. More importantly, they must accept that anything short of a world class manufacturing approach simply leaves them short of where they have to be in order to compete on a lasting basis with the globally competitive onslaught that is now at hand.

It is important to understand that making the kind of correction in course that many (if not most) U.S. manufacturing plants need boils down to more than just using lean concepts and JIT techniques. It requires fearless leaders who are willing to tirelessly demand and strongly encourage the need for total change. This kind of change goes past applying a few accepted tools and techniques. It calls for fundamentally putting a new face on *every* aspect of the manufacturing floor. This doesn't mean the procurement of new or advanced facilities and equipment, but rather an improvement to every existing process, down to the smallest detail.

However, in order to do this, as you will see, you must first start with evaluating everything that currently exists on the shop floor. Then you must apply a system of *absolute and thorough organization* to everything that is deemed necessary. I'll speak much more on this later but at this point in the plant manager's manifesto for total change, it is critical to recognize the serious need to completely change the focus—away from mass production thinking to lean production thinking.

THE CRITICAL NEED FOR RENEWED FOCUS BY TODAY'S PLANT MANAGERS

Let's face it. The United States is no longer great at the art of manufacturing. If we were, we would not have seen such an accelerated trend over the past few decades of a dwindling manufacturing economy and a mushrooming service-oriented economy. If we are to make a successful turnaround of this trend we need a renewed focus by our plant managers. Dale Carnegie said in his book, *How to Stop Worrying and Start Living*:

> If we are going to make things better for others, let's be quick about it. . . . Any good that I can do, let me do it now. Let me not defer nor neglect it, for I will not pass this way again. (p. 25)

In reality, plant managers spend a large percentage of their time dealing with day-to-day problems that are created by an old and ineffective system of mass manufacturing. They generally have little time to address the root cause of problems that are making their factories less than totally competitive. To be more specific, most of the day-to-day problems in traditional manufacturing are created by *wastes* that are commonly viewed as the *cost of doing business*. Thus, competition that views these same costs as unnecessary (as wastes that can indeed be driven out of its operation) has a sizable competitive advantage.

That is exactly what Toyota did in creating its Toyota Production System (TPS). As a result, a company which at one time was seen as just another minor competitor ended up becoming the epitome not only of what an automotive manufacturer should be, but of how manufacturing in general should be performed. Given all this, however, the truth is that U.S. manufacturing has been very slow to respond to the "new" manufacturing system. Although many plant managers can spout popular acronyms and catch phrases that have come from worldwide recognition of TPS, unfortunately this is about as far as it has gone. There are three reasons for this:

1. Many plant managers do not fully understand what globally competitive manufacturing is all about, and have no practical experience with making the kind of change needed to answer the challenge. They lack any real understanding as to how to appropriately apply the new manufacturing techniques required. As a result, they have no appreciation for either the task at hand or the substantial benefits that can be gained.
2. Even among those who do understand, there are some who are unwilling to press forward because they simply do not know which step to take first (i.e., how to establish priorities and how to deal with the many changes that must occur).
3. There are plant managers who are totally unwilling to take a chance because they are controlled by fear of the unknown or have highly self-centered motives for everything they do. They generally believe those who do step out to be different will most often have a very short career.

For any reader who may be in the last category, I would recommend you return this book or better yet, give it to another plant manager who may indeed benefit from it, because the kind of revolutionary change you're about to encounter requires conviction and focus you probably are not able to provide. Moving from a conventional batch production to a waste-free manufacturing environment is not a prescription for the faint-hearted. We are going to need a very high level of good, old-fashioned, patriotic can-do commitment from our plant managers over the next decade if we are going to survive and then compete with the relentless competitive onslaught from the rest of the world. The United States was caught off guard once—and wrongly assumed we had the luxury to ignore it. We are now paying for it with lost markets and are scrambling to survive, let alone compete.

The only solace I can give with any degree of reliability is the fact that *conviction with knowledge is the substance of focus.* Therefore, with a proper focus, results can be swift. With sound results, even those who adamantly oppose the kind of change you will bring will be reluctant to challenge it openly. This need for a renewed focus by U.S. plant managers may have been best expressed by an hourly production associate who, after being exposed to the process of kaizen (continuous improvement), felt the need to compose her thoughts in writing. This was later published in the company's monthly newsletter. In part, she wrote:

> Good fruit comes from a seed planted in good soil. It is no different when we examine what is required to make and keep a company competitive. We need people who are doers ... people who are charged by the message ... people who will set aside personal feelings and emotions to achieve a common goal ... people who are not satisfied with what they see now, but who will strive to be different and better every day ... people who are not content being settlers, but who will find ways to be pioneers. People who can face pressures and trials that come in all shapes, forms and kinds, with dignity and integrity. ... What kind of soil are you?

This message could not be more meaningful. We must indeed have a reawakening, with a heightened sense of commitment, especially from those leading change. Unfortunately, there is no silver bullet for resolving all of the associated problems that may arise, outside of a sharp focus on the things to be done and a willingness, if necessary, to challenge the establishment in making it happen.

Again, it is a medicine (truth) that is not necessarily easy for some to swallow. On the other hand, the disease of destructive complacency, most often created by self-imposed restrictions, can only lead to a continual decline in our manufacturing effectiveness. The question is: If today's plant managers do not assume a personal commitment to, and a lead role in making the journey required to bring the United States back to the forefront of competitive leadership in manufacturing, who will?

THE CHALLENGING JOURNEY FROM MASS TO WASTE-FREE MANUFACTURING

This challenging journey begins with an unrelenting conviction that:

- Everything in conventional mass manufacturing should be questioned by asking why and doing so repeatedly.
- A plant manager has the obligation to quickly eliminate anything that cannot be clearly established as value-added.

Change in itself is never easy and extraordinary change affecting every employee and every function in a factory is extremely hard to implement. With this effort comes the often unpopular need to:

- Evaluate entire departments as to their need.
- Renegotiate contracts with organized labor, which most often need to be entirely changed.
- Undertake massive retraining efforts and heighten communications to a level previously unparalleled in the business.
- Make available time for training and communications.
- Change conventional financial measurements and controls so you can train. Conventional financial measurements and controls can become serious roadblocks.

Pressures will often arise from very powerful functions. There will be those who:

- Make strong efforts to implement needless, yet ever more sophisticated and costly initiatives. This establishes them as an enlightened expert and, therefore, positions them as being indispensable.
- Prefer the status quo and take any implied change to it as a personal affront, for they often see themselves as the protector of both the system and the people who work within it. They view change as

a foolish, self-centered folly and can never bring themselves to accept anything other than the way business has always been conducted.

Then there are:

- Suppliers who will sometimes say they cannot respond to change and from the standpoint of their responsibility to it may try any means of slowing a needed transition.
- Production associates who have long-standing classifications in fields that are recognized as non-value-added and who will fight every policy, rule, or precedent while finding reasons to support the value of their present position.

The only answer to the many types of obstacles that will certainly arise is to keep a sharp focus on the task at hand. That task, again, is to ensure that while you are making these changes the factory remains competitive in the face of a globally oriented business environment, with companies in that environment who know, understand, and practice "unconventional" manufacturing principles. One simply cannot wait until such manufacturers become a rival in a given market to react, because it will then be far too late to adequately respond.

Rest assured that the journey from mass to waste-free manufacturing will not be easy for any plant manager. The path is full of pitfalls and roadblocks. During the journey you will make some strong enemies but once you've put in place the fundamental principles and the organization required to support a true WFM operation, you will have strong supporters. The reason is, you will have amazing results. Most important, you will be in charge of an operation that has much better flexibility in serving the customers' needs, at surprisingly lower operating costs—and you will feel some honest satisfaction about the role you played in making the transition a solid reality.

A man I highly respect said the following to me on my approaching the job of plant manager:

The best advice I can give is to remember as a plant manager you are not the boss. You don't own the operation, literally or otherwise. You will not have this particular post the rest of your career. You're a caretaker—a steward of sorts and you have an awesome responsibility to leave it in better shape than when you arrived. The greatest compliment anyone can give you when you're gone is not that you were a nice guy. The greatest will be for someone to say that you left something of lasting value and that in the process of doing so, you treated people fairly.

I have never forgotten that advice because it says more in a few words than most books on the subject. It is indeed true that plant managers are not normally in their posts for more than a few years. Like race horses, if they are good at what they do, they usually move into a role where they can help perpetuate the breed. In business, this is usually a higher, more formidable position in the company. If they are bad (be this actual or perceived), they are usually moved out to pasture.

His advice was also on target regarding the precise role of the plant manager. He spoke from personal experience, of course, and my own experience proved this. The longer one works at being a plant manager, the more one realizes the substantial *lack* of appointed authority. However, there is little authority a plant manager cannot *assume*, given the will to do so. And enough cannot be said about the need to treat people fairly during the journey of becoming a waste-free manufacturer. Take care, however, not to misconstrue this to mean people's feelings come first above anything else. As you assume the authority (responsibility) for implementing the kind of change required some people will harbor very hard feelings toward you. In some cases, you will be placing a hardship on employees, up to and including eliminating certain jobs and/or positions permanently. The key, again, is keeping a proper focus and dealing with such matters as fairly as possible.

Finally, when it comes to making major changes to a conventional batch manufacturing operation, nothing could be truer in the advice above than the last point. When it is all said and done, and a plant manager moves on, the greatest compliment is to be remembered as a person who brought something of lasting value to the operation. You need two things to accomplish this:

1. A strong desire to position your plant for the challenges of the future.
2. A step-by-step approach to make it happen.

I can't provide you with the will, but I can provide you with an approach that works. But first we need to confront a serious obstacle that may be holding you back.

Overcoming the Conventional Cost of Doing Business

At this point, if it were possible, I would ask you to firmly grasp your head in your hands, remove it from your shoulders, turn it upside down, and shake it very vigorously. The intent would be to rid your mind of all the old, obsolete thoughts and ideas about manufacturing that are embedded within, so you might approach what you are about to read with a clear and open frame of mind. It is also about breaking down what I refer to as the ego barrier. This is the sizable web that has grown, over time, in our mind that drives us toward *inaction*. The web is there to protect us against the one thing our egos fear most ... *failure*.

Any results you achieve during the journey I am about to outline will largely depend on your will in leading such change and your personal fortitude in keeping the process moving aggressively forward. The process of WFM does work, but change of this magnitude does not happen without overcoming some sizable barriers. A good example of the kind of obstacles a plant manager will be dealing with is the typical kind of waste that occurs in conventional mass manufacturing. This is the waste that is usually assumed to be just the *cost of doing business*. Consider just three of these: large raw material, work-in-process, and finished goods inventory levels. In batch manufacturing it is considered necessary to have a standard level of on-hand inventory to:

1. Run so-called economical order quantities that serve to justify the time required to set up or change over equipment or facilities.
2. Produce "just-in-case" stock for potential equipment breakdowns and/or other problems such as the possibility of a supplier not delivering on time.
3. Cover the potential parts and components that could be "bad" as a result of handling damage or improper production techniques, and provide protection against shrinkage due to inaccurate production counts and other unforeseen problems or difficulties.
4. Cover other potential problems.

Toyota and other globally competitive manufacturers would essentially take the following position in opposition to the reasoning above.

1. Reduce setup and changeover to a point where it has no bearing on the level of standard inventory carried in an operation.

2. Maintain equipment at a level where breakdowns simply do not occur.
3. Suppliers should *always* deliver on time, without exception.
4. Use proper production techniques that avoid producing bad parts or at least only producing parts in such low quantities before a problem is discovered that carrying added inventory will not be necessary. In addition, shrinkage due to scrap, rework, handling damage, and the like should *never* happen.
5. Strive to put a process in place that clearly surfaces problems and then fully resolves them—*once and for all*—rather than striving to cover for problems (which in essence means covering up problems).

This one hurdle of overcoming conventional thinking about the cost of doing business, in itself, adequately points out the significant challenges facing the plant manager's desire to bring globally competitive change to his or her factory.

HOW STRONG IS YOUR SENSE OF URGENCY?

Someone once approached me and asked me to sum up in one word what the process I so aspire to is all about. My answer was *urgency*. To some degree, the measure of any success is seizing an opportunity and applying an appropriate sense of urgency. When it comes to changing a conventional style of manufacturing operation to waste-free manufacturing, a strong sense of urgency by the factory's leader is absolutely essential. In fact, you cannot make rapid change without it.

I learned about a sense of urgency—received an equivalent master's degree—from my father. He was a man with an eighth grade education who was a successful, self-made businessman. When I was 16 years old, I was working for him in much of my spare time and I came to recognize the one element of his demeanor that drove everything he did and everything he expected of those who worked with and around him. With my father, it was not just a sense of urgency but what I viewed at the time (now realizing I was wrong) as wanting instant gratification on any and every issue.

If I heard the old adage, "Don't put off until tomorrow what you can do today" once, I must have heard it from him tens of thousands of times. It was one of his favorites and he used it frequently to punctuate almost everything he had to say as well as do about the business. For example:

Son, we offer the same basic products that everyone else does. Why would someone want to give up doing business with others to come to us? The answer is that we offer them something they can't get at the other place. That, quite simply, is much better service, because we don't put off until tomorrow.

We're out of supplies and they can't deliver? Get the owner or someone who's in charge on the phone. I'll let them know we don't put off until tomorrow.

The janitor didn't clean the restrooms before he left? Was busy doing something else? Baloney! You have him see me first thing in the morning. We'll make sure he understands we don't put off until tomorrow...

My father clearly realized the one factor that separated a successful, growing business from those who were just "hanging around and hanging on," as he so aptly put it, was a strong sense of quickly addressing and fully resolving anything that was even the slightest barrier to absolute customer satisfaction. As a result, he quickly addressed inefficiencies that cut into and/or reduced profits.

Good enough, you say, for a small business you own and operate, but in managing a large business where you are working for the other person, this type of approach really isn't practical. In addition, it would not be long before you would be perceived as being a totally unreasonable manager. Unusual, yes. Unreasonable? Not necessarily.

Perhaps it was something that was so frequently drilled into me in my youth that it became second nature, but as a plant manager I had a reputation of having a very high sense of urgency. At first I was certainly viewed as being unusual with my expectations, but later I was approached by numerous employees (including some who went on to bigger and better things) who let me know they had come to clearly understand the importance of accomplishing things in an expedient fashion. The point is, most employees will respect the leader who displays a high sense of urgency because it almost always results in a faster level of accomplishment for the operation.

Although simple in structure, my father's philosophy is most appropriate for any business and certainly for manufacturing. Essentially this means the leader in charge has to establish and drive the following professional conduct through the entire work force:

- *Do not allow someone to table a problem for tomorrow that can be resolved before they go home.* If this means added hours, then so be it. Enough added hours served in addressing nagging problems and it will not be long before those and others start to disappear. However, allowing problems to be dropped at standard quitting time and picked up the next day on regular hours will only send the message that this is the way management expects the business to be run—and that a sense of urgency really isn't important.
- *Rally the entire management team around the problem when a real crisis develops.* Far too often I have witnessed a crisis situation in one area of the plant and the only people involved were people directly assigned to that area. Getting the whole management team involved not only provides a set of new eyes for addressing the problem, but clearly sends the message that overall factory performance is the number one priority, taking precedence over any single department, area, or function.
- *Become personally involved in crisis management.* Do not simply delegate the problem to someone else. Be there. Be active in the process of resolution. It shows you care and are willing to do what you ask and expect of others.
- *Get the message out that missing production schedules by even one unit is simply not acceptable and that employees do not leave until the assembly line, unit, or production department is fully back on schedule.* Even if this means overtime. Why? Because who knows what tomorrow might bring that will complicate a schedule deficiency even further.
- *Ensure that this philosophy applies to all support functions.* This includes things like getting standard departmental reports out on time and meeting established deadlines and schedules for all the other work that goes on within the four walls of the factory.

The factory that begins to apply a true sense of urgency to everything it does will, over time, begin to see some remarkable results. And as this type of thinking spreads into the work force as a standard way of doing business it will probably become unbeatable by its competition.

THE FUNDAMENTALS OF MANUFACTURING LEADERSHIP

Everything I've addressed so far has led to discussing the fundamentals of manufacturing leadership. The reason I feel strongly about this issue is because your best intentions will only lead to failure if you do not have the basic fundamentals in place at the offset of the process. What I have discovered after many years in manufacturing is that the basic fundamentals of effectively involving the management team, tracking performance on a daily basis, and communicating progress to the work force generally are not in place in most manufacturing establishments.

If you are a plant manager or a person in a leadership position with a manufacturing operation, the questions in Table 2-1 will help you determine if your organization has the basic fundamentals in place—the kind needed to aggressively drive the process to become a globally competitive waste-free manufacturer.

The questions point to some of the more meaningful fundamentals that you should have in place if you want to effectively drive the kind of continuous improvement activity that is in line with the criteria for globally competitive manufacturing. Though some of these may seem obvious, as you proceed you will begin to see the importance of how they tie together and become critical components of the process.

Table 2-1. The WFM Fundamentals Checklist

How Globally Competitive Are You?		
Yes	No	
☐	☐	1. Does your organization have a daily business meeting involving the plant manager and his/her entire staff?
☐	☐	a. If such a meeting does exist, is every production area reviewed in terms of customer orders (schedules) and performance to those schedules?
☐	☐	b. If schedules are not being achieved, have you established root causes and made assignments to close the door on the problem?
☐	☐	c. Are in-process defect rates and outgoing quality levels measured and reviewed daily?
☐	☐	d. If problems exist (anything other than zero PPM), have you established root causes and made assignments to close the door on the problem?
☐	☐	e. Is there a daily review of performance to financial forecasts and budgets?
☐	☐	f. If problems exist (anything short of meeting prescribed budgets/forecasts), does the staff immediately address and respond to the issues of bringing things back in line?
☐	☐	g. Are inventory levels reviewed each and every day?

(continued)

Table 2-1. The WFM Fundamentals Checklist *(continued)*

		How Globally Competitive Are You?
Yes	No	
☐	☐	2. Are there regular staff-level reviews, involving both hourly and salaried personnel, geared at identifying and addressing manufacturing wastes? a. If so, have you clearly identified all manufacturing waste categories?
☐	☐	3. Are there clear performance checks, measures, and rewards for waste elimination?
☐	☐	4. Do all members of the management team (staff) visit the factory floor each and every day (at least once, preferably more often)? a. Do they make a point to stop and speak with operators about wastes and to get their thoughts about how to make improvements? b. If so, is there a process in place that allows operators to share and discuss their thoughts/ideas with all other staff members?
☐	☐	5. Have you established in-process defect-rate alert levels for each and every process? a. If so, when a process exceeds this "alert level" is the process stopped and does management collectively go to the shop floor, observe the problem, and make some determination as to what must be done before the process can restart?
☐	☐	6. Does the plant manager and his/her entire staff make regular *waste observation tours*?
☐	☐	7. Does the plant manager and staff perform regular "dock audits" of finished goods? a. If so, are both hourly and salaried personnel, along with the staff, involved in the audits?
☐	☐	8. If a field problem develops with product performance, quality, or workmanship, are 100-percent dock audits performed until it is clear the problem is fully resolved?
☐	☐	9. Does every person involved with written objectives have measurable goals for waste reduction and are these seriously reviewed at least once every quarter? a. If so, do the weight factors for these objectives carry the heaviest weight of all other established goals and objectives?

Revolutionary Pointers

- Most U.S.-based industry still prefers batch (mass) manufacturing. It's a habit they know and understand. As a result, they've been more than just slow to respond to needed change, they've been a most formidable opponent against it.

- To energize for change U.S. industry will have to put aside their old habitual paradigms and stop looking at even the slightest challenge as a major threat to their well-being.

- The manufacturing operation that is wise enough to address the need for change with its work force before it boils down to a loss of business and jobs is an operation that unquestionably has the more difficult scenario in convincing the employees for a need to change.

- Most employees do not like big change because it often requires very hard work, and in today's manufacturing world, with a focus on restructuring and downsizing, employees are already stretched physically and mentally to their limits.

- You need the fundamentals of manufacturing leadership in place before you even begin the process of implementing continuous improvements.

- U.S. manufacturers need a renewed focus and commitment by plant managers and/or manufacturing leaders if they are to become world class. They simply cannot follow the path of others but must effectively and expediently implement world class manufacturing.

- Most plant managers are simply too busy putting out the day-to-day fires created by an old and ineffective system of mass manufacturing to address the *root causes* that are making their factories less than totally competitive.

- To overcome the hurdles of conventional mass manufacturing the plant manager needs the will (focus), a step-by-step approach, and a sense of urgency. With the proper focus, results can be swift and sound and will deflect the challenges from those who adamantly oppose change. Remember, *conviction with knowledge is the substance of focus.*

- The plant manager's journey from mass to WFM begins with an unrelenting conviction that everything in conventional mass manufacturing must be questioned by repeatedly asking why and quickly eliminating anything that is not clearly value added.

3

The New Competition
and the Old Barriers

FOR SOME TIME NOW Japanese manufacturers have been one of the more formidable competitors in the globally competitive manufacturing environment. On the other hand, their successes are no longer limited exclusively to them. Manufacturing operations in countries around the world have begun a relentless commitment to a new system of production that significantly enhances product quality, employee productivity, and customer satisfaction. While this system is built on the key principles of the Toyota Production System (TPS) or the just-in-time (JIT) operating philosophy, understanding and implementing the physical dynamics of JIT is only one small step in the right direction. For any firm seeking to achieve global competitiveness, lasting change must include a complete and absolute reformation to the entire system of production—a change of thinking from mass production to lean production.

The approach differs somewhat, but the premise of globally competitive manufacturing is a system of production that clearly defines wastes, highly utilizes its employees in a battle against those wastes, and constantly strives for continuous improvement. Yet most U.S. manufacturers still see their competition as a direct competitor or series of competitors rather than their system of production. If they focused as much attention on their operations it would be much easier for them to accept the need to completely transform their manufacturing arena and bring it into the lean production era. Instead, many companies continue basing their business strategies on analyzing their direct competition and/or performing what is commonly referred to as benchmarking best in class. Benchmarking in itself is fine, but what I am suggesting is that the time has come to aggressively pursue doing something that is inherently the *right thing to do*—regardless of what a firm's direct competition or the best in class may or may not be doing. The reason is simple. It is nearly impossible to catch a competitor who is already aggressively applying the concepts of globally competitive manufacturing. Every positive step made in the right direction by the company just entering the lean manufacturing process will be answered by an even more effective step from the competitor who is already on the "lean journey."

Does this mean a company that is not into globally competitive manufacturing and has competition who is, faces the possibility of losing a very large amount of market share (if not its entire business, over time)? The answer is: Perhaps. All one has to do is look at the automotive industry. Even though Detroit's Big Three have made some remarkable strides in fighting back, they will, in all probability, never again enjoy the market share they once took for granted. This is all the more reason for U.S. manufacturing to take steps now in the right direction before the new competition forces your response, which could be far too late.

Month One, Day One—A New Assignment

It was a typical Monday. I, on the other hand, was not going to make it to work at my normal time. I had been out of town the week before and had returned home late Friday evening, only to discover that Kathy (my wife, friend, and partner for over twenty-five years) needed my help to drop her car by the dealer the following Monday morning. With this now accomplished, I was finally headed for the office. As I pulled onto Jefferson Boulevard, I checked the time. It was 8:20 A.M., which still left me with a good fifteen minutes to the plant.

Kathy and I were now six months into a transfer with the company and still had unpacked boxes, but our home was gradually taking on some semblance of order. My job as a manufacturing strategic planner kept me on the road much of the time and by the weekend, I usually had no desire to do any settling chores. With the number of moves we had made during my career we had learned, over the years, that it really wasn't necessary to have everything in its proper place the day after the moving van departed, but this particular move was beginning to look as if it might never be fully completed.

As I pulled into the company parking lot, I discovered that finding a spot wasn't going to be easy. Usually when I arrived the lot was virtually empty, but now it was packed. As I was about to give up hope, I spied a spot at the very back of the lot. I hurriedly squeezed into it, just clearing the car on my right, which had taken two feet of the space I was trying to use. I had some difficulty opening the door wide enough to get out, but finally made it, taking mental note that I needed to lose a little weight. As I walked briskly toward the office, I glanced at my watch. It was 8:40.

Kerrie, the executive assistant to my boss, Bill, looked up from the copy machine she was working at and spoke. "Hey, John. Bill wants to see you as soon as you can make some time."

"What luck," I thought as I nodded a confirmation and started toward my office.

"He's really anxious to see you," she interjected politely.

I stopped, turned back to her, and put my briefcase on the floor, beside my feet. "Oh? Any idea what it's about?" I asked.

She shrugged her shoulders and raised her eyebrows. "I don't know, but he said to make sure I got to you as soon as you came in."

"Okay," I replied, picking up my briefcase and continuing on to my office. I took time to check my e-mail, but didn't see anything of great importance, so I picked up a tablet and pen and started back toward Bill's office.

In the office next to mine, Jack was just settling in, and as I passed we exchanged a quick greeting. Before I was more than a few steps past his office, he stuck his head out the door and called after me. "Say, do you have just a minute?"

I stopped and stepped back to his office. "Kerrie says Bill is really anxious to see me about something," I noted.

"I think I know why," he said. "That's what I wanted to talk to you about."

I took a seat in one of the two chairs arranged at a neat angle just in front of his desk. He came right out with it. "I think Bill's going to give you Vince's job."

"What?" I responded, truly taken aback by his remark.

He leaned forward in an implied expression of confidentiality and lowered his voice. "You know all the talk about Vince taking a temporary leave of absence to get his MBA. Well, it's apparently happened. I got word Bill is looking for someone to take over for him on a temporary basis."

"What's temporary supposed to mean? And what about you? Why would he give it to me instead of you?"

Jack played his modest self. "Who knows, but remember I grew up here; and frankly, this operation needs the kind of change that's more along the line you can provide."

(continued)

I said no; he said yes; and we continued playing the "no-you're-much-better" game for a while before I said I should be on my way.

"Good luck," he remarked as I left. I said thanks and, after turning the corner leading to Bill's office, stopped to take a deep breath before entering the small foyer where Kerrie stood guard over Bill's kingdom.

"Ah, you're here," she said. "Go right in. He's expecting you."

Bill sat at his desk, working through a flood of paper. He took time to finish signing his name to a document before recapping his pen and looking up. He then stood and walked from behind his desk, extending his hand as he came closer.

As always, he was wearing a well-starched white shirt, cuff links and a power tie. Bill had a thing about white shirts, and while he never mandated that his subordinates wear them, it was assumed. When he held a staff meeting, it was always in a sea of white.

"Good morning, sir," he said enthusiastically, giving me a warm hand-shake before inviting me to sit down. After I had done so, he took a seat in a chair next to me.

"Sorry I was a little late," I said. "I had to get Kathy's car in the shop and..."

"No problem," he interrupted, "but I've got something I need to run by you."

"Sure. What's that?"

He paused, looking at me very intently, as if silently trying to convince me this was something of special importance.

"I've decided I'm going to give you a shot at being plant manager."

"Really?" I remarked, trying to look surprised, but at the same time not overly anxious about the prospect. "Where?"

"Here." He went on to explain that Vince was taking a sabbatical, as he put it, to get his MBA. He reminded me that the operation was in real trouble, but he didn't feel he should stand in Vince's way, since gaining acceptance to an advanced graduate program didn't happen every day. "I've decided to put you in as an interim plant manager. You know how these things go. If you do a good job you've got a chance of making it a long-term position."

"What about Vince? Would there be some commitment to give him the job back when he finishes school?"

"No," he said flatly. "Manufacturing isn't his forte. He'll come back, of course, but he wants to get into marketing. You shouldn't feel it would have any impact whatsoever on whether or not you continue in the position. It isn't an issue as far as I'm concerned. The way I see it, this gives us the chance to work together and make some very good things happen. From your standpoint, you've been due a shot at a plant for a long time."

I had worked for Bill, off and on, for more than fifteen years in a series of increasingly responsible positions, and had built a solid reputation as a results-oriented individual. My problem, as he had said more than once, was my "ingrained impatience" with others. I had never learned to extend a great deal of understanding to people who worked harder at finding excuses for why things could not be done, than they did at finding ways to make things happen.

This particular "weakness," as some described it, was often overshadowed by the ability to get things done, even when the odds were not always in my favor. I was definitely an individual who maintained a high level of focus on any assignment I undertook. This did not always sit well with some people, especially those who mistook it as a sign that I was far too serious about my work.

Actually, the thing that drove me was a work ethic that could be attributed to being brought up in a family that had its own business. In my junior year in high school, at the age of 17, I had scholastically earned the "privilege" (as we saw it at the time) of participating in a distributive education program. I attended class in the mornings and helped my father run his business in the afternoons. On Saturdays, along with my two brothers, I was typically at work the entire day, and on more than one occasion we accompanied our father to the store on Sunday afternoons after church, to perform stocking chores in preparation for the upcoming week.

Being in a family that operated its own business we didn't think twice about being there on weekends or holidays. Our life was, to a large degree, our work, and we didn't see anything unusual about that. However, it wasn't all work and no play, by any means. We learned how to provide free time for one another by sharing responsibilities. But, there was never a question that the business always came first. After all, apart from our personal commitment, nothing was guaranteed to make it a continuing success.

After I struck out on my own and took a job working for someone else (which led my family to believe I had completely lost my mind), I approached my work with the same type of enthusiasm and it took some time for me to realize that everyone didn't share my zeal for work. While I reluctantly accepted this as a reality I never believed that anyone had the right to give anything less than 100 percent to the company that provided their living.

Now, sitting next to the vice president of manufacturing for a major firm, discussing a relatively high post within the company, I could not help but get a little excited about the chance of being able to approach a job again as if

(continued)

it were my own business. On the other hand, I needed to know more about what he was really expecting of me. I decided to pursue it further.

"I'd be interested in knowing your expectations. On one hand you say this is a temporary assignment, and on another you're talking like it's a permanent post."

"What I'm trying to tell you is that it's definitely going to start out as a temporary assignment, but if you do the kind of job I think you're going to, why would anyone want to remove you? Now, with regard to my expectations, I want us to work together to establish an action plan that will set this factory on the right course; and I want you to use your considerable expertise in bringing some good, old-fashioned order and discipline to this operation. Frankly, it's just about out of control."

Being a member of Bill's manufacturing support team, I knew quite a lot about the factory's performance (or lack of it). I felt it was going to be a stiff challenge for anyone striving to turn it around.

"How long do we have?" I asked.

"I'd say six to eight months, to show some very positive results."

"Is that realistic?"

"It has to be. It's a matter of survival."

OLD BARRIERS TO DEPLOYING WASTE-FREE MANUFACTURING

I've already addressed some of the more common obstacles to change. Most of these could be classified as mental obstacles. There are, however, a number of system obstacles I feel are important to mention because they can sometimes be extremely difficult barriers. These obstacles have been around industry for years and that is why I call them *old barriers*. They are obstacles to any type of substantial, aggressive change but are sometimes very subtle in nature.

One of the first barriers you will encounter is the one associated with taking time away from the task of producing (i.e., making parts, components, and finished units) in order to train, communicate, and physically change the factory. Under most conventional accounting logic, if a manufacturing facility is, *for any reason*, not producing something, it is not absorbing its costs. The production of parts, assemblies, and finished units means the generation of credits (sometimes called earned hours), which in turn serve as a positive indicator against the actual expenses incurred. Thus, credits become the yard-stick to measure factory performance. In essence, when credits or earned hours equal or exceed operating expenses, the plant is *perceived* to be fully absorbing its costs. But nothing could be further from the truth.

Given a little time, an eighth grader could see the senseless logic of such a measurement and could dream up ways to beat the system. This is because if the sustaining measurement is output, expressed in earned hours, all one has to do is find a way to inflate the hours. How? Since hours are only provided for work that is classified as direct labor, if one could find some reasonable logic to transfer certain portions of indirect work in the factory to direct (and establish standard hours for that work), the plant would receive additional earned hours for the same amount of overall throughput.

For any reader who may think this could never happen, because businesses just would not allow it—think again! It happens in every manufacturing firm that uses an earned hour approach. What is the corresponding result? Most larger manufacturing firms use earned hours to establish labor costs, which, in turn, they apply to the price customers pay for the goods produced and delivered. Even in much smaller businesses, some form of labor-hour value, based on typical (or standard) production output, is commonly applied for pricing purposes. When hours are inflated, costs are inflated, and subsequently price is inflated. Thus, the customer is often forced to pay for the non-value-added costs (wastes) the plant is incurring—at least up to the time a competitor without those wastes comes on the scene.

I have seen plants celebrate at the end of the month when they "over absorbed" their costs by producing product that was not in tune with real customer requirements. Overproduction resulting in added hours for absorption may be well and good, but it is basically immaterial to the true task of manufacturing. That task is meeting customer requirements. Nothing more and nothing less.

This whole matter is a major barrier to making needed change, yet the financial community generally frowns on any effort that might seriously lessen attention to earned hours. Therefore, the person leading change must be prepared to face up to and deal with this issue, because it is certainly a barrier that will, in one form or another, surface.

There are numerous other operating practices that can pose serious stumbling blocks for the factory trying to deploy waste-free manufacturing. A few of these are:

- *Quality measurements.* Those measurements that serve to guide an operation toward active *inspection* throughout the plant—of goods received, of first piece and last piece produced, and the like.
- *Economic lot sizing.* Measurements tied to producing large batches of parts that, in turn, theoretically reduce the piece part cost associated with changeover of equipment and facilities.
- *Indirect labor costs.* Measurements that look at indirect labor as non-value-added (true in itself), but which can become an accounting barrier as more and more people are moved from direct to indirect (for at least a period of time) as the process of implementing waste-free manufacturing progresses.

These are only a few of the standard measurements that tend to drive many manufacturing operations toward absolutely the wrong goals and objectives, and more important, away from doing the right kind of things needed for change.

System barriers do indeed vary from company to company, but the person leading change toward waste-free manufacturing must realize they will arise. You may have to apply some creative thinking in addressing and satisfactorily resolving such issues.

However, these system barriers are minor in comparison to the mental barriers that will indeed affect any effort to change the existing system of production. The more damaging are found in any operation, in varying degrees, regardless of product or service. Table 3-1 shows the worst of these.

Table 3-1. Damaging Mental Barriers

Five Primary Barriers to Change
1. The 'justification' barrier
2. The 'not invented here' barrier
3. The 'done that before' barrier
4. The 'don't rock the boat' barrier
5. The 'it's not my job' barrier

In addressing and pursuing the mental barriers to change, it is good for the plant manager to keep a couple things in mind. The first, as I have mentioned before, is that the entire work force must be actively engaged in any effort directed at moving an operation to a waste-free status. The second is that in doing so, one must come to the recognition that not everyone is a "manufacturing expert." Outside of some notable expertise in the finer mechanics of manufacturing—such as in the management, engineering, and supervisory ranks—there are many other vital roles in a typical manufacturing organization (administrative, clerical, and the like) that have a difficult time associating common manufacturing lingo with the task at hand.

In my consulting ventures, my colleagues and I repeatedly worked through the frustrations associated with fully establishing how prevalent and deeply imbedded mental barriers can be. But, most important was striving to do this in a manner that everyone could clearly understand, regardless of their particular manufacturing expertise. As a result, we constructed a "tale" of sorts and called it "The Legend of the Loaves." While it may appear to be somewhat juvenile, it very adequately served its intended purpose. In its typical use, participants were first asked to read the story and then to gather in small groups and identify where each of the specific barriers were at work. Perhaps not so surprisingly, in almost every case, the participants were quick to identify the barriers and to better associate how they could be at work in their own areas. I include the tale for those readers who may find an appropriate place for it in the future.

The Legend of the Loaves

Once upon a time in the kingdom of Locks, a young baker named Barren accidentally invented a unique recipe for yeast bread that became the rave of the kingdom. His loaves became so popular that he had to labor each day, from dawn to dusk, preparing as many loaves as he possibly could. Yet he found demand far outweighed his ability to supply.

One day the Governor of Locks came to Barren and said, "Sir Barren, I have an idea as to how you can produce many more loaves of your wonderful bread. If you agree to do this, we can spread the demand to the neighboring

(continued)

kingdoms of Axon and Manuan and others. We shall call it Locks' Loaves and this will make our kingdom famous and you a very rich man."

"But how shall this be done?" asked Barren.

"Well, you mix your concoction in a very large pot, right?"

"That is right, Your Excellency. The only one of its size in the kingdom."

"Then the kingdom will build you many such pots and help you teach the citizens of Locks how to make your wonderful loaves, for which you will pay them a decent pittance. We will build onto your bakery to make room for more pots and carry your loaves each day to the surrounding kingdoms by horse and hitchery. Our kingdom will become famous, and our citizens will enjoy the benefits of the work we have provided them, and again, sir, you will become a wealthy man, beyond your wildest dreams. In turn, I will become the governor of the most prosperous kingdom of all kingdoms."

Barren agreed with the governor and in the years to come he did indeed become a wealthy man and the kingdom of Locks prospered and became renown for its Locks' Loaves. Almost everyone in the kingdom worked for Barren, and each year more expansions were made to his shop and many more pots were added. Everyone in Locks was delighted and convinced their prosperity would continue forever, for no one else made Locks' Loaves and no one else ever would.

In the kingdom of Axon, a bright young man named Gaven gave much study to Locks' success, and decided to see if Barren would allow him to visit his bakery. This was agreed upon and in doing so Gaven saw much opportunity to reduce the considerable waste that was inherent to the process of preparing the loaves. He proceeded to share his thoughts with Barren. Barren said he really wasn't interested. He was already richer than he ever imagined he would be, and most everyone in Locks was working in his shop and prospering as never before. Why would he want to change anything? he asked.

"Sir Barren," responded Gaven, "the reason you should consider change is to guard against someone else taking your business in the future. Someone who could produce the loaves for less by eliminating the wastes that exist in your bakery. This way, you help ensure that you stay where you are today, and that the people of Locks continue to enjoy the work and prosperity they have today."

"All right, I will listen to what you have to say. So what sort of wastes are you referring to?" quizzed Barren.

"Well, as an example, I observed how long it takes to change from one pot of mix to the next. It took hours, and almost half a pot of mix was thrown away. If we could devise a means to use the mix faster so it did not harden to a point it could not be used and then find a way to cut the time to change the mix in the pot, you could save a considerable amount of..."

Barren interrupted, "Young man, our loaves are a tradition and they are only made in Locks. The people of the kingdoms buy our loaves because of what they are, not what they cost. I'm sorry, but there is no way anyone is going to take my business away. It just isn't possible."

"Sir Barren, what if someone found a way to make their loaves just as flavorful as yours, and could produce them in larger quantities and deliver them faster? Do you not think they would have the chance of getting some, if not most, of your business?"

"We plan to expand again this year and I need the money I have available for that. How can I justify spending money for such things as you suggest when it is needed in order to expand my shop and deliver our loaves to other kingdoms?" Barren replied.

"Well, again, Sir, perhaps if you spent your money on what I'm suggesting there would be no need to expand further. Perhaps you could get many more loaves out of the pots you now have."

"Perhaps, perhaps. You say perhaps! I cannot operate on the basis of perhaps. I know what has worked in the past, and I'll have no part of some foolhardy scheme."

Seeing that it was useless to continue, young Gaven went his way and Sir Barren continued with his way, and Locks' Loaves indeed continued to grow and prosper even further.

As the months went by, however, Gaven went to work on his "scheme." With the help of a local baker who was able to prepare a recipe that tasted just as good as Locks' Loaves, Gaven was able to prepare a plan and get counsel with the governor of Axon.

Suffice to say, it did not take much convincing to get the governor of Axon to give his full kingdom's support to helping Gaven start Axon's Loaves and they went about this on a rather grand scale. Within months they were in business, directly competing with Locks, at a price that was less expensive and with a flavor that was comparable in taste.

When Barren learned of this, he summoned his head bakers and with samples of Axon's loaves at hand, they proceeded to study the competition and form conclusions.

"Without doubt, they are selling some of their loaves in the kingdoms, but only to people who have saving a penny in mind," Baker One remarked.

"Most certainly, citizens of the kingdoms will try it out of curiosity, but no upstanding citizen would ever decide to switch forever to Axon over a proven product like Locks," Baker Two said.

"It's only a matter of time before they're out of business," Baker Three chided sarcastically.

(continued)

"They're just buying their way in, and can't keep the cheaper prices going forever," Sir Barren remarked.

In the end, they convinced themselves they really had nothing to worry about and proceeded with business as usual. In the meantime, Gaven was busy with ideas as to how to reduce wastes. He developed a process that allowed him to use batches faster by flowing the loaves, one after another to groups of workers who did pieces of work to the loaves, rather than each worker making an entire loaf as was the method in Locks. But he went even further. He made sure no worker started his portion on another loaf if he had one that had not been picked up by the next worker. He did this because he did not want workers building and stacking loaves that weren't ready to be used by the next worker in the line. This way he could ensure there would not be wasted loaves at the end of the day. He had learned, with the product being bread, that anything left to be finished tomorrow usually ended up in the scrap pile—something he could ill afford.

Later, one of the workers suggested that with this type of approach they did not need such large containers. They could produce and use the mix in much smaller batches, thus eliminating dealing with the hardening of the mix in the bottom of the pot.

One improvement built on another. One idea followed another and within a relatively short period of time Axon dropped the prices of its loaves even further and became the loaf of choice throughout the kingdoms.

As business began to decline substantially, Barren once again summoned his head bakers. What were they to do? Certainly, it was evident they could no longer keep everyone on, so they decided they must first reduce the work force. This was done, much to the chagrin of both the governor and the workers.

They further decided they had to cut prices to match Axon, and find ways to reduce cost and offset the impact of the price reductions on profits. They agreed that for some time they were going to have to operate at a loss in order to ensure there would be no further decline in share of the kingdom.

They decided they would hire an Axon baker to determine what Axon was doing to reduce prices. They did this, but when the baker told them what they had to do in order to compete with Axon, many of the head bakers scoffed at the suggestions. Get rid of their larger pots? How absurd. Have the workers build only a portion of a loaf? Indeed, in some cases, tell them to slow down? They did try a smaller mixing pot, but being unwilling to change the method in which workers made the loaves, they found the smaller pots simply did not function for them. There never seemed to be enough mix available when it was needed. They soon collectively convinced Barren that the newly hired baker was planted by Axon to lead them astray, and it was not long before he was released.

Further business declines followed for Locks, which were followed by further reductions in the work force. Employees at Locks became extremely unhappy, and they expended much time and energy in gossip and discussions about leadership or the lack thereof. Many had left and sold their farms to join Locks and now had nothing to return to. While the coffers of Locks had substantial funds from its many years of success, the governor was seeing them starting to dwindle rapidly. He took up the chant that the problem was with Sir Barren. He just wasn't foresighted enough. After all, it was he, the governor, who had to show Barren how to get the business started. Within a few short months, Barren was released and replaced.

A group of Axon workers had left the bakery to form their own group of "Show-Hows" and were spending time on the road teaching the principles of Axon to other businesses—and not necessarily to those in the bread business. Locks decided to hire the "Show-Hows." Business by now continued to slip rapidly and profits were slipping even faster. The work force was only half of what it had been at one time, and in many sections of the bakery, mixing pots sat idle, starting to rust away.

The Show-Hows tried desperately, but resistance was great. It was greatest among the head bakers, who simply could not accept the new way. But they did show compliance by making small changes in some areas of the shop so the work force could practice the new methods and become comfortable with them. Yet it was clear to the Show-Hows there was no intention on the part of the head bakers to make a complete and absolute change. When the head bakers scoffed at the suggestion of smaller pots and said, "We have tried that and it does not work for us," the Show-Hows, once alone, laughed among themselves and called the head bakers "Brick Heads." But Locks was paying them a decent wage for their service, so if that was the way Locks wanted to be then so be it.

Time marched on. Business at Locks continued to decline. Business at Axon continued to grow, and a day eventually came when all the workers at Axon were called together and informed that Locks' Loaves, the first and the original, had officially closed its doors.

The moral of the story? *Clinging diligently to practices of the past can often blind one to the requirements of the future!*

Finding the Damaging Mental Barriers

Of course all five mental barriers can be found in this legend. But when and how frequently did each of them occur? Let's take a little time to explore them a bit further.

- *Justification.* This barrier was at work when Barren told Gaven he could not spend the money required to do the things Gaven was suggesting because he had to expand his shop and needed any capital he might have available for that necessary task. Do you suppose that he would have taken a different position had he known at the time what he was later to discover?
- *Not invented here and done that before.* These two very destructive barriers were in place throughout. Remember the head bakers informing the Show-Hows, who were suggesting the use of smaller mixing pots, that "We've tried that and it just didn't work for us"? In every case both Barren and his head bakers aggressively fought (and mentally justified) any proposal aimed at changing the way things had always been done.
- *Don't rock the boat.* This damaging barrier came into play when the head bakers eventually complied regarding the use of smaller mixing pots, but only in a manner that didn't serve to effectively change the existing system of production.
- *It's not my job.* Do you not suppose the head bakers, at one point or another, discussed among themselves that they were there to cook and not to worry about the size of the pots and other so-called wastes, wastes they were now being asked to deal with? This damaging barrier is an insidious worm buried deep within the rot of the mass production system.

The person leading change in any organization that has enjoyed a minimal amount of success from its old system of production is going to be faced with these barriers to some degree or another. The person dealing with bringing dramatic (revolutionary) change to an organization that has enjoyed a *great* deal of success from its old system of production will generally see these barriers persistently raising their heads in a multitude of ways.

Therefore, leading change, especially significant change in the way a manufacturing operation goes about doing business inevitably boils down to a strong dedication to the task at hand and a willingness to be extremely persistent—at least until the results start to far outweigh the criticism directed at those managing the change. However, one should not fail to recognize that leadership is not a popularity contest, but rather the assigned task of bringing the kinds of things to a business that serve to make it more successful tomorrow than it is today.

Month One, Day Eight—Getting a Clearer Picture

Bob fidgeted with the edge of the folder he was holding as he listened to my opening comments. I had cleared my calendar so we had most of the morning, if required, to probe further into the matter he had brought to my attention the previous day.

"Bob, allow me to give you a quick overview of what I see, after only a very short time on the job. Then you can tell me if I'm on target or just all wet."

He nodded his approval, and I continued.

"To begin, we have to face the reality of the situation. This plant is in big trouble. It's losing market share. It hasn't operated anywhere close to budget for the last five years. It has a reputation of having a hard-nosed union. Let's not forget they took the factory out on a 13-week strike a few years back. Now, in addition to all that we're thousands of units behind schedule on the new CS series. That is more than enough for any management team to deal with. But regarding our management team, I'm already starting to have some serious concerns, especially after what I went through yesterday."

I paused briefly, then continued. "I met rather late yesterday afternoon with Ray, and he brought me up to speed on our scheduling policies. Gosh, do we ever need some change in that area. But he left me with the strong impression that more than one person on the staff was uncomfortable with my rather probing style and this is only a few days into the job."

I continued: "I have to understand what I'm dealing with here, and I don't have months before I start being a decision maker. If this were a simple transition of plant managers, I could afford to take more time, but it isn't. We have to get this operation back on track quickly, and that's going to call for doing things differently. I really need your take on all this."

"Would you be offended if I brought something up about your situation that does have an impact?" he asked.

"Of course not, go ahead."

"Please don't take this the wrong way, but everyone knows you're here in what has been defined as a temporary role. I hope it works out to be something permanent for you, but the question you need to ask yourself is

(continued)

just how much change you think you can effectively make under those conditions."

"So, you think I'm moving too fast, given that people view me as someone who might only be in this position for a short period of time?"

"To some degree, I suppose, but I must say there's no question some things need to change or we're going to continue the unfortunate slide we've been experiencing. The truth is people here are looking for strong leadership, and it appears you might be able to bring that. The question becomes how fast you can make it happen and what kind of support you can expect since most everyone sees you—at least at this time—as temporary."

He went further. "I probably don't have to say this, but you've got another small problem, and it rests with being from another division. You're seen as an outsider of sorts, so it's my guess you wouldn't get a lot of votes from the troops for a permanent slot ... if it ever came down to that."

"Fortunately, Bob, companies don't hold elections for leadership posts, and while I appreciate your candor, it just supports the fact there are two ways I can approach the situation. The first would be to *act* like an interim plant manager ... don't offend anyone, don't make waves, and hope I'll eventually be offered a full-time position. The other is to forget about that and act like a plant manager. I've chosen the latter, and that's the way I intend to operate. I may not have held the position before, but I know manufacturing, I've been a successful manager, I've proven I'm a good leader, and I know something about considering the big picture in getting things done. Now, with that in mind, I'd like to get back to what this meeting was intended to address."

"All right," he said, straightening in his seat. "Let's do it."

"Good," I replied.

We proceeded to discuss the management team and he gave me his "H.R." perspective on the various members of my staff, taking time to go over their background as he shifted through the personnel folders he had brought along. I made notes and asked questions where I felt it was appropriate, but for the most part he talked and I listened.

"Are they all that good?" I quizzed after we had gone over a performance rating profile on each of them.

"Look. I'm smart enough to know everyone is on trial here, including both of us. I've been here twelve years, but before I start giving you opinions about other people's performance, especially my peers, I have to prove to you that I'm someone you can trust."

"Thanks for recognizing that, Bob, but allow me to say I think we're making some reasonably good progress toward doing that today."

He smiled. "Thanks. That's good to know."

He then continued. "It's one of those things, again, where many managers and supervisors just don't feel comfortable facing up to serious performance problems. The end result is that subordinates sometimes get rated higher than they should, and problems outside of meeting clearly stated individual objectives are never fully addressed and resolved. One of the bigger issues is people who simply do not meet their stated objectives."

"I think it may be more a matter of the objectives themselves than the methods used in meeting them, but that's another story and we can address that later," I replied.

We shifted gears, getting into a discussion about the union. He brought me up to date on the latest labor contract, which had been negotiated only a few months prior to my coming aboard. He talked some about the current union leadership, his perception of their hot spots and the general feelings of the work force about union/management relationships. Essentially, in his judgment, the work force had been hardened against management; and the union leadership had proven they were "savvy" and not afraid to take management on, if and when they felt the need.

It was clear that I was facing some exceptional challenges. These included an operation that needed some fast change for the better, a work force that was displaying less and less confidence in management's general ability to lead, and a union that could be as tough as they come.

We ended the meeting with an agreement that Bob and I would spend more time together over the next few weeks to try to establish just how much flexibility we really had in structuring things for the better. As I was going to discover, I had absolutely no idea, at that time, of the number of challenges that lay ahead.

STEPS TO OVERCOMING OLD BARRIERS

The person leading significant change in a manufacturing operation is going to face both physical (system related) and mental (people related) obstacles. The key to success is:

1. Getting employees and others to both realize and buy in to the fact that without change the operation stands to gradually become less and less competitive. And, in addition, getting them to understand

that there indeed becomes a "competitive saturation point" where even the best of efforts will probably be too little, too late.

2. Getting employees to understand there really are no substantial barriers to change other than their own mental barriers. If employees can get past this, it is remarkable what they can achieve in a relatively short period of time.

How does one effectively go about doing this? Well, there are a number of ways, but one of the best is putting employees through training sessions exclusively focused on the subject matter. It works something like this:

1. Hire someone qualified to conduct the training, or if you have a full-time training manager, have this person put together a training package *for all employees* directed at the subject of mental barriers.

2. Start the training with an overview of the strengths of the operation and something about the competition (or just as important, the competition that has not yet arrived).

3. Use the Joel Barker paradigm tapes. This is an excellent tool in getting people's attention and setting the stage for addressing mental barriers.

4. Have the group go through an exercise noting everything they can think of as a barrier to making change for the better. Once this is done, have the group decide for each item (barrier) listed if it is a *physical* or a *mental* barrier.

5. Have the facilitator go through an exercise of addressing each barrier and helping the group decide if the barrier is how they initially viewed it (physical versus mental).

The group will usually insist that most of the barriers are physical, in other words, beyond their power to influence. A good facilitator will lead them out of that impression and help them recognize that most, if not all, barriers are actually mental. Something that almost always shows up on the employees' list is the lack of expense and capital required to get the job done. The group usually sees these as physical barriers. The company, in their judgment, will not allow the expense and since any capital required would in all likelihood be out of plan, this becomes a physical barrier. The talented facilitator will get the group to recognize that money is usually available, given decent justification for the expenditure. Since achieving this justification is associated with salesmanship, the group then comes to recognize this is, if anything, a mental rather than a physical barrier.

Who the Heck Is Management?

Lack of management support is usually one of the first barriers that end up on any group's list. Employees almost always perceive this as a barrier, regardless of the situation. I also believe it just so happens that this barrier is an easy one to throw out because it is generic in nature. This particular issue sets up one of my favorite group exercises, which I call, "Who the heck is management?" Allow me to give you a brief synopsis as to how this works.

I start with examining the bottom of the ranks and ask the group to help me determine who they view as management, and then proceed to work my way up to the top of the organization (see Figure 3-1). Starting with the operator on the shop floor, I ask: "Who do these employees truly see as their management?" The instant reply is usually their supervisor. I write this down on a flip chart, then ask: "Who does the supervisor see as management?" We eventually identify this as their direct

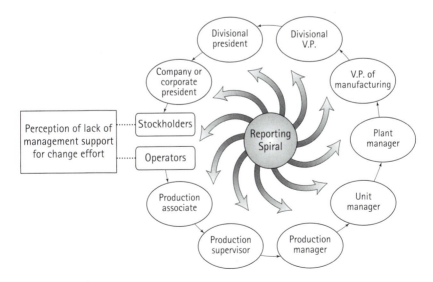

Figure 3-1. Who the Heck Is Management?

boss, usually the production manager or superintendent. I draw an arrow from the operator to the supervisor and another from the supervisor to the production manager, and then continue doing this as other positions are listed.

Following notation of the production manager, I then ask who these people see as management and what's usually established is that it's a person on the plant manager's staff of direct reports. I then continue from there up the chain, through the plant manager and various corporate positions until we have worked our way up to the president of the company. The question is then asked: "Who does the president see as management?" Surprisingly, perhaps, many employees see management terminating at the president level. But then it is quickly pointed out that if nothing else, the president sees stockholders as management. You finally ask the question: "And who do the stockholders see as management?" Of course, we now come to the end of the spiral, and end up where we started because the stockholders can also view, like many employees, that the resistance to change stems from a total lack of management support. This is very common, especially during bad times when the need for change is really necessary.

This exercise vividly points out that the perception of who's actually in charge of any particular situation—especially any change initiative that can substantially improve an operation—is gray, to say the least. This perception is strengthened during the exercise by asking the following questions: "We currently operate in a batch mode. Who, if anyone, actually demanded that we operate in this manner? Was it the president of the company? The answer is no and that we in manufacturing decided to operate in this fashion. So if we decided this, can we not decide to change? The answer is yes. However, regardless of the particular approach you take the point is to get the work force's attention to the need for change and that change is within their power, given they understand why and are willing to try to make it work.

This chapter has highlighted some of the old barriers facing those working to change their operation from an obsolete method of mass manufacturing to world class, waste-free manufacturing. We have concentrated on various barriers and ways to deal with them, but of course, there is no cookbook to cover every possible challenge. But a better understanding as to the things the leader and the work force must deal with will make the task of removing these obstacles somewhat easier. In the next chapter we will deal with the principles that drive such an effort. Without well established and deep rooted principles that the work force can understand, accept, and adhere to, your change effort will have no definite focus and will realize little success.

Revolutionary Pointers

- It would be much easier for U.S. manufacturers to accept the need for total change in the manufacturing arena if they saw their enemy as their *system of production.*

- The leader needs to be cognizant and prepared to handle the many system obstacles—old barriers—that will inevitably surface during the change effort. These old barriers usually center around creating policy for earned hours to establish labor costs, quality measurements, economic lot sizing, and indirect labor costs.

- System barriers are minor in comparison to the mental barriers that bar the way to changing the existing system of production. The five most damaging are: justification, not invented here, done that before, don't rock the boat, and it's not my job.

- Before you can significantly change a manufacturing operation you will have to overcome and remove these system and mental barriers. Along the way you will be faced with a great deal of criticism. But leading change is not a popularity contest. It boils down to a strong dedication to the task at hand and a willingness to be persistent.

- Like employees, stockholders often hold the view that resistance to change stems from a lack of management support. But who's actually in charge of any particular situation—especially any change initiative—is not always recognized. This is one of the few mental barriers to change that you can usually easily overcome.

4

Waste-Free Manufacturing–
Changing the Rules

TODAY, THERE IS A SET of new manufacturing principles that are key to eliminating wastes and achieving and maintaining global manufacturing competitiveness. Toyota, seen as the father of these manufacturing principles, adheres to three key principles, which serve as the foundation for its Toyota Production System (TPS). These are:

1. Takt time
2. One-piece flow
3. Pull production

Waste-free manufacturing (WFM) uses four principles or what I refer to as *drivers* to help companies become world class manufacturers in a very rapid manner. But before outlining these I want to make a flat statement that may astound many who are currently working in the field:

> Although the principles of the TPS were unquestionably effective for the time frame, approach, and culture under which they were developed and utilized, they are far too complex and much too difficult for most U.S.-based manufacturers to adopt and implement in a relatively short period of time.

If there is any truth whatsoever to the preceding statement, this leaves two clear choices. One is to accept the major difficulties (and length of time) required to follow the principles of the TPS to become a world class manufacturer. The other is to devise a way of moving more rapidly to world class manufacturing.

I am convinced that U.S. manufacturers have no other choice but to do the latter and the key lies in understanding that *the issue is not whether a plant installs one-piece flow, takt time, and pull production—we know these are important—it is knowing* when *to implement them.* For U.S. manufacturers there are important conditioning steps a factory must go through first before it can systematically apply and accept the concepts and tools of TPS. This requires a totally new focus than what we have been hearing from JIT consultants/gurus since the 1980s. What U.S. manufacturers need is a new set of manufacturing principles—a new model that is in sync with our times and culture. And it must be a system that can move a factory as fast as possible to a waste-free environment. I call this new method the *rapid deployment of waste-free manufacturing.*

Even insinuating that you must change the established rules of the game will be viewed by many JIT purists as sacrilegious. But rules do change. Evolution does happen and adaptation (change) is one of the rules. To understand that changing the rules doesn't mean changing the name of the game we can look at a couple of the rule changes that have occurred in the sports world. James Naismith, the father of basketball, may not have rolled over in his grave when someone first brought up the idea of the three-point shot, but many purists in the sport had great difficulty accepting it. It has since proven to be the great equalizer, because it has allowed teams without tremendous height to be competitive. Football purists initially went into shock when the NFL installed the two-point conversion, but mathematically it has increased the number of ways a game can be won or tied.

It is no different with the needed change to the fundamental principles surrounding the deployment of waste-free manufacturing. What worked in one era or culture may not apply to the current demands or situation. Currently there are many U.S. companies that need a way to change quickly if they are even to survive. Specifically, they need a set of new rules (approach) to give them an edge in moving from conventional batch manufacturing to waste-free manufacturing, because what they are doing today is neither fast enough nor effective enough to get them aboard the lean manufacturing revolution. The United States is lagging and we need to introduce a three-pointer or a two-point conversion to give us a better chance of catching up with the competition.

FOUR KEY DRIVERS FOR WASTE-FREE MANUFACTURING

In changing the rules I've created four drivers to help companies rapidly deploy waste-free manufacturing. To better understand them I will discuss the similarities and differences between these drivers and the three principles noted for the TPS. The four drivers for WFM and what I call the *compressed production system* are:

- Driver one: Workplace organization
- Driver two: Uninterrupted Flow
- Driver three: Error-free processing
- Driver four: Insignificant changeover

Although similar sounding to the basic JIT tools created by Japanese manufacturers, each of these drivers is utilized quite differently in WFM. Using a compressed production system, the rapid deployment approach provides the steps for a much faster insertion of the overall JIT process. This chapter provides a brief definition of these four drivers. In Chapter 5 we will explore the compressed production system and provide an in-depth examination of these drivers that will further show the differences in approach between TPS and WFM.

Driver One: Workplace Organization

As you will see in the "Ten-Step Road Map" and in the "Continuous Improvement Pyramid" discussed later in this work, workplace organization (WPO) is the foundation for establishing and maintaining a waste-free manufacturing environment. Additionally, it is the driver that will yield the single greatest return on investment. For now it is important to understand that WPO means more than cleaning the floor, neatly arranging things, and painting equipment. In practice, it involves an extremely disciplined approach for the organization of literally everything that touches the shop floor.

Driver Two: Uninterrupted Flow

Uninterrupted flow (U-flow) ensures that the entire process of manufacturing is performed in a manner that has fewest breaks possible throughout the entire processing cycle. Striving for one-piece flow, the

JIT way, is an admirable goal but I do not consider it a *driving* principle in WFM. Concentrating too much on this distracts from a much more important objective—to place as many pieces of support equipment as close as physically possible to (or in) the final assembly process and to produce in a flow that has the fewest number of interruptions possible.

When a manufacturing firm tries to adopt the key principles of TPS and waits until it has one-piece flow in place before it moves to the next process, it will usually find that the barriers of the existing mass production system will not allow enforcement of the overall process. In truth, you can work to eliminate disruptions in flow in a batch environment. And, as more and more of this is successfully accomplished, reducing the number of pieces in the flow between operations becomes much easier to do.

An interruption in flow is any occurrence in the production process that requires parts, assemblies, or components to *stop* before they can be completed. The better an operation flows in an uninterrupted manner, the fewer parts required in the overall work-in-process chain. The fewer parts required in the chain, the less scrap, rework, and obsolescence required. When you've done enough to eliminate disruptions in flow, one-piece flow becomes a result of the process. *Applying this driver is an extremely important step in the journey to a waste-free environment.*

Driver Three: Error-Free Processing

Errors are very common in manufacturing. You can often attribute these to operator fatigue or lack of attention, or because equipment has not been engineered to fully eliminate mistakes. If we think hard about the typical wastes in manufacturing, we will find a path that leads us directly back to the people, machines, equipment, and facilities used. However, the mass production system tends to cover up big problems and, as a result, these problems are often never recognized for what they really are—*hidden wastes.*

The error-free processing driver deals with putting appropriate controls in place in every process that allow a factory to achieve an advanced level of waste reduction. As the Japanese often aptly advise: "Inventory is the root of all evil." Enough inventory in the system and the need to address and resolve hidden waste becomes unimportant. Take the inventory out and these begin to serve as tremendous roadblocks to plant throughput. The scope of error-free processing involves a concerted effort directed at eradicating recurring process problems and/or those problems that can potentially develop because methods, tooling, and fixturing have not been engineered to fully and completely produce in an error-free manner.

Driver Four: Insignificant Changeover

Changeover (frequently called *setup*) is probably the most sizable waste in conventional manufacturing. Additionally, it is one of the more shameful, because it is one of the easiest to address and resolve. The insignificant changeover driver strives to make the work required in changing from one part (or product) to another so insignificant that it plays no role in the decision-making process. In other words, it covers so small a segment of time that it is absolutely no factor in the total lead-time required to produce.

Japanese manufacturers (and in particular those using TPS) ignore the issue of changeover in their cycle and lead time formulas. This implies changeover of equipment and processing has already been eliminated or has been engineered to a level so small it is of no significance. In the United States we simply cannot make the assumption that manufacturing engineers and others will attack changeover with the same zeal that Toyota has obviously done. Therefore, we must make it a driving principle.

By definition, changeover is the time for *all* activities that occur between the last piece produced (for a given part, component, or finished product) and the first *good* piece produced for the next part, component, or finished unit. Ideally, changeover in any process in the factory would be little more than a simple push of a button. In most cases you cannot fully accomplish this at the offset of pursuing a significant reduction in changeover time. Regardless of current conditions, with the application of the proper tools and techniques, you can most often reduce changeover to a matter of minutes. Japanese manufacturers call this approach SMED (Single Minute Exchange of Dies), but you can use the techniques employed in any manufacturing process and they are in no way limited to equipment that utilizes dies and fixturing (machining processes, power punch presses, etc.).

SOME VERY IMPORTANT DIFFERENCES BETWEEN WFM AND TPS

So what are differences between the principles outlined for TPS and the drivers for WFM, other than perhaps the number of drivers (four vs. three)? Though the two production systems are covering some of the same territory it is the *approach* that makes the biggest difference.

First, there is no reference in the WFM drivers to takt time. This is because under the new drivers it becomes a tool rather than a guiding or driving principle. However, just in case anyone is wondering if I am so bold as to imply takt time may or may not be utilized, depending on circumstances, the answer is an emphatic yes.

Takt time is a means of displaying customer requirements in terms of time, rather than the usual method of expressing those requirements in volume. The theory is that operators and others can relate to this approach much better. Additionally, takt time serves as a gage or marker in the utilization of what the Japanese manufacturers call *standard work*. I will cover standard work in some detail later, but it is an attempt to simplify scientific work measurement to a point where *anyone* can perform it, given a few hours training. While this is admirable, it simply is not very practical. The fallacy of standard work is that it boldly ignores performance rating, which has to do with operator skill, effort, and/or work pace, and suggests that regardless of the cycle time an operator gives a person conducting work measurement, it should be considered a normal (good) time. This is like saying: Trust a race horse to give you an adequate (or average) performance whenever you may decide to casually proceed to the track with a stopwatch in hand.

I also do not mention pull production and one-piece flow as specific principles in the rapid deployment of waste-free manufacturing. That's because these become tools (based on certain conditions) for the implementation of WFM. A better understanding of these drivers and how they support the rapid insertion of WFM will become much clearer as we proceed through the course of this work. Right now let's take a look at some of the tools that support WFM.

TOOL BOXES TO SUPPORT THE FOUR KEY DRIVERS

Figure 4-1 represents the four key drivers and a tool box of techniques that apply to each driver. The tools listed in each respective tool box are not intended to represent every possible technique that can or should be applied in order to effectively deploy a given driver. However, all those listed should definitely be utilized in pursuit of the particular WFM driver noted.

I will address each of the specific tools, to one degree or another, throughout the course of this book. If you need to learn more about these techniques (tools) I highly recommend you check out the numerous

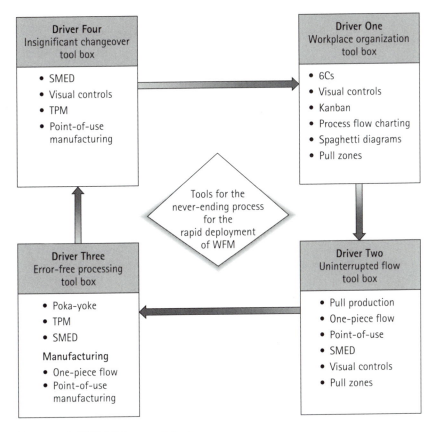

Figure 4-1. WFM Drivers and Tools

instructional works and books on the market. Also there are seminars and the like that can further your education on the application of these tools and techniques. The WFM tools I'll be discussing in this book are:

- Kanban
- Poka-yoke
- SMED
- Process flow charting
- Spaghetti diagrams
- TPM
- Visual controls (Andon)
- Pull production
- Point-of-use manufacturing

I will be providing some very specific instructions regarding two other tools:

- 6C
- Pull zones (supermarkets)

6C replaces the TPS 5S approach. Pull zones are another special technique I have effectively modified in operating what is usually referred to as supermarkets. In Chapter 5 I'll be addressing all of these tools separately. But since 6C and supermarkets require some special notations, I'll briefly describe them now.

Steps and Levels for 6C

Toyota uses what is referred to as 5S. Over the years there have been various translations of the S's in the 5S system. Below I provide two.

• Sort	• Sort
• Set in order	• Straighten
• Shine	• Sweep
• Standardize	• Sanitize
• Sustain	• Sustain

The 5S tool is specifically designed to help establish effective organization of tools, equipment, etc., and to ensure a neat, clean, and orderly work area. What I have found is that many manufacturers in both North and Latin America, as well as Europe have a difficult time associating with the definitions of 5S and putting an effective scoring or measurement system in place that clearly defines where an operation stands in the process. Plus, I believe that with good workplace organization there is an important step that is not included in 5S. Therefore, these two factors led me to devise 6C (see Table 4-1).

Whereas 5S tends to be used as a group of things to do, with no special order as to which is prescribed first, second, or third other than what might be assumed, the steps and levels noted are an extremely important factor in applying 6C. Unlike 5S, the scoring approach is absolutely critical for determining the effectiveness of each of 6C's steps. What you typically do with 5S is go through a checklist of approximately 50 items, rating each on a scale of 1 to 5. You then establish a base score by taking the sum of the ratings for each item on the checklist and dividing it by 50. What often happens is that the particular area of the plant being examined is good enough in certain categories that a bottom line, composite score of, say, 2.5 (on a scale of 1–5) is established. This can be very misleading, for in essence it is saying the area examined is already *half as good as it needs to be.* Usually, nothing could be further from the truth.

For any plant or operation that has not gone through the process of putting true workplace organization in place, the initial 6C score will always be *zero.* That is correct, zero! Therefore, imagine how a group charged with this task would perceive the job that lay ahead if they were looking at a score of 0 as opposed to 2.5.—obviously, with a greater sense of urgency.

Why do I take the position that your 6C score will always be zero when you go through the checklist and analyze an area for the first time?

Table 4-1. 6C Steps and Levels

Step one	Clear	Level I
Step two	Confine	Level II
Step three	Control	Level III
Step four	Clean	Level IV
Step five	Communicate	Level V
Step six	Continue	Level VI

Because I believe the process is a series of steps and not just separate activities that can be performed at the whim of whomever is charged with the task of workplace organization. In other words, there is a definite time and place to "shine" or in the case of 6C to "clean." In either case there are definitely other things you must accomplish before you take this step.

In Chapter 5, I discuss achieving workplace organization through staircasing 6C. The point is that the process should be a very disciplined, step-by-step effort, rather than something resembling a scatter-gun approach. Most important is coming to understand and accept that in order to make this a lasting initiative a plant must learn to take one step at a time, in a very precise order. Like climbing a staircase in a careful, adult manner this requires firmly hitting each step and taking caution against trying to leap over one or two steps in an effort to hurry to the top. The latter, of course, can sometimes result in a serious and injurious fall (see Figure 4-2).

I have found that staircasing 6C is much easier for employees to understand than 5S, and that it is more effective in getting the job done in a meaningful and expedient manner. From a measurement stand-point when the first step is fully completed, an area would then achieve a level I rating. The next objective would be to do what is necessary to carry the area to a level II, then to level III and so on up the staircase. This helps provide focus and further helps the group working on such an initiative to clearly understand what to do first, as well as last.

Pull Zones Rather Than Supermarkets

Chapter 5 details the when, where, and how relating to pull zones, but as with 6C, I want to point out a major difference in approach in the use of

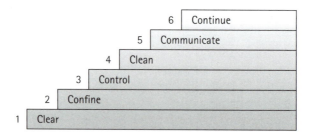

Figure 4-2. Staircasing the 6C

this tool as opposed to standard JIT manufacturing. The purpose of supermarkets as applied by most consultants in the field is a means of setting up a pull system where material (both purchased and fabricated) is staged very close to the final assembly process. The intent is for each operator in the process to go to the supermarket and pull only what they need, as needed. Theoretically, this sets up the principles of pull production, even in a factory that is currently operating in a batch production mode. And, again theoretically, this starts to help condition employees, managers, and others to a pull system of production. This is great in theory, but it's not very practical in approach. Here is what usually happens.

Batch manufacturing production systems most often have material handlers. It is the job of material handlers to pick material, as projected by the order system and schedules in place, and to carry (or push) material onto the next operation. Operators, in most cases, are not used to stopping production work and being mini-material handlers. Production supervisors are not conditioned to this approach either, and usually are not inclined to let the line operators stop what they are doing to get material. The end result most often is that management relents and places a storekeeper in charge of the supermarket. This person is most often one of the previous material handlers. In essence, what then happens is that nothing really changes, other than perhaps increasing indirect labor support due to now having another inventory staging area in the factory to manage and control.

There is a time and place for supermarkets, without question. In fact, I contend that without some type of similar approach, a factory cannot truly become waste free. But, again, you must take care as to when and how this is accomplished. Further, the title *supermarkets* sounds almost humorous to most workers in U.S. factories. It just isn't something most U.S. workers associate with serious business. During training they, of course, come to understand that it was derived through the Japanese fascination with U.S. supermarkets.

It works like this: A customer goes to the supermarket, picks up the goods (food and such) they need and then checks out. As the purchase (or pull) is noted at the cashier counter an electronic flag is raised noting to resupply or restock at a certain point, depending on the level of inventory the store chooses to keep on the shelf. Simple, straightforward, and effective.

This observance led to a brilliant idea by Japanese manufacturers. Why not run a manufacturing operation in somewhat the same manner by having operators control inventory by pulling only what they need, when it is needed, rather than having someone push inventory on them? In turn, create levels (kanbans) as to when to resupply or restock inventory, always keeping it as "lean" as possible and supplied on a "just in time" basis. And with some adaptation for a manufacturing firm (rather than a supermarket) this approach came to work very well for them.

But given all this, the average U.S. worker still has a hard time relating to something on a manufacturing shop floor called a supermarket because, after all, the supermarket is a place they've gone to since they were a child to pick up food and household goods. However, while they may have difficulty relating to a supermarket in a factory, with proper training they can very easily relate to *pull zones*, which apply the basic concepts and techniques of supermarkets.

A pull zone is a place with a clearly established level of inventory and it essentially begins the process of eliminating *all* centralized stores areas in the factory to the point that material is brought, in the smallest quantities possible, directly to the point of use without any intermediate storage. In Chapter 5 we'll discuss the details of establishing, running, and maintaining pull zones. You will see how through the use of the four new drivers and pull zones, you will be able to derive all the benefits of WFM.

Month Seven—Not So World Class

Prior to my tenure as plant manager, a decision had been made to invest a large sum of money in a world class manufacturing process for one of our premium product series. It was designed to flow the production of products through a series of highly automated processes. The line itself wound in a serpentine fashion throughout a rather large portion of the factory, with supporting equipment and facilities built into and/or adjacent to the main line. On the surface it was a very impressive facility, but in reality, it had some major problems that made it a production nightmare.

I had asked Ken, my production manager, and his engineers to take me through a detailed tour of the process, and had scheduled the entire afternoon. I wanted to carefully examine each station on the line to better understand how the process was designed to function, and to get a feel for the reason we were experiencing some serious throughput problems. These problems were leaving our customers very unhappy, creating added expense for the factory, and establishing the need for excessive overtime.

I was weary of hearing it was only going to be a matter of time before all the bugs were worked out, and decided if I was going to be held ultimately responsible for the delivery of products off the line, I needed to have a much better understanding of the entire process. I was not totally unfamiliar with it. I had, in fact, spent quite some time walking through, conversing with supervisors, operators, and others—but there was much I did not know, and I intended to correct this lack of knowledge.

Ken and I were accompanied on the special tour by his chief manufacturing engineer, Martin, and the foreman of the first shift operation, Darrell. I asked that we begin at the head of the line, which was an automated series of interconnecting processes that not only blanked but pierced and fully formed the casing for the unit. After allowing Darrell and Martin to give me the particulars, I asked them why the process seemed to have so much downtime.

"Actually," Martin replied, "it doesn't have that much downtime."

"It doesn't?" I responded. "It seems like a lot to me. The last report I looked at indicated we were down almost 50 percent of the time."

"It isn't the process," responded Martin, "it's the material."

"Tell me more," I requested.

"Actually, it's a long story, but in essence the material we used to prove the process was very expensive, so after we started production the purchasing department was able to find another supplier who offered a cheaper cost per pound. The problem has been our new supplier has had difficulties with consistency in material thickness."

"So, what are we doing about it?"

"Doing about it?"

"Yes. What's purchasing doing about it?"

"I have no idea," he replied.

I looked at Ken who had been standing to one side listening to the conversation.

"I've been fighting a running battle on this," he responded.

"Excuse me, Ken, but why didn't you let me know?" I asked.

He paused before answering, "I don't make a practice of running every production problem up the flagpole."

"Little problems I can understand, Ken, but this looks more like a major problem to me."

(continued)

Ken smiled and chuckled just a bit, and then following his lead the other two joined in as if silently understanding a common point, with some obvious humor in it. Ken then explained: "We're laughing because we've just started the tour and have only scratched the surface on the problems we're experiencing on this line. You're going to find a lot more as you get further into it."

"I hope not," I said.

"Believe me, you will," he reflected as we moved on.

I was next to irate by the time we finished. It seemed at almost every station there was one problem or another. First it was with material, then product design, then equipment, then maintenance, then people—and/or some combination thereof. What was especially disturbing to me was that I had to request a special tour of the process in order to get the problems surfaced. Ken was starting to feel my frustrations before the tour was over. My guess was, he was happy it was coming to an end.

WHERE TO BEGIN—UNDERSTANDING THE HIDDEN WASTES

Conventional wisdom typically identifies manufacturing wastes in terms of scrap, rework, and obsolescence. Things such as equipment downtime (due to long setup and changeover requirements, or because equipment repeatedly breaks down) are usually seen as standard operating inefficiencies—inefficiencies companies feel obligated to pass on to the customer as the cost of doing business.

What conventional mass manufacturers see as wastes are actually a *result* of the production system itself, but more about that later. It is the manufacturing wastes that are not so obvious that are costing many U.S. companies a rightful place within the ranks of globally competitive manufacturers. These are the *hidden wastes*. They are hidden because mass producing manufacturers are simply blind to them. In fact, they are so accustomed to these wastes that those working in and around them most often perceive them as being normal. In reality, they are a sign of a dysfunctional factory.

I believe that many companies who have started a lean manufacturing initiative and are using words and phrases such as *poka-yoke, kanban, SMED, takt time, one-piece flow* and the like are distracting the average U.S. worker from the real purpose of such an effort. The purpose, simply put, is to enlist the work force in driving *wastes* out of an operation. To achieve this, first and foremost, the work force must clearly understand what to look for. The true goal is not to implement single-minute exchange of dies (SMED) or to insert kanban or any of the other tools typically used in the process. Again, the goal is to make an operation as waste free as possible.

You can liken what is occurring in many manufacturing firms to teaching someone who knows nothing about sports how to kick a football without providing the understanding that in the end, the primary objective is to kick the ball over the crossbar between the two posts in a game called football. Becoming the best kicker in the world without understanding the whole game, or where and when to kick to make it count, falls far short of making the person an NFL-caliber football player.

Working at having the very best application of kanban, for example, without a good understanding as to how, where, when, and why this should be applied, makes the mission the implementation of kanban rather than the elimination of wastes. The truth is, I have seen factories become so obsessed with kanban that their entire focus filtered to this, while wastes continued to run rampant throughout their facility.

The key, again, is to help the work force clearly understand and begin to see wastes through a commonsense approach designed to help them analyze each and every possible form of waste—without all the fancy bells and whistles that are typically used in such an effort. A method I use for achieving this centers on having a group of managers and/or employees make a tour of an area in the plant (or the plant as a whole), and to make both observations and notations based on the following set of waste-finding questions (see Table 4-2).

Once you've answered these questions, which usually does not require more than a couple of hours, at most, have the group report findings. I assure you, they will have identified many wastes. It is usually very easy for the members of the work force selected for this exercise to both see and understand something that is making their operation inefficient. You should repeat this type of exercise until every employee in the plant has an opportunity to find and analyze wastes. Once you fully accomplish this, the work force can more easily relate to how tools such as kanban or poka-yoke can and should be applied. Most important, based on their own waste analysis, it will help

Table 4–2. The Hidden Wastes Checklist

		Finding Hidden Wastes in a Work Area
Yes	No	
☐	☐	1. Is there a place for everything and is everything in its place?
☐	☐	2. Is inventory sitting idle in the shop, not being immediately utilized?
☐	☐	3. Are there visual aids/controls in each process that identify how the operation should be performed, that limit production volumes to what is needed by the next operation in the chain, and that provide operators with clear, precise operating instructions?
☐	☐	4. Are there devices on equipment that eliminate the chance of production and/or assembly errors?
☐	☐	5. Are only a few minutes spent, in any process, to set up or change over the equipment?
☐	☐	6. Is a pull system used for the movement and control of material and components?
☐	☐	7. Have preventive maintenance procedures been established for all equipment that clearly identify operator obligations to the process?
☐	☐	8. Are there owner-operators for key equipment and procedures?
☐	☐	9. Is there any scrap, rework, or obsolescence?
☐	☐	10. Does the workload of all operators appear to be about equal?

them determine which tools they should apply first, second, and third (prioritization) and which tools would be of the least benefit at that particular time.

The Connection Between Hidden Wastes and World Class Manufacturing

To help you understand how these questions uncover *real wastes* and how it affects your pursuit of applying the principles, concepts, and techniques of world class manufacturing, I'll go over each of the 10 questions for finding hidden waste.

> 1. *Is there a place for everything and is everything in its place?* I have already addressed workplace organization as one of the four

drivers of WFM. In Chapter 5 under "How to Begin Implementing WPO," I'll further discuss the wastes associated with not having a place for everything and everything in its place.

2. *Is inventory sitting idle on the shop floor, not being immediately utilized?* Most Japanese manufacturers see inventory as the root of all evil. It is quite visible to employees within organizations, such as Toyota, that a plant with inventory that is not being immediately used is almost a shocking waste. However, this is usually hidden in the eyes of employees and managers who are used to seeing large batches of parts produced and stored, often for excessive periods of time. Thus, the wastes associated with not fully resolving question one are the wastes of overproducing.

   As a result of overproduction, scrap and rework always occur, the production associate's time is not utilized effectively in meeting customer demand, and you incur carrying costs for unneeded inventory. Plus, quite often you must then use over-time to produce something that is not immediately needed—to point out just a few of the more common wastes created with overproduction.

3. *Are there visual aids/controls in each process that identify how the operation should be performed, that limit production volumes to what is needed by the next operation in the chain, and that provide operators with clear, precise operating instructions?* The wastes associated with a lack of appropriate visual controls may not be as obvious as the waste of overproduction, but much time and effort is wasted by employees when they do not clearly understand what is expected of them—in terms of the job to be done. This is not meant to imply that large volumes of written text should be given to each operator. As a simple guide, operator instructions should be at least 90 percent visual in nature.

4. *Are there devices on equipment that eliminate the chance of production and/or assembly errors?* Equipment devices designed to eliminate mistakes guard against the wastes associated with producing defective parts, assemblies, and components and, thus, the potential of scrap or rework.

5. *Are only a few minutes spent, in any process, to set up or change over the equipment?* Setup and changeover requiring anything other than only a few minutes create wastes in the form of under-utilizing an employee's time, and adding absolutely unnecessary costs to the products due to gross inefficiency in the operation.

6. *Is a pull system used for the movement and control of material and components?* Knowing if a pull system of production exists relates to the wastes associated with batching and pushing material through the factory versus a flow that calls for material as required and in the exact quantities needed. Obviously, with this type of approach there is absolutely no room for defective parts or materials, thus the requirement to fully address and resolve any inherent quality problems and/or issues within the process.

7. *Have preventive maintenance procedures been established for all equipment that clearly identify operator obligations to the process?* Maintenance procedures that call for active involvement of the operator (generally termed TPM, total productive maintenance) help drive out the wastes of equipment downtime by doing the kinds of things that serve to keep the equipment well maintained and operative—at all times.

8. *Are there owner-operators for key equipment and procedures?* Owner-operators are employees who have the ability to do more than simply run parts. They, in essence, own the equipment and have a well-defined set of tasks and responsibilities. The concept of owner-operators is discussed in more detail later and will provide a better understanding as to the type of wastes this approach was designed to eliminate.

9. *Is there any scrap, rework, or obsolescence?* Any scrap, rework, or obsolescence is a waste that most workers can understand without extensive explanation. The key becomes assuring the work force that this is no longer acceptable and that every effort will be made to insert the kind of initiatives (tools) that help to drive most, if not all, of these considerable wastes out of the operation.

10. *Does the workload of all operators appear to be about equal?* If the workload between employees is not about equal the waste is the inherent loss of balance and the inefficiencies this seems to create. Efforts have to be applied (and tools are available) to balance work as equally as possible between operations.

There is one other subject I will briefly address regarding hidden wastes. In a typical mass manufacturing operation an interesting mindset exists when it comes to making a gain on the competition. It is that any win must come in quantum leaps, and that the one key factor in doing this is through huge capital investments in so-called leading technology. The facts are that a considerable amount of the expensive showcase equipment in U.S. industry should be thrown out and replaced with much simpler production processing. Much of this expensive technology does little to assist in eliminating wastes and in some cases actually creates additional wastes, because the people who specify the equipment are blinded by a conventional wisdom that prevents them from understanding what hidden wastes really are.

THE NEED FOR NEVER-ENDING IMPROVEMENT

If you ever hope to make continuous improvement a lasting process you need to make sure that all employees understand it as a journey with no end and that they need to be fully involved and substantially empowered. Additionally, you cannot have employees who proceed to make the right kind of improvement, unless there is a clear understanding of the wastes they should concentrate on eliminating. On the other hand it is impossible to reach a final pinnacle and thus, the objective becomes helping your employees to understand that each day is an opportunity for just another step in the right direction.

Unfortunately, while U.S. companies are daily launching new programs for continuous improvement, there are just as many programs gasping their last breath, and once again disappointing all those involved. This is why you must view continuous improvement as a process for survival—not a program—one that employees come to accept as a challenging task that is never ending. This underlines the point that the mind-set of lean manufacturers is exactly at the opposite end of the spectrum from mass manufacturers and it will take a total change in the conventional mind-set to move from batch processing to world class manufacturing. Without lean thinking you will continue to go from one floundering program to another. This is not meant to imply that lean manufacturers are more adept or dedicated than mass manufacturers, only that they see things very differently.

The continuous improvement cycle mass manufacturers need to institute does not evolve around installing new and expensive production equipment, but rather around deploying continuous improvement to their existing processes. Over time this approach begins to change the face of the factory—and the way you think about production itself. Your thrust is to continually strive to enhance product quality and customer satisfaction through a collection of small, yet powerful changes—the kind that center on the *total elimination of wastes.*

Becoming Knowledgeable in the Lean Tools and Techniques

What could be running through a person's mind at this point who has had little or no exposure to lean manufacturing? It should be: How do I go about learning more about these lean tools and techniques? Well, there are countless books, seminars, and consulting services available that deal with how-to, all of which are primarily based on the utilization of the basic principles and tools established in the TPS. There is also bountiful information and professional services available regarding how to deploy specific tools such as kanban, SMED, poka-yoke, and TPM. I strongly urge you to use this information and the professional services to learn more about the process. But, take care against getting yourself locked into any process until you learn about the *rapid deployment* of the process itself. Return to the first page of this chapter and reread what I consider to be a very important statement regarding implementing these processes.

For the person who has had little exposure to the principles, concepts, and techniques discussed in this chapter but who is already itching to seize the opportunity to begin the change process, I offer the following advice:

1. Find out all you can about what is currently going on with the different approaches being used in lean manufacturing—about the tools, techniques, and results (or lack thereof) that other operations have experienced.

2. Hire a good consultant in the field. Have this person(s) teach you and your people about lean manufacturing, the applied tools, various approaches to continuous improvement, etc.

3. Try your utmost to become the best expert in your unit, especially if you are the leader. The leader, of all people, needs to become very knowledgeable.

4. Don't try to become "lean" by purchasing the expertise and turn the responsibility entirely over to others. Remember, the change process will ultimately come back to you and your staff to construct, lead, and implement.

In Chapter 6, under "The Ten-Step Road Map for the Rapid Deployment of WFM," I discuss the details of how the plant manager and his or her staff need to be first to learn about the tools, concepts and techniques of WFM. This road map is specifically designed to give you an effective step-by-step approach to implementing WFM. I can guarantee you that it works—without exception.

As you begin identifying waste and deploying WFM you'll find that the tools and techniques specified for each step are very common-sense oriented and very easy to use. SMED may sound strange and foreign, even somewhat technical (you definitely won't find it listed in Webster's), but in essence it consists of nothing more than using a simple set of procedures that are constructed to measure setup and/or changeover. This requires that you understand what is actually happening by observing and making some notations during an actual setup. Following this, you apply some basic logic to reduce the overall time required.

Just as applying SMED doesn't take an engineering degree, those other terms that may sound a little foreign, like poka-yoke, TPM and kanban, will be equally easy to learn and not hard to apply. Actually, as we proceed, the tools and techniques will become the easy part. It's getting people to fully buy in—to change their thinking—that is the difficult part.

THE ULTIMATE CHALLENGE FACING U.S. MANUFACTURERS

Assuming your company buys into the need for changing its system of production your ultimate challenge will not be learning how to use the tools of lean manufacturing nor applying them on the shop floor and in the office arena. The ultimate challenge will be:

- Fully convincing senior management of the company of the need to make this the absolute top priority.
- Learning how to go about the job of implementation in an effective manner and, most important, understanding how to deal with the things no textbook on the subject, until this one, has addressed.

I would like to cover the latter issue first, which can help in better understanding what needs to be done in successfully accomplishing item one.

While there are untold numbers of consultants, advisors, and such who are currently involved with helping manufacturing operations implement the tools created by Toyota, what factories are *not* being taught is how to put it all together—what to do first, second, and so on and, most important, how to deal with the issues certain to arise as you go about changing old habits. The following example illustrates my point.

Once I was involved with a kaizen session conducted by a number of ex-Toyota employees (all of whom were Japanese). An issue arose as to how we should handle operators who would be displaced because of the productivity improvements that were being discussed. Were they to be laid off? Given work elsewhere? If elsewhere, what kind of work? What did they recommend? The answer was—no answer!

In fact, the Japanese consultants seemed rather perplexed by the question. A friend of mine insisted they knew, but it was the one secret they intended to keep to themselves. That way we Americans would never know how and, therefore, there would always be plenty of work for the Japanese consultants. I was not so sure. I was almost positive they *did not* have the answer, which posed a special problem for U.S. industry, because here were people who were teaching and directing U.S. manufacturing in a new manufacturing approach but with no advice as to how to handle the consequences of change. Basically the answer they did end up giving us, by giving no answer at all, was: "If it is indeed an issue, then you as management must figure out what is best to do." Therefore, U.S. manufacturing managers are typically being left on their own to address such serious questions as:

- How do you work with the union to make it a partner in the change required?
- How do you get employees to actively participate in a process that may eliminate their jobs?
- How do you justify the expense of the change with accounting measurements that aren't designed to justify such actions?
- What organizational revisions and/or resources are needed?
- What do you do when other company or corporate initiatives get in the way?

This list of questions could go on but I am sure you get the picture and probably have heard a few horror stories about plant managers struggling with these issues—with no help in sight. This is why for conventional mass manufacturers the ultimate challenge in changing the system of production concerns *the issues that arise when deploying the overall world class manufacturing process.* Obviously, an effective approach needs to include such issues as communication, organization, measurement, etc.—things that plant managers just do not get in a typical kaizen consulting venture given by *anyone* in the field.

There are many specialists in the field of kaizen or continuous improvement who are selling TPM or kanban and/or other tools as an ultimate solution for implementing world class manufacturing. What the conventional mass manufacturers must recognize is that the answer to changing their system of production is not necessarily how effective any given tool of the trade is, but in taking the appropriate steps to make changes to the *entire system of production*—using the tools and techniques *when needed*. More importantly, are the principles you're embracing able to take on the task of total change?

This is why with the rapid deployment of WFM I step back from the theory and provide the manufacturing manager in charge with the four major drivers and precise sequential steps necessary to organize, construct, and implement this revolutionary change. I successfully applied this approach in two separate manufacturing facilities—both in a two-year period or less (see Table 4-3).

- *Plant operating cost.* The total cost to operate, including all labor, expenses, and overhead.
- *Space required.* The space required to perform standard production work.
- *WIP inventory.* The standard work-in-process inventory normally carried to operate.

Table 4-3. Percent of Improvements from the Rapid Deployment of WFM

	Plant one	Plant two
1. Plant operating costs	35%	45%
2. Space required	30%	25%
3. WIP inventory	60%	75%
4. F.G. inventory	55%	35%
5. Direct labor	20%	25%
6. Indirect labor	30%	45%
7. Outgoing product quality	50%	60%
8. Manufacturing lead time	40%	30%

- *F.G. inventory.* The standard finished goods inventory normally carried to operate.
- *Direct labor.* The number of direct labor employees required.
- *Indirect labor.* The number of indirect labor employees required.
- *Outgoing quality.* The outgoing quality measured in terms of customer returns/rejects.
- *Manufacturing lead time.* The lead time specified to customers to produce requirements (once material is made available from suppliers).

These are only a series of key improvement indicators and there were, of course, others specific to the operations. But these improvements were of major proportions. Why? Because I changed a few of the rules for applying JIT principles and adapted them to the needs and present reality that is occurring on every shop floor of any conventional batch-producing U.S. manufacturer.

Month Nine—The Awakening

We were within hours of shutdown for the holidays, and I was busy trying to get around to the various departments to wish everyone a merry Christmas. For the first time in almost a year, I was going to have a little discretionary time on my hands during the holidays, although I knew I would have to spend some time in the plant in preparation for the upcoming year. This, unfortunately, meant Kathy and I could not plan to make a trip out of town to visit relatives. However, at least I was going to have some time for something other than work, and I was really looking forward to it.

Everyone had the Christmas spirit, it seemed, and although it had not been the best of years for the plant, morale appeared to be reasonably high. I was certain this had more to do with the magic of the holiday season than anything else.

I passed on a number of invitations to join various groups after work at some of the local watering holes, pleading that I had a lot of work to wrap up before the holidays. I did, however, do a considerable amount of visiting with the troops . . . much more than I had ever done in any one day, and it left me with the feeling that I had to make more of an effort at this kind of interface in the future. I decided to change some things in the coming year, but little did I know at the time just how much change was actually going to occur.

At home during the holidays, with the weather being cold and dreary, I became restless and found myself spending more time back at the plant than I had intended.

As I sat in my office one afternoon on the factory mezzanine, which provided a good view of the factory floor below, I was reflecting on where I had taken the operation at the end of my first year on the job. I kept trying to tell myself we had not done so badly, but down deep I didn't feel good about where we were. Something was missing, and I was having a hard time putting my finger on it. I was becoming seriously frustrated with my inability to move the factory on to a much higher level of accomplishment.

As I was contemplating what my next step would be, my attention was drawn to a book lying on the top shelf of my bookcase. I retrieved it with the intention of setting it in its proper place, upright and neatly aligned with all the other business books and articles in the aging metal cabinet.

For some reason, I returned to my desk with the book and studied the cover momentarily before leafing through the contents. The book was entitled *America Can Compete*, by Michael George, a consultant and lecturer on a production system he called Continuous Flow Manufacturing. I had received the book while attending one of his seminars some years back, and I remembered I had been impressed with the success stories that had been related to turnarounds in a number of diversified industries as a result of implementing his approach.

Nonetheless, I began reading the book again and somewhere in the middle of the second chapter, it hit me like a ton of bricks. Here was the answer! What I had been guilty of was getting so wrapped up in trying to run a good conventional batch manufacturing operation that I had forgotten something Mr. George so aptly advised . . . *There is no such thing as a good conventional batch operation in today's global market.*

I suddenly became excited about the opportunity of making the change to some type of continuous flow operation that would incorporate the benefits of JIT manufacturing. However, I needed something that would move the process along quickly and started visualizing in my mind how we might go about making it happen.

We could start by moving as much fabrication equipment as possible to point-of-use and then transfer all associated inventory to the general area the equipment occupied. Forget standard work, process mapping, and all the other databasing tools typically used before making machine and equipment moves. We would "just do it." As a result we would expose our massive inventory levels and begin to work them down to a more manageable size, and as a further initiative, we would begin to downsize our centralized stores areas. Our goal would be to eventually get rid of them, and to fine-tune our processes so we could produce as needed. It would be a different, bold approach, but the speed of implementation could be dynamic. Suddenly, the

(continued)

little people that live in everyone's head surfaced and began to carry on a conversation.

First with an outburst was the little red devil of doubt. He hissed, "You idiot, how could you possibly do that? You have a union to deal with. You have labor classifications. The union wouldn't support you. You would be flooded with grievances if you attempted such a thing. It would be impossible... impossible."

Then, in all her glory, the little white angel of hope appeared and spoke: "Don't listen to him. Of course you can do it. If you don't, who will?"

"Oh yeah," Mr. Red retorted. "What happened the last time you took Miss Goody Two-Shoes' advice? Remember, you wanted to give everyone on the shop floor ice cream, but forgot the second shift. Remember their reaction? I told you to forget it, but you wanted to be a nice guy. See what it got you?"

"That wasn't his fault," responded Miss White, emphasizing the point with a wag of her finger. "He specified the second shift be included, but someone dropped the ball ... and he did correct it later when he did something very special for the second shift."

"Bah!" shouted Mr. Red, ignoring her comment. "It got you nothing but misery, and now you want to really upset the apple cart. Take it easy, pal. Don't rock the boat. You haven't finished a full year on the job, and you're not the most popular guy on the block as it is. How about the layoff? They still hate you for that ..."

I was drawn out of my fantasy by a tremendous crash on the shop floor. I wheeled my chair around and peered out the window at the factory below. Across the main aisle, in one of a number of in-process stores areas, a forklift had caught the edge of a section of containers and they had come tumbling down, spilling hundreds of parts over the floor. As I clambered out of my chair and headed for the door, I couldn't help but think, "Gosh, Miss White, what a way to make your point."

Revolutionary Pointers

- The principles of the TPS are far too complex and much too difficult for most U.S.-based manufacturers to adopt and implement in a relatively short period of time.

- For the rapid deployment of WFM you need to implement the tools and techniques of the four new drivers: (1) workplace organization, (2) uninterrupted flow, (3) error-free processing, and (4) insignificant changeover, *when needed*.

- There is a significant difference between TPS and WFM. Among other things, WFM uses takt time as a tool rather than a driving principle. Additionally, it's not practical for U.S. manufacturers to use takt time as a marker in the utilization of standard work—so that anyone can perform it—because this ignores the performance rating for each operator. Also, under WFM, pull production and one-piece flow become tools for implementation rather than specific TPS principles.

- Staircasing the 6Cs (Clear, Confine, Control, Clean, Communicate, Continue) provides focus and further helps the group working on such an initiative to know what to do first. It is much easier for employees to understand than 5S.

- WFM takes the basic concepts of supermarkets and creates pull zones. This is a place with a clearly established level of inventory and is a way of eventually eliminating all centralized stores areas in the factory.

- What conventional mass manufacturers view as wastes are actually a *result* of the production system itself. They are hidden because most conventional manufacturers are simply blind to them.

- The key in uncovering hidden wastes is to help the work force understand, see, and analyze wastes. WFM uses a method whereby a group of managers and/or employees tour an area in the factory and make observations and notations based on a set of 10 waste-finding questions.

- WFM deals with issues that standard JIT implementation often has no answers for, such as working with the union, handling displaced operators, justifying the expense of the change with old accounting measurements, what to do when corporate initiatives get in the way, and so on.

- You must include all of your employees in the continuous improvement process and they must understand it as a journey with no end. To make continuous improvement a lasting process you must also substantially empower your employees so they can participate in the journey.

- There is no way you can simply purchase the expertise to change your system of production (process) and then turn the initiative entirely over to others. Remember that this kind of change process is ultimately dependent upon your people to construct, lead, and implement.

5

Examining the WFM Drivers

IN EXAMINING THE WFM drivers it is important to reiterate the major difference between waste-free manufacturing's approach and all the other world class manufacturing systems. By making a significant change (changing the rules) to the guiding principles of TPS (JIT manufacturing), WFM provides companies with a way to rapidly deploy and implement a waste-free process—or at the least *a much accelerated implementation process*. U.S. manufacturing must realize that following the same structured path of Japan's companies, and more specifically Toyota, in pursuit of JIT manufacturing will simply leave us treading in the dust of those who have gone before. We need to do much more than catch up with the leading world competition; we need to pass them by. And as I've repeatedly said, this is something that WFM gives you the potential of doing.

How do I know this? Because I personally led the extremely successful turnaround of three separate manufacturing facilities, using the approach outlined in this book. However, you might be interested in knowing how I formed my strong conclusions about changing the JIT rules and creating the four new drivers. Let's return to our ongoing story and find out a little more.

Month Twelve—Learning the Truth

After shaking hands with Art and introducing myself, I took a seat across the table from him, next to Jack, who had arrived a short time before me. Art, as I was to learn, was a consultant who was a friend of the new president of the company. Art was in the plant at the request of Bill, who I was certain had volunteered my operation for his review. He took little time getting to the point:

"Your plant is terrible!" he proclaimed, waiting for my response.

I was utterly astonished by his statement, and my initial reaction was to shrug my shoulders slightly and turn to glance at Jack, who was staring back at me.

Art decided to continue: "But . . . I suspect you're probably no worse than most of the plants in your company."

The truth was we had begun to move equipment to point-of-use, had cleaned the factory up and put in some organization, and were starting to make some progress on better meeting customer demand. In fact, I was beginning to think we were doing reasonably well. I finally responded: "I know what you're trying to say. We've started the process, but we have a long way to go."

"Started?" He quickly challenged me. "I think not."

Suddenly I was beginning to feel a little irritated with his stiff criticism, but he continued before I could think of how to respond.

"Bill asked me to get with you and pass on my observations. As I think you know, I've been asked to look at all his plants and provide him with some recommendations. There are a lot of problems in your factory . . . John, is it?"

I nodded. I couldn't believe what I was hearing. Here was a person who had made a quick trip through my factory and was making some very strong accusations and, he didn't even know my name. I always considered myself to be a straightforward individual, but I was convinced I was a "pussy cat" compared to Art. I couldn't help but notice a smirk of disgust on Jack's face as he fidgeted nervously in his chair.

"You've got inventory running out your ears," he continued. "You've got far too many people. They're totally unproductive. You score zero for flow in the factory. There's waste everywhere."

Now I was really getting irritated, and I was beginning to think I didn't like this man. "Wait a minute," I responded. "I think you're making some very strong accusations based only on a very short time in the factory. We know we have problems, and we know that we need to make some changes. We're in the process of doing it."

"You are?" he quizzed.

"What is this, the third degree?" I retorted. Jack decided to chime in.

"I agree with John," he said. "We've got problems but . . ."

Art interrupted again. "Look, gentlemen, I admit I'm outspoken, but I told Bill about this and he said he wanted me to be honest and forthright when it comes to what I observed. I don't mean to be rude, but I do know what I'm talking about. I grew up in Toyota and we were taught to have absolutely no patience with waste. The facts are, if you really understood what world class manufacturing was all about, you wouldn't be taking such a defensive position. You would be in total agreement with my observations. I didn't have to spend as much time as I did in your factory to form my opinions. I can walk through any factory—just walk through—and tell you what they know and don't know about world class."

I couldn't figure out if he was the most obnoxious person I had ever met or one of the most brilliant. As I was later to discover, there was no question about it being the latter. He continued for a good fifteen minutes, often walking to the chalkboard that hung at the far end of the conference room, scribbling on it words like takt time, poka-yoke, and kanban. He rambled on about one-piece flow and the terrible lack of it in the factory. He said the plant was dirty (I was thinking he should have seen it a year earlier), and that there was a total lack of order.

Bill entered the room somewhere in the middle of what Jack and I were viewing as a tirade, and he couldn't help but notice the look of utter astonishment on our faces. Bill listened politely as Art continued for a few more minutes, then decided to take command. He started by telling Art that he appreciated him sharing his observations, but wanted to cover a few things with us in private; then let him know he would meet him a little later in his office. Art excused himself and closed the door as he exited.

It did not take a genius to know that some type of prior arrangement had been made between Bill and Art ... and, that we were now going to get an understanding as to what it was. As soon as Art left, I jumped to my feet and began pacing back and forth. I was hot and Bill knew it.

"What the hell's going on?" I asked. "You have some self-professed expert walk through the factory and then have him unload on us like we're idiots. He isn't the only one who knows about takt time, one-piece flow, and all the other concepts he's spouting," emphasizing my comment by pointing at the chalkboard where he had left those and other terms.

"Settle down, John," Bill said, "and have a seat." I reluctantly complied. "Look, I know there was some shock-treatment in all this, but there's a reason for it. Art is a past associate of Carl's and Carl has him visiting the various business units to see if anyone wants to use him. I met with him a few weeks ago and I was very impressed with his credentials. I asked him to visit our plants and let me know what he thinks. He's the first to admit that his techniques are different." He paused before proceeding.

"Now, with regard to your point, you may know the words and think you know JIT manufacturing, but he's lived the experience in Toyota, and you

(continued)

should listen rather than get defensive about the matter. I knew how he was going to come across, but there's a reason for it. He wants to get a feeling as to my plant managers' mind-sets, to see if they are open to new thoughts and ideas."

I was waiting for him to give us the bottom line, and he did.

"What it boils down to is this. I've contracted Art to do some training in our division. He stipulates he won't go into a factory where he feels the plant manager will not give him strong support. You're the first he's met with, John."

"Training?" I inquired further.

"Yes, in the basics of the Toyota Production System."

"I've got my own game plan for that," I replied, somewhat stiffly.

"If that's the case, then what you and your people can learn from him should be in tune with your game plan. Right?"

I saw it was hopeless to argue. Bill was not about to back out on any agreement he had made with Art, and the facts were, most of the time I had found Bill was generally right about his feelings.

"So what does this mean, in terms of any commitment we have to him?" I asked.

"Nothing right now. As I've said, to a large degree he will decide where he'll go after he's met with all the plant managers."

"What if he thinks we're all too defensive?"

"Then I've got big problems, don't I? You're one of the more forward-thinking plant managers in the company, John, and I would like Art to work with you. Would you like to spend some more time with him before he leaves?"

I knew it was not a question as much as a serious request, so I agreed.

Jack and I had lunch with Art, and later we spent an hour touring the factory together. He pointed out a whole litany of problems ("opportunities," as he called them). Jack, who had been rather quiet during most of the proceedings, opened up and got into a running conversation about operational procedures and such. I could see he was beginning to believe Art knew his business.

Later, Art and I spent an hour together in my office discussing the situation. I told him about my plan to move equipment to point-of-use and to decentralized stores, etc. He said that was good, but far short of what was needed. By the time the afternoon was over and I was walking him back to Bill's office, I think we both had a much better feeling about one another.

After returning to my office, I called Jack and asked him to stop by. We spent the rest of the afternoon discussing the matter and by the time the day had ended, we both agreed if we put aside Art's rather biting personality, he definitely had something to offer us. Little did we know it was going to be a gigantic step in the right direction.

Two months later, Art conducted his first session in the plant. It consisted of one day of classroom training and two days of making change on the shop floor. The results, in terms of a reduction in inventory, improved process flow, enhanced productivity, and shortened processing time, was impressive, to say the least. It clearly demonstrated the considerable benefits associated with the Toyota Production System.

While I was pleased with the results, I did not like the formality of the process as it pertained to the process of data gathering and shopfloor observations before change could be made. I saw it as taking entirely too long to meet the type of restructuring our entire factory critically needed. I was still convinced there had to be a better way.

However, the techniques we learned in Art's session were important. There is unquestionably a place for their utilization in the quest for waste-free manufacturing, but not on the front end, as was being prescribed. At the end of the training, I asked Art to meet with my entire staff and to provide us the benefit of his counsel. He was never short on advice and agreed.

This turned out to be an important stepping stone, because my staff was hearing about the need to make big changes from someone other than me. In fact, it was such inspiring counsel that in the months to come, many of them repeatedly referred back to "our session with Art."

It had also reinforced and solidified my commitment to making a complete change in the way we did business. One thing he certainly convinced me of was the need to set up a highly visible promotion office for the process and, additionally, I was impressed with the 5S aspects of kaizen and began to wonder why we had to wait until a kaizen session was conducted to do much more of this in the factory. However, there were things I was convinced we needed to put in place before we started an aggressive in-house training process and, at the risk of ignoring Art's advice, I decided to take some other steps first.

Seeing a Better Way to Apply TPS

As a result of this unique experience (you'll find out what happened to the factory at the end of the book), the way to a waste-free factory became clear to me. Most important was the realization that a means existed to change a factory from conventional batch manufacturing to world class in a short period of time without:

1. Changing existing MRP and/or other business systems.
2. Huge capital investments in equipment and facilities.
3. Increases in the salaried work force (in fact, with reductions).

Again, the key was understanding the guiding principles Toyota used in bringing about the type of substantial improvements it made over the years, as opposed to the conventional and supposedly tried-and-true mass method of operation most industries around the world were using at the time. I then followed up on this by structuring a new approach that indeed calls for using the tools applied by Toyota, but with *priority-based management* inserted into the decision-making process. Put another way, first understand what the ultimate objective for a tool is, then understand how this fits on a priority basis with the particular wastes that need to be driven out.

For example, SMED (single-minute exchange of dies) is a tool invented by Toyota that stands high on their list of things to concentrate on. Under the Toyota Production System (and with regard to how most consulting firms approach the matter of training and implementation), SMED would be something the work force not only must learn, but would have to take the time to apply, as a specific exercise of learning the new system in its entirety.

On the other hand, given an operation that does not have significant setup and changeover as part of its product and process designs, the application of resources for the full insertion of SMED becomes somewhat meaningless from the standpoint of the specific impact it would have on improving overall performance. This is not to say SMED is not a vitally important tool, only that, in the case noted, it would be like forcing yourself to take insulin shots when you're not a diabetic!

If the guiding principles of the TPS process are takt time, one-piece flow, and pull production, as most U.S. manufacturers are being taught, the focus will obviously be on these. If, however, the principles (drivers) are workplace organization, uninterrupted flow, error-free processing, and insignificant changeover, the focus (and outcome) will be quite different.

Regardless, the most important step in your WFM journey is to first understand that *every* mass production facility has serious hidden wastes, and that you must find them and drive them out of your operation to stay competitive. Only then are you ready to apply the tools, when *necessary*, to successfully implement the new WFM drivers. We've already discussed the importance of hidden waste in the last chapter and will discuss them more in Chapter 10, under "The 15-Point Checklist." Now it's time to go into the heart of the compressed production system, which becomes the forum, or fast track, to implementing the WFM drivers.

DRIVER ONE: WORKPLACE ORGANIZATION

To really focus on what workplace organization (WPO) is, it is probably important to start out with an examination of what it isn't. Many people who have had some exposure to the TPS, lean manufacturing, or other world class initiatives that primarily use the tools developed by Toyota might think that workplace organization is just a fancy name for what Japanese manufacturers call 5S. The truth is, workplace organization is much more. In waste-free manufacturing it is the foundation for all continuous improvement. In fact, you must fully deploy workplace organization if you are to have any chance of rapidly deploying the other drivers and creating a continuous improvement process. It doesn't come second, third, or somewhere else down the line. It has to absolutely be the *first* area of focus and concentration. 5S is indeed a tool used in workplace organization, but it is only one of a number of tools. Part of gaining and maintaining good workplace organization (WPO) is:

1. Deploying and maintaining appropriate visual controls.
2. Deploying and maintaining appropriate kanbans.

The point is that you can fully insert 5S in your plant and WPO would still be woefully incomplete. This obviously indicates the first area of training and the first use of the many tools has to be 5S, in conjunction with kanban and visual controls (often referred to as *andons*). Until you do this, learning and exploring other tools only results in *slowing down the overall process of full and total implementation.* In the most fundamental of terms, what I am driving at is that the work force in general and the key implementors and champions in particular must realize that the waste free process must start with a *solid foundation* and that foundation is workplace organization. Any other area of work and use of JIT (or lean) tools will bring some results, undoubtedly, but will not serve the purpose of pushing the overall improvement process forward at an aggressive pace.

Just as important is that by thoroughly and effectively deploying WPO you can achieve considerable improvements—*without changing your system of production (batch operation) on the front end.* This is very important because in most cases a conventional factory is not ready to accept one-piece flow or pull production right off the bat. Being pressed to insert these tools into a system of production that is not prepared to accommodate it, and which many people in the organization have not yet come to value, most often results in one common conclusion: "This just doesn't work!" Or what many manufacturers wrongly think, "JIT just doesn't fit!" This takes us back to the most crucial question. How are you deploying these tools? You have a much better chance of success if instead of rushing headlong into all the JIT bells and whistles, you concentrate on deploying WPO while the factory is still operating in a batch mode. The employees will readily see the value of it, and most often they will energetically support it.

How to Begin Implementing WPO

In the 10-step road map outlined in Chapter 6, I recommend that you establish a WFM promotion office early on and staff it with a small number of talented people whose job it is to lead, promote, educate, and follow up on this initiative—*on a full-time basis.* Typically, you would establish a series of ongoing events for training and WFM implementation. Table 5-1 shows a window diagram noting how you would conduct a typical WFM event. In this case, the window diagram indicates a training outline for a two-week session or what is most often referred to as an "event," although in some cases a one-week exercise is sufficient. I will speak more to this particular subject later. These events give specific training in WPO to a group of selected participants, ranging from 20 to no more than 40 employees, which should include hourly as well as salaried employees. Note that on the second day the team begins implementing WPO.

Table 5-1. A Waste-Free Manufacturing Event

Overview of Week One			
Day one: Tuesday	Day two: Wednesday	Day three: Thursday	Day four: Friday
• Course introduction • The change paradigm • Understanding the hidden wastes	• Introduction to JIT • Push-pull exercise • Workplace organization (6C)	• Tools of WFM: - SMED - Visual controls - Poka-yoke - Standard work - Takt time - Flowcharting - Kanban	• Obstacles to change • Vision Statement
Lunch	Lunch	Lunch	Lunch
• Floor work - Waste analysis • Team reports • Wrap up	• Floor work - Begin implementation of workplace organization (6C) • Team reports • Wrap up	• Floor work - Analyze current process - Workplace organization (6C)–(cont.) • Team reports • Wrap up	• Floor work - Analyze current process–(cont.) - Workplace organization (6C)–(cont.) • Team reports • Wrap up
Overview of Week Two			
Day one: Monday	Day two: Tuesday	Day three: Wednesday	Day four: Thursday
• Develop team goals and objectives • Develop communication plan • Floor work - Communications - Perform standard work	• Floor work - Finalize standard work, action plan, and team assignments	• Floor work - Continue change	• Floor work - Prove new process
Lunch	Lunch	Lunch	Lunch
• Floor work - Standard work and prepare for change–(cont.) • Team reports • Wrap up	• Floor work - Begin change • Team reports • Wrap up	• Floor work - Continue change • Team reports • Wrap up	• Floor work • Team reports (Final results)

- *Day one.* After some initial training in the hidden wastes the group is asked to proceed to the shop floor and perform a waste analysis in a select area of the factory. This sets the stage for recognition of the opportunities that exist for improvement.
- *Day two.* WPO is covered in detail and the group then spends the afternoon on the shop floor analyzing the situation. Here the group determines where the area that has been selected stands in relationship to workplace organization, establishes a plan of action to correct any deficiencies, and rates the area on a scale of 0 to 5 (5 being the best possible rating). Most often, the group will come to the conclusion that the area selected for review is currently at a zero rating, because the first and most fundamental piece of the 6C (Clear) has not been accomplished. Clear in this case is intended to make sure that anything in the selected area not immediately needed for production is removed.
- *Day three.* After the introduction to some JIT tools, the group begins removal of anything not perceived to be needed. This includes an examination of everything—file cabinets, inventory, chairs, tables, work benches, smaller equipment and facilities, etc. Nothing is considered exempt, with the exception of large equipment and facilities, which cannot be readily removed and/or which can be very expensive and time consuming to remove.
- *Day four.* After a discussion of some of the obstacles to change, we begin to chart a vision statement. Then in the afternoon we pick up where we left off the day before.

Establishing a Disposition Zone

To ensure that no one can readily bring back anything removed, a most important step is taken before the WFM exercise even begins—the establishment of a *disposition zone*. The disposition zone is an area that is cordoned off and identified beforehand as the place where everything the group removes is taken for control and future disposition—*without a single exception.* "Future disposition" in this case means before the event is completed.

Once this group exercise is accomplished, the department or area involved will *immediately* take on both an improved appearance and efficiency. However, this is only the first step in overall WPO. You cannot accomplish the full deployment of WPO during a one- or two-week event but it does establish a basic foundation from which WPO can be effectively launched. In fact, it is the first step in the fundamentals of the 6C approach discussed in Chapter 4. After this, to complete WPO and maintain it at all times in the future you must:

- Define a place for everything.
- Make sure everything is in its place.
- Establish and operate pull zones.
- Insert the appropriate visual controls throughout the area.
- Put in place the appropriate *initial* kanban applications.
- Establish audit procedures to guard against any slippage.

The important rule here is: *There has to be a defined place for every-thing and everything has to be in its place.* This includes tools, fixtures, and inventory even down to an identified spot on the floor for the trash can sitting next to the foreman's desk. Once this is fully and absolutely achieved, it only takes a glance to know something has been placed in the department that doesn't belong.

Now that the first event is underway, this first exercise should put the initial steps of WPO in place. The result will be a cleaner, more orderly and efficient area or department in the factory. This will get the favorable attention of employees and, most often, it is not long before other areas of the plant will be asking when they are going to get their turn. One important point about workplace organization is that it usually will get very little, if any, resistance from the work force. In fact, it usually gets relatively strong support. Why? Because it provides a better overall workplace for employees, a place that is much cleaner, safer, and more orderly—yet does not change the exist-ing system of production. The only flack typically received about WPO is from employees who have a "pack rat" mentality and want to keep everything that is currently in the department (and more if possi-ble) just in case there should ever be a need for it. However, these people are generally in the minority.

Implementing 6C

After the initial step of sorting out everything not immediately needed or required, the next thing to do is to follow the other five steps of the 6C. Before proceeding I want to point out a common error made by most manufacturers first trying to apply 5S. As mentioned in Chapter 4, most U.S. manufacturers' 5S efforts have been for the purpose of establishing a checklist of roughly 50 items that examine and rate each particular step of the 5S on a scale of 1 to 5. The participants are then asked to average the results and this in turn becomes the score. As a result, many U.S. manufacturing firms are gathering faulty information as to where they really stand in this crucial process. For example, in rating all the five different categories of the 5S on a scale of 1 to 5, a score of, say, 2.1 or 3.2 could result.

What I have taught and feel very strongly about is that regardless of how good an operation is in any one area, it is impossible to be a two (2.0) if you're not a one (1.0), and there is absolutely no such thing as a fractional rating. As I see it, the six separate categories of 6C are *six separate, distinct steps to six separate and different performance levels* (see Figure 5-1). In order to get to step two, step one has to first be fully in place and so forth all the way to the top level. Therefore, under this scenario where the category of clean is intended to represent all the things associated with excellent housekeeping, a factory could be clean enough to eat off the floor, but if it had not fully implemented step number one (Clear) its WPO rating would be zero!

I take this position because operations have to take care to avoid misleading employees as to where they actually stand in the process. Many batch manufacturing factories are very clean and have done a reasonably good job of straightening things, regardless of whether they are all needed or not. In an averaging exercise, a plant might then find it had rated itself 2.5 on a scale of 0–5. This would say that the plant

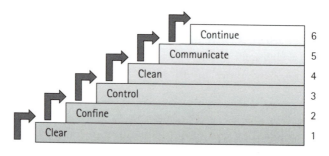

Figure 5-1. 6C Steps to Six Different Performance Levels

was already halfway there in its 5S effort. Nothing could be further from the truth, because the truth is that step one is far more difficult to accomplish than steps two and three. Plus, rather than giving recognition to some past housekeeping and straightening effort that ended up improving nothing, operationally, other than perhaps perceived appearance, it is far better for the work force to clearly understand it is at a zero level and has far to go in taking this initiative to its ultimate, intended purpose.

Achieving WPO Through Staircasing 6C

To create six separate categories with six separate, distinct steps to six different performance levels I've come up with a method of staircasing them and then linking this staircasing to the other three drivers. But before we get ahead of ourselves it's time to take a closer look at the six levels (6C) of workplace organization.

- *Level I*: Clear addresses the issue of removing things not needed or required to perform the intended production function. In order to achieve performance level I, the chosen process or production department must have removed anything not immediately being utilized. This means inventory of all kinds, all unused equipment and facilities, tables, chairs, work benches, tools, fixtures, gages, file cabinets, and so on—again, anything that is not absolutely needed. In addition, full disposition must have been made of anything removed (scrap it, sell it, give it to another production area as needed, etc.). I can't stress strongly enough just how difficult it is for many employees to take this first step to its ultimate conclusion. Some will see the light. Others simply cannot or will not buy in. The latter are usually people who are blinded by what they have been used to in the past. They are comfortable living in and around a cluttered and confusing production environment. They like things the way they are and they generally hate change of any kind. They see a need for things that may have never been used, perhaps for years, but have always been there. Thus, in their mind there must be a genuine purpose for it being there. Therefore, taking this initial level of the 6C to its ultimate often ends up being one of the tougher challenges for rapid deployment of WFM. So, you must be sure that you do not allow any slack as this first and most important step is taken. This, in fact, is the place where the plant manager must be most adamant about his or her expectations.

- *Level II*: **Confine** addresses confining everything to a specific place within the area or department. This means *everything*, down to a spot on the floor for a wastepaper basket next to the foreman's desk and a "shadow diagram" on each work bench for every tool, fixture, gage and the like. Again, *everything with absolutely nothing excluded!* Therefore, if there is not a spot for something, it clearly does not belong in the area.

- *Level III*: **Control** addresses fully controlling all inventory near, at, and in the production area or department. This is primarily achieved through a pull zone approach, which is addressed in detail in the closing section of this chapter. More specifically, however, fully achieving a level III would mean that only a very specific quantity of raw materials and work-in-process inventory would be allowed in the department at any time and that it must enter and exit through some very disciplined and controlled channels of distribution to and from the workstations involved.

- *Level IV*: **Clean**. It is not until you fully implement levels I–III that work begins on cleaning floors, painting equipment, etc. Usually this is one of the first things people do when performing standard 5S work. But, given that steps one through three are indeed in place, now is the time to take the step to clean the area or department. This, however, must go further than sweeping and painting because you cannot achieve a level IV until equipment leaks (oil, grease, water, etc.) are also clearly addressed and fully corrected (eliminated).

- *Level V*: **Communicate** addresses adding needed visual controls in order to clearly communicate where things are located and how the area is performing to customer requirements. In addition, visual controls would be in place that address safety and/or environmental issues, along with a whole litany of other special visual aids specific to any given production area.

- *Level VI*: **Continue** addresses what is required to ensure a continuance of the process. Here, you usually require a management audit procedure along with some sort of measurement and recognition and reward process. The key being: Keep the improvement process going and never allow it to slip back in the slightest.

Remember the following steps regarding how to deploy WPO:

1. Proceed only after you have put a qualified WFM promotion office in place, staffed with a small but well-trained group of professionals who are experts in using lean tools. Those selected for this task can receive training from a number of sources. Remember, there are numerous consulting and training resources available to help firms learn how to use the basic tools of world class manufacturing (kanban, SMED, poka-yoke, and the like).

2. Select a small area of the factory to pilot the approach. Put a group of both hourly and salaried people together (20 minimum to 40 maximum), with as close to a 50-50 split, hourly versus salaried personnel.

3. Ensure the first pass achieves, at a minimum, a level I 6C rating. This is to say that you have totally cleared the selected department of anything not absolutely required to perform its intended production function and that you have made disposition on anything removed from the area (scrap, sell, give to another area, etc.).

4. Continue with another group, using this same area of the plant, and ensure this group takes the area to a level II, at a minimum. Then use another group to take the area to a level III or level IV and so on until you finally have one area in the plant that truly has workplace organization fully in place and absolutely sustained.

There are a number of important reasons for using this particular approach at the offset of deploying WFM:

1. It provides a waste-free training format for many employees. Consider that it indeed took four separate sessions, with four separate groups, to put your first WPO into a selected pilot area. This would mean 8–10 weeks to finish the complete area, but you will have also trained up to 160 employees in the process.

2. It allows you to make the first pass at WPO about as perfect as it can be (although absolute perfection is never fully achieved). This is important because you want to make sure your first effort can be viewed as an absolute success.

3. It shows employees that the process has a systematic rather than scatter-gun approach to continuous improvement.

An Imaginary Tour of a Fully Deployed WPO

We are now ready to take an imaginary tour of the first area in the factory where we have fully deployed workplace organization.

Clear

We find an area that has been cleared of absolutely everything that is not required in order to perform the intended production function. Where in the past there was unused equipment and facilities scattered about everywhere, today there is nothing in the department that isn't absolutely required. Further, the group has eliminated the disposition zone that was used to house the equipment and facilities that the group removed from the department. In achieving this, appropriate disposition was made of everything placed in the area.

When questioned, people provide assurance that nothing is to be brought into the department without a clear understanding as to its intended use and if it is to become a permanent fixture, that it must have approval of the department manager and the head of the WFM promotion office.

Confine, Control, and Communicate

We find a well-defined place for everything and everything in its place. On work benches, the group has outlined shadow diagrams for every tool, fixture, gage, and so on. Therefore, when a tool or gage is not being utilized by the employee or not in its designated spot we can assume it is lost—or most certainly out of place. And we are told if and when this happens, that the entire department stops work and finds (or in the worst case, replaces) the lost item.

Anything sitting on the floor, including inventory, has a defined place. Even a corrugated waste container has a taped outline on the floor that fits its dimensions. The same goes for a file cabinet and a wastepaper basket next to the foreman's desk. At assembly stations, the group has designated and placed in convenient locations small parts bins for items like screws and nuts. Simple horizontal lines inside each container (using red adhesive tape) identify at what level the bins should be refilled.

A pull zone is in place, with a clearly established level of inventory. In this particular case, it is four hours. Upon checking with the zone manager, an ex-forklift driver, we find the prescribed level of inventory is being maintained. The group has clearly marked and appropriately color coded aisles to indicate whether they are working aisles (white) or travel aisles (yellow), and we see nothing on aisle lines or stacked within the aisle markers.

Departmental control boards are in place. On the boards the group has prescribed areas for general information (postings, etc.), schedule reliability charts (customer satisfaction indices), quality performance indices and the like, and most important, a place for employees to jot down suggestions for further improvement. Also, in this general area, an employee *skills matrix* is in place and maintained, noting the name of every employee, all the possible skills (or classifications) utilized in this particular work area, and how each employee stands in relationship to having full capability of performing each of the tasks.

Clean

Everything is extremely clean and orderly. The area is entirely free of trash, dirt, oil, and grease. All the equipment has a fresh coat of paint in an entirely new and different color to indicate the new way—the way the entire factory will eventually look. All equipment has had any type of leaks repaired. Splash guards for equipment using oil or water-based solvents are in place. Floors have been cleaned and polished and are free of dirt, dust, and grime of any kind. Brooms, dust pans, vacuums and such have a place on a *cleaning stand* (or numbers of stands within the area), and all employees in the department (hourly and salaried) share a role in general housekeeping, for there are no janitors assigned to the area. A sign posted in the center of the department reads: "If something does not have an established spot in this department, it doesn't belong and *shall* be removed!"

Continue

It will now be up to you, as management, to establish a process that provides the type of audits, measurements, awards, and recognition that will ensure the workplace organization put in place is built upon and steadily improved. In doing so, you must remember there is no such thing as a perfect department when it comes to WPO, and there is always room for further improvement.

Carrying the Momentum of WPO into the Office Arena

It has been my experience that once an operation starts to put effective WPO into the production arena, it is not long before it becomes somewhat contagious. As a result, someone in the salaried ranks, who has been exposed to the process and recognizes this as something management truly values, will generally set out to pilot WPO in a select office area. If and when this occurs, go out of your way to show strong support and great enthusiasm for the effort.

However, should no one come forth, then seek someone out. Find a person on your staff who has shown some real enthusiasm for the process and ask him or her to pilot an office WPO for the plant or operation. Here the same steps are followed as when addressing WPO on the shop floor. Later in this book I will address carrying all the drivers of waste-free manufacturing into the office environment, but pursuing WPO in the office is actually no more complicated than is expressed in this brief explanation.

Common sense will prevail when it comes to the extent visual controls are utilized in the office and in clearing the areas selected of things not absolutely needed. But in the end the purpose will be to begin a process that serves to rid the office of inherent wastes. Just as in the production arena, the first step to take is workplace organization, which, as I hope you are beginning to see, is the foundation for all continuous improvement.

WPO as the Foundation for Continuous Improvement

Why am I so adamant that WPO is truly the foundation for continuously improving an operation whether it be on the production floor or in the office? There are five reasons:

1. Without WPO, you can exert wasted efforts in dealing with things that are not absolutely needed, thus expending time and energy that could be better applied elsewhere.

2. Until an area is rid of things not absolutely required, it is impossible to see the real workplace, and then to understand the extent of what you are actually dealing with.

3. Time wasted trying to find things, whether in the office or on the shop floor, distracts from productivity, sometimes quite significantly. As well, new employees come up to speed much quicker in an office environment that has good organization in the workplace (visual aids and controls, etc.).

4. A tidy and orderly work area, regardless of whether it is in an office or on the shop floor, provides an appearance of efficiency. This can have a positive influence on the perception of the operation by customers who visit the plant and on the attitude of employees who work there daily.

5. Applying WPO in an area of a factory where it has not existed before provides a stark contrast to the way things are run in the rest of the factory, thus visually indicating the level of the change underway.

Regarding the last point, you could start work in a production area on applying tools such as SMED or poka-yoke (mistake proofing) and a wonderful job could probably be done without ever pursuing WPO. However, the visual impact of change would hardly be noticed. It is these visual aspects of WPO that makes it very easy for anyone to see the magnitude of change being undertaken factorywide—along with the efficiency gains as a result of eliminating waste, which make it the absolute first principle of WFM.

LINKING THE FOUR WFM DRIVERS

I want to pause before proceeding to the second driver, uninterrupted flow, to reflect on an important point. The process of rapidly deploying waste-free manufacturing is a series of events and/or actions that sequentially link its four drivers. As you move the linkage process forward throughout the operation, the level of implementation and the subsequent results pick up considerable speed. The first task is getting a selected area in the factory up to a level II in workplace organization, and then to begin to link the basics of driver two, uninterrupted flow, to what has thus far been accomplished in workplace organization. Next you need to move forward with a linkage of driver two to three (error-free processing), and finally driver three to four (insignificant changeover). (See Figure 5-2.) Remember, we are striving to build a foundation for continuous improvement, from which you can make dramatic, significant, and rapid change.

By the time the first pilot area is at the point mentioned above, it is then time to start the same process in another selected area of the factory. In essence, by the time the first area is brought up to full speed on all the drivers, tools, and techniques of WFM, most areas of the factory will have at least started work on the first driver (WPO). This is a totally different approach than is commonly used in implementing world class manufacturing techniques in a factory stuck in an old batch manufacturing mode. Usually the practice is to select an area and try to put all the major tools and techniques in place before going on to the next area—if indeed it ever gets that far.

Shock Treatment Is Not Lasting Treatment

You must condition a factory into the required change rather than shock it into submission. This shock treatment, which tends to be the method many consultants suggest to management, simply has not proven to be very effective. In fact, it generally builds resentment and resistance along the way. While it is, in theory, a fast track to change,

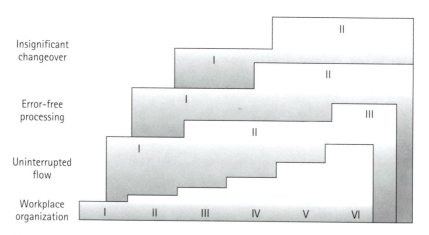

Figure 5-2. Levels and Linkages of the Four Drivers

in actuality it is a slow and cumbersome means of implementing the process.

I do believe there is a time and place for the shock treatment, as long as this does not become the sole means of implementation. Usually, this is best done by a group of outsiders (consultants) for the very first effort in an operation, with the intent being to clearly demonstrate the magnitude of change required and to show the kind of results that can be achieved. From there, however, you must make efforts to quickly internalize the process and to begin a change process that conditions the employees to *embrace* the effort rather than shell-shocks them into a state of submission, or worse, apathy.

The key to conditioning the factory to embrace the change is a series of sequential actions that build, one upon the other, throughout the factory, to a point where change to the new system of production becomes a *natural way of life*. As we proceed, you will get a much clearer picture of how this works. But, in examining Figure 5-2, it should be obvious that in using this approach, each department or area of the plant selected for implementation of the WFM process can be measured in relationship to where it stands; along with measuring how the factory, as a whole, is progressing. The ultimate goal, of course, is to fully achieve the very highest level prescribed for every one of the four drivers. Realistically, however, since the job is never entirely done or absolutely completed, the first step in the journey is for a factory to thoroughly convince itself that every area of the plant has, at a minimum, clearly achieved the following levels of accomplishment:

- Workplace organization—Level V
- Uninterrupted flow—Level II
- Error-free processing—Level I
- Insignificant changeover—Level I

Under levels of accomplishment for the plant as a whole, you could proclaim that an operation has moved from a conventional batch manufacturing approach to a level I in WFM (see Figure 5-3).

Achieving a level I significantly positions a plant to become globally competitive. At this point, you've realized substantial improvement in all aspects of performance, and it is from this stage that an operation could rapidly springboard to a level II and then ultimately level III. But

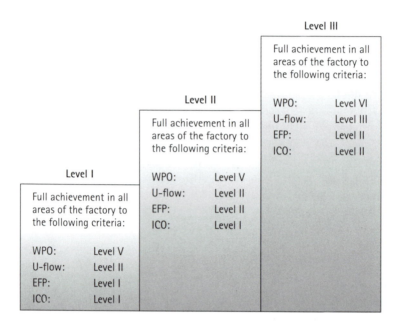

Figure 5-3. WFM Levels of Accomplishment

it is important to remember that at any of the prescribed levels, no plant or operation can ever reach the point where it can consider itself perfect. There is always room for further improvement, even though it may be less than quantum in nature. Therefore, you should look upon the performance levels as only being *relative* to where a particular business stands in relationship to market demands, competitive pressures, and the like. However, without some sort of idea (measurement) as to how one stands in this most important journey, it is very difficult to know just how far a plant has come and how much further it needs to go in the process. I believe, with such an approach, that any manufacturing plant can achieve the following levels of factory performance in WFM in matter of two to three years (see Table 5-2).

Essentially, a factory on a fast-track implementation schedule should be able to attain a level II rating in as little as a year. But a typical implementation would normally result in taking an operation somewhere between one to two years, depending on a number of factors

Table 5-2. Types of Implementation

Level	Fast Track Implementation	Typical Implementation
I	8 to 10 months	10 to 18 months
II	12 to 18 months	18 to 24 months
III	18 to 24 months	24 to 36 months

(training needs, communications, working relationship with the union, other). For a plant with absolutely no exposure to the process, to reach a point where it can say it is meeting all the criteria of a level II waste-free factory would almost always require 1.5 to 2 years. But for those who have had some training and exposure to the techniques and principles, this time frame can, of course, be shortened.

There Is No Such Thing as a Perfect Factory

The question may arise in the reader's mind as to which level constitutes being classified as a globally competitive and/or world-class operation. The true measurement lies in taking a snapshot of both the market one serves, as well as the competition. Certainly any manufacturer in the automotive industry, competing with Toyota, could never consider itself a true world-class operation unless it was clearly at a level III and aggressively pursuing further continuous improvement. On the other hand, the achievement of a level II, with continuing efforts to reach a level III would position most U.S. manufacturing operations as world class in their particular fields of endeavor.

The bottom-line objective has to be to aggressively and continuously pursue world class practices without ever becoming even the slightest bit complacent or assuming the job is done, because the truth is, the task is never entirely finished—unless of course an operation can proclaim it is a perfect factory.

Let's take the time to examine the perfect factory. Here, there would be zero setup or changeover on all equipment. There would be no chance of any mistakes ever being made, in any process or at any operation. There would be very close to zero inventory carried throughout the factory. Every operation would be fully point-of-use oriented. There would be no scrap or rework produced under any circumstances. Every bit of work would be equally balanced between operators. Everything would be perfectly arranged and in perfect order at all times.

Get the picture? There just isn't such a thing as a perfect factory, any more so than the perfect human being—nor will there ever be. If one can accept this, then it becomes obvious that the task is to continuously strive to get just a little better today than yesterday. Put another way, assuming an operation did indeed achieve a level III (which is noted as the epitome in this work), it would then proceed to do what was necessary to establish its own criteria for a level IV, and then aggressively proceed in striving to accomplish it!

DRIVER TWO: UNINTERRUPTED FLOW

Uninterrupted flow (U-flow) is the second driver of WFM and its basic intent is to eliminate as many breaks in the flow of work required to complete a product as physically possible. What normally happens is that you must relocate equipment and facilities to support the effort. However, it is important that you do not do this in a helter-skelter manner. Again, at the offset, this usually calls for a pilot area approach. But before getting into how we would go about that, let's further examine the concept of uninterrupted flow.

An interruption in flow is any occurrence in the production process that requires parts, assemblies, or components to *stop* before they can be completed. The more an operation flows in an uninterrupted manner, the fewer the parts that are required in the overall work-in-process chain. The fewer parts required in the chain, the less scrap, rework, and obsolescence required. When you have done enough to eliminate disruptions in flow, one-piece flow becomes a *result* of the process.

A stop generally implies that an intermediate storage of some kind is required. For example: Part AA flows from its first operation, going from raw material to the formation of a completed part and proceeds through operation 1. Then on to 2, then finally 3, where the part is finished. However, the part is used in sub-assembly BB, which also requires other parts and components. Subassembly BB is put together elsewhere in the factory so Part AA is sent, in completed form, to a storage or staging area, where it remains until it is later picked up along with the other four components required, transferred to the area where subassembly BB is made and then used. How many stops have occurred? Well, if you consider that the other four components required probably went through the same process, the number of stops would be four since one intermediate storage was required on each of the four components used. But, if you also consider that subassembly BB is only one of a dozen subassemblies required to make a finished product, then you can begin to see the potential number of interruptions in flow in the process of making a finished unit ready for the customer.

Consider the waste, because it is often of the magnitude that can be alarming. Every time a part, component, or subassembly is stopped and/or the flow interrupted, someone has to assume the job of caring for the parts. They have to be placed in containers, most likely transferred to a prescribed area of the factory and then tagged, counted, stacked and booked, among other things. Then when it is time to use them, they have to be unstacked and most likely retagged, recounted, rebooked, and then transferred to another area of the plant for use. Then when that particular subassembly is done, it goes through the same process as the parts that made it up, as do all the other subassemblies, before they finally come together to become a finished product ready for the customer. Often what we see, as someone so aptly said, are parts and components being given "a grand tour of the factory."

Japanese manufacturers see inventory as the "root of all evil." What employees must also come to see as evil are storage areas of any kind. Japanese manufacturers, of course, also see storage areas, overhead conveyors transporting parts and the like as waste, but this is not always well understood by U.S. manufacturers. All this is not to say, as for inventory in general, that some storage isn't needed, only that employees should come to view these as a clear waste reduction opportunity. But you would be surprised how many employees in firms that have come to accept the JIT philosophy regarding inventory do not consider storage areas to be in the same category. In fact, many have completely misunderstood the intention behind TPS when they established supermarkets. In reality, what Japanese manufacturers were asking for and purposely doing was creating a *conscious waste* in order to eliminate supermarkets with the disciplines of pull production. On the other hand, I've seen firms set out on a course to make supermarkets *permanent* fixtures in their operation—rather than working at things that could serve to eventually eliminate them.

I have also seen this happen with kanban applications. Kanban, much to some U.S. manufacturers' chagrin, is another method to consciously create waste. You must be constantly working to find ways to eliminate kanbans—where feasible. But what is happening in many U.S. firms is that kanban has become the single principle of focus and, as a result, exotic kanban plans and initiatives are being driven forward, which are doing little other than perhaps more effectively managing a batch manufacturing approach and not in any way working to eliminate waste.

The First U-Flow Effort—Pick the Low-Hanging Fruit

Once you have accomplished the minimum of a level II with workplace organization (i.e., having implemented the clear and confine elements of WPO), you should begin concurrent efforts on the principle of U-flow. In fact, once you have accomplished a level II with WPO, you should delay levels III–VI until you make the first effort (or step) in establishing U-flow for the area involved. I say first effort because work on U-flow is actually a never-ending process.

The first effort or first pass at U-flow is usually to pick the low-hanging fruit. Here small machines, equipment, and facilities used in other areas of the factory to produce parts and components for the area are typically moved to the area and set up as point-of-use operations. Someone once asked me: "How can you justify moving such equipment to a given department, if it is furnishing parts for other areas?" The answer is simple. Just do it! The machine doesn't know it is occupying a different place on the shop floor and, of course, anything you can do with a machine in department A, you can do just as easily in department B.

But beware of the obstacles that are sure to arise. I once had an excited accountant rush to my office to inform me a machine had been moved across the aisle to another department and as a result product cost was going up because the receiving department "had a higher burden rate." My response was: "Sam, then you have the task of doing some creative accounting work." The facts were that costs certainly didn't change just because a machine was moved 30 feet. But getting back to my point about work being performed just as easily regardless of location of the equipment, assume we have two small power presses located in a press department (along with all the other power presses in the factory) that make parts for area A where the plant has implemented its first application of workplace organization through level II. Area A is a final assembly department. The presses in question also make parts for areas B, C, and D, which are other final assembly departments. When we move these particular presses to area A, the requirement for the other departments obviously doesn't go away; therefore, the presses must continue, at least for some time, to satisfy those needs. What then is the value of moving the equipment to area A?

Well, while the parts made for the other departments would still be required (for the time being at least), and must be produced in batches and transferred to storage areas, just as before those parts produced for area A could be made on an as needed or JIT basis. In order to do this, however, engineers assigned to the department would have to begin work with SMED to reduce setup and changeover on the equipment, in order to avoid negatively affecting established equipment capacity. Now, let's examine what is actually occurring when you take this kind of step:

1. In area A, we have a department where we have begun the process of WPO and have carried this through a level II, which means the department has been cleared of all unneeded items and everything remaining has a clearly identified place. As a result of this effort, space was freed.
2. By moving the two presses into the open space provided in area A, along with some other minor rearrangements to get the presses as close as possible to point-of-use, the factory has now demonstrated its intent to pursue a new way of doing business.
3. By establishing the need to reduce setup and changeover in order for the presses to provide area A's parts on a JIT basis, the plant has actively started to insert the tools of waste-free manufacturing.
4. As a result of all the above, cost and efficiency for Area A will start to improve.

After you've made such an initial move don't be surprised to hear complaints. The press shop will usually see this as an effort to destroy their department and, after all, "What does an assembly area know about power presses?" In the assembly area, some will be offended about bringing the noise, dirt, and grime normally associated with press work into a department that is typically much cleaner and quieter. Also, those of you who have been around manufacturing for any period of time will probably be quick to conclude that this initial move of some select presses to point-of-use in area A might not be the last move these and other equipment will have to make as you carry the U-flow process throughout the factory and you learn more about where equipment should be located. Of course you would be precisely on target! This is an extremely important issue relative to the commitment required to change a manufacturing operation from a conventional mass manufacturing approach to a JIT, world class operation.

> You may have to move equipment and facilities numerous times in pursuit of fully achieving a true WFM environment. Although WFM doesn't require expensive capital, but rather places emphasis on improving existing equipment and facilities, the full deployment of the process is *not free*, by any means. Equipment relocation is a must and over a period of time this can become a major operating expense. But the rewards will more than justify any of the associated costs.

Basically, the premise of U-flow is to insert a continuous, ongoing effort by the work force to identify and eliminate stops, wherever feasible, in the flow of the production, starting with parts and components and continuing through everything done to complete the finished product. The fewer stops, the less waste. The less waste, the more profit a manufacturing firm will realize. However, profit is not the only reward. As a result of keeping the U-flow driver high on the list of priorities and concentration, you can significantly reduce manufacturing lead time, along with improving overall product quality.

How to Implement U-Flow

As with workplace organization, there are also three levels of achievement in U-flow.

- *Level I.* This is the first attempt at uninterrupted flow, where you pick the low-hanging fruit. This calls for moving some select equip-

ment or processing from other areas of the factory to the department or area that was the first to pursue WPO. This would normally
be equipment that was exclusively dedicated to the production of
parts or components for the pilot area or which was *primarily* dedicated to the production of such parts and components.

- *Level II.* Assuming the first pilot area had satisfactorily achieved a
  level II in workplace organization, the next step would be to
  achieve a level I in uninterrupted flow. Again, this is accomplished
  by moving some equipment and facilities located in other sections
  of the factory to the pilot area. You would achieve a level II when
  the first pilot area had, over time, moved all or most supporting
  equipment into the pilot area and any following areas that had
  been selected. Therefore, as the process proceeds, one area of the
  factory could be at a level I in uninterrupted flow and another at a
  II. However, you cannot achieve a level III on an independent
  departmental basis because it is meant to measure the factory as a
  whole.
- *Level III.* You can only achieve a level III when the plant has done
  all it can reasonably do in rearranging equipment and facilities for
  point-of-use manufacturing and U-flow and all centralized in-
  process stores areas have been eliminated. Some processes that
  could be considered exempt from this activity would be painting
  facilities, plating facilities, and the like. However, a plant cannot
  usually hope to achieve a level III in U-flow until it has been into
  the overall process of WFM for at least 12–18 months.

Perhaps you are now beginning to better understand the point I mentioned regarding linkage and the fact that the whole process of WFM
can be a step-by-step approach to more effective and rapid deployment
of the process. What you see in the application of the linkage between
drivers one and two will also apply to drivers three and four. Figure 5-4
presents a graphic description of this. The shadowed portion represents
a scenario where a selected area of the factory has satisfactorily
achieved a level II in WPO and a level I in U-flow.

Again, if you are now getting the picture, the very next thing this
area would do after achieving such a scenario would be to begin work
on taking the department to a level VI in workplace organization. They
would follow this by striving to achieve a level I in error-free processing, which would be followed by taking U-flow to a level II, then taking

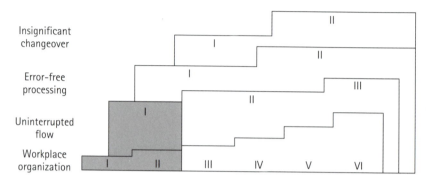

Figure 5-4. Levels and Linkages of the Four Drivers in One Factory Area

insignificant changeover (ICO) to a level I, and so forth, until all four drivers were being utilized to some extent. Usually the time frame for your pilot plant to get to the point of using all the drivers, from one degree to another, is between 4 and 6 months. In actual practice, what will happen is that as the work force learns more about the entire process and begins to value it, speed and momentum will pick up significantly. In fact, what usually starts to happen is that change becomes so fast that management simply can't keep up with it.

In implementing U-flow, you should use two separate approaches. The first is selecting someone and giving him or her unusual authority to make decisions regarding equipment moves to point-of-use. The second is a team-oriented approach, which obviously is a more scientific technique.

Aggressive Pursuit of Point-of-Use Manufacturing Applications

This is when you need to appoint a person to lead or champion an initial effort in quickly and effectively getting at least *some* equipment and facilities to point-of-use. This would normally be a top-level manager in the plant who reports directly to the plant manager and who clearly values the benefits of waste-free manufacturing. His or her basic mission is to set the stage for eventually eliminating, to the greatest extent possible, all back shop or feeder-type departments. This would include areas in the plant like a press department, a subassembly area, or a welding shop, as just a few examples.

The reason for your initiative beginning here is because back shop or feeder operations, because they are separate and independent departments in the plant, *always create stops in flow*. They always require (at a minimum) at least one intermediate storage before they can make the parts, components, or subassemblies used in the final product. Therefore, any efforts that, over a period of time, served to eliminate such departments can only help in setting the stage for even greater improvement. Certainly, by simply moving equipment from the press department to the final assembly area, as an example, will not in itself establish bona fide U-flow in a plant. But it will set the stage so you can complete this more effectively over time.

Believe me, many manufacturing managers have great difficulty accepting both this philosophy and approach because the thought of appointing someone who has absolute freedom to make choices about eliminating well-established areas in the factory, and who can move equipment around at his or her whim, is often next to frightening. I say again, as I have said before, that the ultimate leader of the overall process has to be the person at the very top of the plant's chain of command. Most often, this is the plant manager. The person selected for this task would obviously have to be someone the plant manager highly respected and someone who, more importantly, shared a common vision of the job to be done. Therefore, just by the nature of this alone, the plant manager and the champion would be forced to spend much time together and to agree on the specifics—the what, when, where, and how—of deploying WFM.

Remember, in the process of pursuing the radical change we're examining here, *there must be demonstration of clear management intent* because the type of change I am prescribing will set into motion a rapid deployment of the process. This obviously means a business-as-usual approach simply will not work. But, when employees begin to see you moving equipment to point-of-use and demolishing old operating ways, it will not be long before they will all come to agree on at least one thing, whether they necessarily like everything about it or not, and that is:

> Clear and irreversible change in the way management intends to go about doing business is underway and, over time, it will most definitely

affect every employee and every area of the factory in one manner or another.

Here, I would like to point out something that was mentioned in Chapter 2 under "The Critical Need for a Renewed Focus by Today's Plant Managers":

> This most definitely is not a prescription for the fainthearted. We are going to need a very high level of good, old-fashioned, patriotic can-do commitment from our plant managers over the next decade if we are going to survive and then compete with the relentless competitive onslaught from the rest of the world.

The only solace I can give with any degree of reliability is the fact that *conviction with knowledge is the substance of focus.* Therefore, with a proper focus, results can be swift and with sound results; even those who adamantly oppose the kind of change you will bring will have some reluctance to openly challenge it.

Team Approach to Analyzing and Implementing U-Flow

The team approach for U-flow is usually best carried out through a group activity (a WFM event) involving both salaried (management) and hourly (production) personnel assigned to a particular area. Table 5-1 will help guide a group of employees in how to go about analyzing a particular area of the plant. This exercise normally requires from one to two days to complete. However, if the number of parts is overwhelming, the first pass should be for those parts, components, or assemblies that make up the highest volumes. There are four steps you must go through to accomplish this team exercise:

1. *List every part or subassembly that requires a stop, where it occurs, and why it occurs.* Here, the group collectively establishes a list of the fabricated parts and subassemblies used in their area that require a stop of any kind. Fabricated means any parts that are manufactured from raw materials somewhere inside the four walls of the factory. Subassemblies mean any two or more fabricated parts or purchased components that are physically assembled or put together somewhere inside the four walls of the factory.

   Again, a stop is an intermediate storage of some kind *before* a part or subassembly is fully completed and/or before it is used in the final product. It is important to remember in this study that the group will normally have to venture to other areas of the plant to understand how parts made for their area are processed and if and when stops occur. This means they must talk with operators, supervisors, engineers, and others throughout the factory to fully understand the process used to produce their parts. This is a valuable learning experience for most employees, who often have little if any knowledge about how the parts they use every day are processed. In the end they usually establish a better appreciation for the job others have to do in supplying parts for their work.

2. *Decide what the three to five most important parts/assemblies are.* Obviously, this first exercise is not going to serve to resolve all the uninterrupted flow issues throughout the factory. Therefore, it is important that the group size the list of parts/assemblies down to something they can effectively deal with. The group usually achieves this by determining the three to five parts/assemblies that are most heavily used by their area.

3. *For the top three to five parts/assemblies listed, brainstorm all the potential options that would eliminate any of the stops identified.* This is usually a matter of the manufacturing and/or industrial engineer (or engineers) who have been selected to participate with the group to provide some sound advice, since many of the other participants will not have the technical skills and expertise to understand the overall impact of different options. However, everyone will have good ideas and these should be drawn out. The engineer(s) involved play an important role in this process and should be tutored beforehand on waiting to offer their particular ideas until everyone else has had the chance to provide theirs.

   Further, as ideas are generated, the engineer(s) should indeed quickly step in to respond if an option poses an obviously insurmountable problem. But you must take care not to embarrass any of the participants or to give the impression the engineers are the only ones suitable to determine processing options. Most important, the engineer(s) must have a positive attitude about the process of U-flow or the exercise will quickly deteriorate.

4. *Sell the best idea(s) to management.* At this point, the exercise becomes one of the group selling its ideas to management. This is accomplished by having the entire factory management team, including, of course, the plant manager, attend a meeting where the thoughts, ideas, and recommendations of the team can be

heard. And most importantly, where *immediate decisions are made as to whether to proceed with the team's recommendations or do something else.*

How Management Should Deal with Team Recommendations

Step four is an important juncture in the process implementing WFM because it sets the stage for the work force to feel they are indeed actively involved and it is also the place where the plant management team has its first real chance to show they are willing to fully support the process. The wrong move by management at this point can be most damaging. Therefore, how management both hears and responds to what the team has to recommend is crucial. Some very important things to remember at this juncture are:

- Although management has the responsibility to ensure that nothing "dumb" is allowed to happen, anything short of this should be very strongly considered for implementation—*without a tremendous amount of debate.*
- Responses by the management team to the suggestions given by the team should, without exception, be provided in a tone of counsel rather than debate or challenge.

The reason for this is probably obvious, but the idea is to show employees that management truly supports empowering its employees to bring about needed change. To do this effectively, management must also show it is willing to accept something less than what might be perceived as the perfect solution. After all, the process of WFM (or for that matter any other world class effort) is to learn by doing. Therefore, mistakes and/or coming up short of the ultimate or very best option should, if anything, be applauded rather than condemned or criticized.

In addition, it is also critical that management make immediate decisions at this point. Avoid any temptation to table suggestions or to take any of them outside the meeting for further deliberation. Make a decision, one way or the other, and once you've reached a go decision, demand that the team do it now! Show them that a sense of urgency is expected by taking away all excuses and providing them with the flexibility and support that is needed for action.

However, situations can and often will arise where management must not hesitate to correct the team, of course in a polite manner. The more significant examples of this would be a recommendation requiring:

- Hard capital to implement.
- Extensive outside services to implement.
- That someone other than the team take ownership.
- An extensive delay in implementation.
- That nothing be done.

Let's examine each of these in some detail.

Recommendation for Hard Capital

Remember, the basic intent of WFM is to improve *existing* equipment and processes. Therefore, as a general rule you should strongly discourage capital investment proposals. As I've mentioned before, however, you will need expense money for moving equipment and facilities around in the plant in the pursuit of deploying U-flow and the other WFM drivers.

Recommendation for Extensive Outside Services

You should make every effort to utilize existing (internal) maintenance and building services rather than outside contractors. There is an important reason for this. It starts with the need for you to project the message that waste-free manufacturing is now a standard part of doing business, and that the equipment and facilities maintenance groups must become aligned to actively participate in the process. Only if the physical size of the equipment absolutely requires you to use special rigging should you give any consideration to using outside contractors. Using internal maintenance always goes down better with unions, who will insist (rightfully so) that the company should use its own people, when and wherever possible.

Recommendation for Someone Else to Take Ownership

Sometimes a team will decide that the responsibility for implementation, even though it was their idea, belongs to another group, department or function. *Do not allow this to happen.* The team must understand that the ultimate responsibility lies with them to manage and see everything through to completion—not someone else.

Recommendation for Extensive Delay

There will be cases where the team will propose what they feel is a good solution, but will then convince themselves that nothing can be done for, say, months down the road. If a team feels this way, you need to help them devise a means of getting the job done immediately. Again, a sense of urgency is critical to the process of WFM.

Recommendation That Nothing Can or Should Be Done

Once in a great while the team will come up with a number of reasons why no changes can be made. This is a point where management has the right to express at least some frustration and disappointment and send the group back to the drawing board. It is management's responsibility to insist that the team make some recommendations for improvement and that anything short of this is simply unacceptable.

As one of the four drivers of WFM, you must keep a sharp focus on U-flow as you proceed down the path of continuous improvement. U-flow, to a large degree, is a never-ending process but these initial efforts can yield some of the more significant long-term benefits in terms of inventory reductions and improvements in operating efficiency. What you need to do is to get to a point where you have identified every stop in the plant and post these in places where they will receive a high level of attention. Take the opportunity to speak about U-flow whenever possible and the opportunities that still exist. Help the work force get to the point where they too are thinking about U-flow and seeing stops as a waste they are obligated to resolve—as quickly as possible.

DRIVER THREE: ERROR-FREE PROCESSING

There are two levels of achievement in error-free processing. Level I is achieved when you have initiated and successfully implemented *at least one* mistake-proofing initiative in all areas (departments) of the factory where production work is performed. Mistake-proofing is accomplished by using the established techniques of poka-yoke. Level II is achieved when you have applied mistake proofing to *every key process* in the plant, again using the established techniques of poka-yoke and most important, when you've established a means to continuously review, audit, and keep the key process list fully up to date. The following examines the purpose and intent of the distinct levels.

- *Level I error-free processing.* The purpose of level I is to start the process and to provide the learning and first hand experience required to become proficient at mistake proofing (poka-yoke). Here you need to apply at least some error-free processing throughout all the production areas in the factory. It is very important to have some plantwide exposure to the process of error-free processing before taking it to some ultimate application. Like the other three WFM drivers you need to have some successful applications in place early on in the process. Clearly, if done right, the benefits of this driver will be most obvious to all concerned.
- *Level II error-free processing.* The purpose of level II is to ensure that you have fully applied error-free processing to all critical or key processes in the plant. This starts by clearly identifying each and every key production process, plantwide. Further, you must put in place a system that keeps a sharp focus on updating, tracking, and maintaining this list, which should include (1) reasons why the processes noted (equipment, facilities) are considered key, (2) schedule for the application of mistake-proofing (priority based). Some hints in creating this key process list are to:
  - Identify the processes in the factory that generate the largest volumes of scrap and/or rework.
  - Identify the processes that tie most directly to past field warranty claims and/or customer rejects.
  - Identify the processes in the factory that are the most troublesome from the standpoint of keeping them fully in control.

Generally when you establish one of the above, you will find that all three are evident, from one degree to another. A process that has a history of not being fully in control at all times is usually a prime candidate for mistake proofing. However, a word of caution: *You cannot successfully achieve error-free processing unless at the offset you perform appropriate root cause analysis.* One of the worst mistakes that you can make is to carelessly proceed with mistake proofing without first clearly understanding the cause of errors to begin with. In each and every exercise associated with mistake proofing, keep at the forefront of the issue what created the need and what factors truly established the problem. Otherwise, considerable work, effort, and cost can go into mistake proofing a process with the end result being that you never fully establish a solution or eliminate the *real problem.*

DRIVER FOUR: INSIGNIFICANT CHANGEOVER

In every manufacturing operation, equipment and facilities must be changed from one setup to another. The reader who may be savvy in world class manufacturing concepts and techniques may wonder why I haven't used one of the more common terms in addressing this matter such as quick setup or SMED (single-minute exchange of dies) when addressing this subject. The reason is because SMED and other such techniques are, again, tools rather than drivers or principles. What manufacturing operations must recognize is that since setup and changeover *is one of the more substantial wastes* in manufacturing they need to methodically go about making setup and changeover insignificant in terms of the length of time it takes to process parts, components, and finished units. Consider the following:

> If most manufacturing operations could completely eliminate all their setup and changeover, they typically could reduce their assigned manufacturing costs by up to 20 percent or more.

Assuming there is some truth to this statement, how does a manufacturing operation go about reducing setup and changeover and at what point is setup and changeover deemed to be insignificant? I'll briefly address the latter question first and then move into a broader discussion on how to get started in reducing setup and changeover.

When Is Setup and Changeover Deemed Insignificant?

You can deem setup and changeover insignificant when it has almost no bearing on the cost of the product produced or when it has little, if any, impact on an operation being totally flexible and responsive to customer needs and demands. Over the years I have seen setup and changeover become a considerable barrier in responding to changing customer needs. In this era of companies being customer-driven, this is a serious obstacle. If U.S. manufacturing ever hopes to be a viable competitor with the rest of world it must become the most flexible of all those that are in the race to satisfy the customer! Since U.S. companies can no longer compete on the basis of cost and/or price alone, they must become more effective in meeting customer needs by developing better products and services *at a faster rate.* One way to be more responsive to your customer demands is to make changeover an insignificant factor in the delivery of your product.

This is such an important issue that I strongly recommend that colleges establish special curriculums in manufacturing and industrial engineering aimed at making graduates experts in the field of setup and changeover, especially since this is a full-time position for most operations, or at least a small staff of qualified engineers. Just as important is for the work force to view changeover as a waste that is making the operation less than competitive. This obviously has to come as a result of appropriate and ongoing communications and training on the subject. There are two levels of insignificant setup and changeover:

- *Level I.* In achieving this level a plant must have set a program in place, using the tools of SMED and other such techniques, and have reduced changeover at least 50 percent on at least one process, in each area or department within the factory.
- *Level II.* To achieve a level II status, a plant must have fully inserted SMED on every identified key process in the factory and must have an ongoing program of setup and changeover reduction, with a bona fide system for measuring and tracking progress.

Recognizing Your Key Processes

Since I have brought up the subject of key processes on a number of occasions, it is important I address it. Key processes are the production equipment and facilities that essentially control the factory's capability (and the timing required) to deliver finished product to the customer. This generally includes such specialized processes as painting or coating facilities, one-of-a-kind equipment (for example, a piece of unique equipment specially designed for a specific type of fabrication and/or assembly), heat treating processes, and the like. The degree of key processing varies widely from factory to factory, but it is absolutely essential that a manufacturing operation clearly recognize what its key processes are, for it is here that you must apply considerable effort in making setup and changeover insignificant in nature.

Getting Started with Insignificant Changeover

First, you approach this initiative in the same manner as implementing U-flow. Start by selecting a group of both salaried and hourly personnel and giving them specialized training in quick setup and changeover. Then have this group of people select a key process and apply what they have learned. The techniques of SMED are an excellent tool for this activity. In this initial effort, expect to see resistance to change, because in most cases the participants will not readily see a means of effectively reducing changeover time. In addition, in many cases it is the livelihood of some workers to spend 100 percent of their time changing over equipment. When you make efforts to reduce changeover, they can view it as a threat to their jobs. But, if you maintain a proper focus throughout the process, the end result will be a refined setup and changeover method that requires considerably less time and effort.

After the initial session, continue the training effort for as many employees in the factory as possible and ideally build this into an overall training program that addresses all of the principles and utilizes all or most of the tools in each training event. In conjunction with this, have one or two of the plant's engineers take advanced training in SMED and assign these individuals to setup and changeover reduction on a full-time basis.

At the offset, do not worry much about where the efforts are specifically directed, but rather have those assigned to work on the issue simply make as much setup and changeover reduction they can, on as many production processes as possible. Over time, the work force will begin to see the value of the efforts undertaken and at that point it will be appropriate to implement a formal program for WFM's insignificant changeover driver.

A SECOND LOOK AT PULL ZONES

In Chapter 4 we discussed in some detail the concept of pull zones. Now that we've gone through the four drivers you may better appreciate how essential it is that you establish these zones. It has been utterly amazing to me how many efforts in applying pull zones (or supermarkets) falter and then fail and how many consultants and plants pursuing globally competitive manufacturing simply choose to ignore this most important step. You must implement these zones at the outset of your change effort (pull zone is a tool in both WPO and U-flow) or most likely all your efforts will come tumbling down like a house of cards.

First, it is important to remember that pull zones are not meant to be some long-term initiative, though they are often required for some time. Essentially they begin the process of eliminating *all* centralized stores areas in the factory and they end when the factory has progressed to a point that material is brought in the smallest quantities possible directly to the point of use—without intermediate storage of any kind required.

But achieving this often requires a considerable amount of time and effort and usually is not fully accomplished until a factory has achieved at least a Level III in WFM. Therefore, pull zones become a necessity for a factory trying to move from a conventional mode of operation to waste free. There are a number of ways to set up pull zones but in every case, you should establish zones as close as physically possible to the production process or processes they serve.

What I have found to be the best approach to constructing pull zones is actually a very simple method. It starts by marking off with tape or paint a box or square on the shop floor for each part number that is used—in the size of the largest parts container utilized in the factory (see Figure 5-5). Notice the line in the middle of the Pull Zone separating incoming stock from stock about to be utilized. When stock is pulled from the back of the zone to the front it means the material is about to be used. This becomes a clear signal for the material handler to fill the blank space with more material or in some cases different (new) material for the next product series scheduled to be run.

To make a pull zone work properly, you must assign a pull zone manager to each zone established. The size of the zone will, of course, vary depending on what a factory is producing and the number of parts, components and/or raw materials required to produce a finished product. Normally the pull zone managers are hourly production personnel who have been displaced as a result of improving the efficiency of the operation (through the performance of standard work analysis,

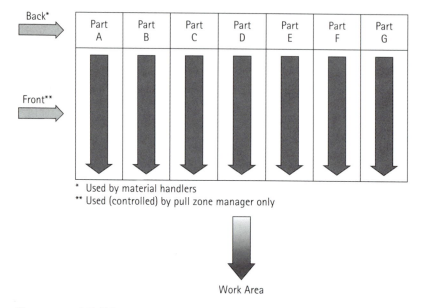

* Used by material handlers
** Used (controlled) by pull zone manager only

Work Area

Figure 5–5. A Pull Zone Example

which will be covered later). Obviously, the pull zone managers must clearly understand the principles of pull production and the production schedules that need to be achieved. Therefore, they have to be one of the better trained and educated employees in waste-free manufacturing.

Material handlers, whose job it is to load and unload transportation vehicles and move material throughout the factory as needed, are instructed not to place material, under any circumstances, in the front section of the pull zone. They are to fill only the back section of the zone as parts or components are called for by the zone manager. The pull zone managers are responsible for moving material from the back of the zone to the front. In fact they are the only persons authorized to move material into the front section of the zone.

The establishment of pull zones throughout the plant requires floor space that may not be readily available at the offset of pursuing WFM. This is another strong reason why it is important to quickly implement workplace organization throughout the factory, so you can provide plenty of space for this important step in the WFM process.

Revolutionary Pointers

- The four drivers of WFM, workplace organization (WPO), uninterrupted flow (U-flow), error-free processing, and insignificant changeover, differ from other approaches in that they provide you with the means to *rapidly* deploy the waste-free process.

- In the most fundamental terms, the work force, key implementors and champions, in particular, must see that the process of WFM starts with a solid foundation of continuous improvement and that foundation is WPO. You must fully implement this foundation for WFM to have any chance of being rapidly deployed.

- Unlike 5S, 6C, with its six different performance levels (rather than lumping all five categories of 5S on rating on a scale of 1 to 5), will give you the kind of measurement that can't mislead employees as to where they stand in the process. Furthermore they cannot move to the next step until the previous one is fully in place.

- The better an operation flows in an uninterrupted manner, the fewer parts required in the overall work-in-process change. The fewer parts required, the less scrap, rework, and obsolescence required. When you eliminate disruptions in flow, one-piece flow becomes a result and you accomplish U-flow.

- Equipment and facilities may have to move numerous times in pursuit of achieving a true WFM environment. Equipment relocation is a must and over a period of time can become a major operating expense. But the rewards will more than justify any of the associated costs.

- You cannot successfully achieve error-free processing unless you perform the appropriate root cause analysis at the offset. Otherwise, considerable cost and effort can go into mistake proofing a production process without ever fully establishing or eliminating the real problem.

- If most manufacturing operations could completely eliminate all their setup and changeover, they typically could reduce their assigned costs by up to 20 percent or more.

- Levels are used to link the four WFM drivers so you can use a step-by-step approach to more rapidly deploy the waste-free process and change your system of production.

- You must condition a factory into the change required rather than shock it into submission.

- Many manufacturing managers have difficulty appointing someone who has absolute freedom to make choices about eliminating well-established areas in the factory, and who can move equipment around at his/her whim. This is why the appointed leader (champion) has to be the person at the very top of the chain of command *and who clearly values the benefits of waste-free manufacturing.*

- With proper focus you can bring about results swiftly. With sound results, even those who adamantly oppose the kind of changes you are making will have some reluctance in openly challenging it.

- The most important juncture in the process of implementing WFM is when the group sells its implementation ideas to management. This is the time for management to step back and strongly consider every recommendation and to respond to all suggestions in tone of counsel rather than debate or challenge.

- It is essential for a conventional mass manufacturer to use pull zones to begin the process of eliminating *all* centralized stores areas in the factory. You will no longer need pull zones when the waste-free process has progressed to a point that material is brought, in the smallest quantities possible, directly to the point of use—without intermediate storage of any kind.

6

Beginning the WFM Journey

IN TODAY'S WORKPLACE, there is a rapidly spreading cancer called complacency, because employees have not seen a positive focus, nor effective results, from the continuing barrage of new programs, new organizational structures, and new operating philosophies they have been forced to absorb. These new ventures have been chock-full of talk about the need for empowered employees, for more open and forthright communications, for the self-directed work force, for team- and data-based management and so on. However, employees have seen little, if any, real change to the thing that is the springboard for any lasting correction in course—the existing system of production.

They have been asked to apply new and advanced concepts, such as SPC or TQM, while the business of manufacturing continues to trod along a single, unchanging course called batch production. This is somewhat like entering Indy-style cars in a quarter-mile, dirt track race. The power of the cars will never be realized, and the end result is a machine that cannot perform up to expectations. It is little wonder that the average U.S. manufacturing employee is frustrated to the point where complacency is the only way to cope. To change this, we must have leaders who are capable of projecting a clear, concise vision, and what is needed most is a road map to steer the requisite priorities.

In this chapter we will examine how to begin your journey into waste-free manufacturing (WFM). Included is a road map that sets forth a step-by-step approach for rapidly implementing WFM. However, before striking out on any journey it is important to think through a series of questions, such as:

- Do you know where you want to go?
- Do you know when you expect to be there?
- Are you going to take anyone with you?
- Do you plan to return and, if so, how and when?

Surprisingly, many businesses begin journeys without so much as ever addressing even one of these questions. Instead, it usually happens like this:

The purveyors of the most recent "program of the month" come to the factory. They let everyone know they have the blessing of senior management to put a new program in place. The factory follows along blindly as a pilot is set forth. From there a champion is identified and later the process of implementation begins, which continues until the next program of the month.

Why does the process of implementation fall short so often? In most cases, if you were to ask the employees how they felt about the journey, many of them would say they wandered rather aimlessly, without any real understanding as to where the process was ultimately taking them or the business.

THE WFM JOURNEY IS A NEVER-ENDING PROCESS

In beginning a journey into WFM, it is critical that the leader let the work force know the journey is definitely not a program, but rather a never-ending process that simply will not allow business as usual. The leader must point out that everyone in the factory is expected to go along on this journey, and must let them know when he or she expects to "be there" (at least fundamentally) with them during this journey. Most important, the leader must let everyone know there will be no return trip, and that they are embarking on journey with no end. Beware of starting the journey into WFM without this type of front-end planning and communication. Otherwise, you will be asking people to follow blindly. While it may be possible to make the trip with blind followers, the journey will be far smoother by putting appropriate communications in place at the very beginning.

The Will to Change and the Pain Threshold

Once you have satisfactorily communicated to your employees, you are ready to begin the WFM journey. However, before addressing the road map and other essential tools for the trip, it would be helpful to briefly examine what I call the *pain threshold*. This deals with a factory's will to change. We should not lose sight of the fact that the driving intent of JIT manufacturing is to increase competitive ability through the elimination of wastes that come in numerous shapes and forms. As a result of waste elimination, a factory becomes the skilled opponent who can run faster, jump higher, and throw farther than its competition. This compares somewhat to the will required to completely recondition the human body, for there is often some pain involved in the process.

When a grossly out of shape person starts to work at getting in condition, the first few efforts will be extremely painful. There are times when the person may decide it is just far too difficult and quit. However, for the person who has the will to stick with it, the conditioning starts to get easier and easier as time goes by. It is no different with a business pursuing the kind of substantial (revolutionary) change associated with waste-free manufacturing. Rest assured the initial conditioning is very painful. On the other hand, the farther one goes, the easier change becomes.

Learning From Each Other

Toyota went through great pains (conditioning) in making its Toyota Production System (TPS) a reality. They had repeated failures over the course of many years, but never lacked the will to continue. Some readers might wonder how and why Toyota came to the conclusion that their "lean" system of production was far superior to mass production's traditional manufacturing techniques.

Not unlike many other Japanese firms at the time, Toyota spent a great deal of time in the United States observing various manufacturing operations. Those who were around during the steady trail of business executives coming here from Japan in the late fifties and early sixties to "learn about American manufacturing," will remember them being welcomed with open arms by most firms. They were encouraged to use their cameras to photograph processes and work techniques. Essentially, we were made to feel like a big brother teaching a younger brother all the tricks of the trade.

Today, we know this was not the case at all. Their version of world class manufacturing had already begun to take shape. No doubt they were here to learn everything they could about manufacturing from the unquestionable leader in the world at the time. The mission indeed accomplished more because it verified what they believed to be true. That belief was that waste within manufacturing in the United States and Europe was excessive and because the U.S., in particular, was so engrossed in its unwavering mind-set about how to manufacture, it was totally vulnerable to a new and more effective system of manufacturing.

This observation is not meant to be critical of Japanese manufacturers. They were indeed fighting for survival—to change their reputation at the time of producing shoddy, cheap products. On the other hand, had they been rich in cash and natural resources like the United States they might have simply copied our approach. Being rich in neither, however, they were forced into fulfilling another, if not new, approach to manufacturing, and to their credit, they were not too proud to look back in order to move forward.

The backward glance they took was at the first true flow manufacturing operation in the world—creating a factory where considerable thought was given to every kind of waste and where considerable effort was made to utilize every ounce of raw material that entered the facility. It was a place where each production operator inspected the work of the prior operator, where material handling was kept to an absolute minimum, and where visual shopfloor controls were used to dictate what needed to be done. The place they copied was the Ford Motor Company and the man behind the manufacturing scheme was none other than Henry Ford himself.

Since that particular era, most U.S. manufacturers veered from the true flow manufacturing operation and convinced themselves that batch manufacturing was the only answer to mass production, and that wastes were simply an inherent cost that you passed on to the consumer. This worked well until a paradigm shift suddenly occurred and the new pricing formula became: *The customer sets the price and the difference between that price and a manufacturer's cost becomes ... profit!*

Toyota seized the opportunity to take the original Henry Ford approach and over almost four decades built into it a highly advanced application of JIT tools, which seek out and eliminate wastes. As a result, they lowered operating costs, greatly enhanced product quality, and most important, greatly reduced the time required from order to product delivery. Few would argue that unlike Japan, the United States does not have 40 years to make the change required to return to Henry Ford's original flow approach. We, in fact, probably have no more than a decade, at best. Whatever the timetable may be, it is indeed a short horizon for the gigantic task that lies ahead.

Some may ask, how can we hope to do in five years what took leading manufacturers in Japan 40 years to accomplish? The task is actually rather simple: Learn from Japanese manufacturers. This is partly what the term "lean manufacturing" is about—taking what has been effective from the Toyota Production System (TPS) and adapting it to our culture, using old-fashioned American ingenuity (approach) to forge our own path. This is also what waste-free manufacturing is all about. Again, it is important to stress that WFM is not an ultimate achievement, but rather a journey where some are farther along the path than others. Clearing the path, getting out of old mind-sets, and jettisoning old habits of producing is still our biggest challenge while Japanese manufacturers, specifically Toyota, have, over the course of many years, already gone far beyond these "barriers."

This is why U.S. manufacturers must use their ingenuity (building a better mousetrap) to make up the distance Toyota and other manufacturers have gained in getting an early start in the lean system of production. To achieve this leaders must once and for all get away from their arrogant disregard for adopting "Japanese-style" production, and see that it has nothing to do with nationality and everything to do with the new paradigm of using a waste-free approach to transforming materials into goods and services. From my perspective what U.S. manufacturers must do is akin to what this country went through in World War II when it had to finally face up to the realization that it had to rebuild its military might. Some may see this comparison as being a bit theatrical, but we are in an economic war and the enemy is not Japan. The enemy is an old, obsolete system of mass manufacturing. Although we have the right to choose not to take an aggressive offense in this economic war, we must then be willing to accept the consequences of this decision—because there is no turning back the clock to the "good old days."

On the other hand, Toyota established and refined the principles of JIT manufacturing over many years so U.S. manufacturers do not have to reinvent the wheel. They simply have to trust in the techniques and begin to work on implementing them in a way that works most effectively for us. If a typical manufacturing operation does this it should be able to make a transition from conventional mass manufacturing to a fundamental level of lean manufacturing in as little as one year.

Old Habits Don't Die Easily

As I have mentioned, conventional thinking by U.S. management could be the single biggest stumbling block to regaining a competitive manufacturing edge. In a conversation with a seasoned plant manager on the topic of employee empowerment, he said to me:

> We would never allow production employees to stop one of our assembly lines. Our lines must run continuously, from the start of a shift to the end, with the exception of breaks and lunch. We're here to satisfy customer needs, and we can't do that by allowing people to shut down a line anytime they see fit.

This is a very different attitude from Taiichi Ohno's thoughts on the subject. He says in his book, *The Toyota Production System*:

> A production line that does not shut down is either a perfect line or a line with big problems. When many people are assigned to a line and the flow does not stop, it means problems are not surfacing. This is very bad! (p. 128)

Table 6-1 examines the most fundamental differences in TPS and conventional mass (batch) manufacturing.

Table 6-1 could go on, but perhaps the point is established. The differences are dynamic and changing to waste-free manufacturing cannot be done until the industry concerned faces the challenge of addressing and potentially changing *its entire operating scheme*. And to do that it must change conventional thinking, which is one of those early hurdles management must overcome in their conditioning program.

Table 6-1. Differences Between TPS and Conventional Mass Manufacturing

Toyota Production System (TPS)	Conventional Mass Manufacturing
1. TPS believes in and encourages employees to stop production when problems occur.	Conventional thinking stands firmly against this concept.
2. TPS believes in and encourages visual management.	Conventional thinking neither understands nor appreciates the benefits of this and, therefore, would typically oppose most efforts and the resources required to make it happen.
3. TPS believes in and demands that kanban be an inherent part of the production scheme.	Conventional thinking opposes kanban (another sight management tool) in favor of MRP and other economical order techniques.
4. TPS believes in striving to mistake-proof as many operations as possible through the use of poka-yoke, sometimes called baka-yoke, which refers to devices for the prevention of defects.	Conventional thinking believes that defects are just going to happen, and that the answer is to cover them up with waste (inventory).
5. TPS believes in arranging processes so that workers can readily see other work within the process and can move from machine to machine in a flow that adjusts people and equipment.	Conventional thinking is one person/one machine, the theory being that this reduces learning curves and improves individual efficiency.

Takt Time—Producing to the Beat

Another part of your conditioning (moving from flabby to lean) is understanding some of the fundamental JIT tools. For instance, one of the more difficult tools to implement at the start of your journey is takt time (pronounced "tack"), which is a German word referring to beat or rhythm. Initially it is difficult for conventional manufacturers to accept that it's possible to produce only for those customer orders needed within a given shift and/or day. Conventional wisdom tells management that if they are going to do this they must keep their people and equipment busy at all times. Therefore, what they consider waste is an employee or group of employees standing around with nothing to do. This is indeed a form of waste, but not in the sense most perceive it to be. It is far more wasteful to have these employees producing parts and components that are not immediately needed than to produce only what is needed and then cease production—*even at the expense of operators having nothing to do for a period of time.* The real waste is not utilizing operators who have time available for things that would further improve the operation, such as serving as "fill-ins" for other employees so as to enhance the employee training process (just one example).

More critical, perhaps, is that typical batch manufacturing processes are structured for production employees to more or less perform at their own pace. Allow me to explain the principal shortcoming of this approach. A symphony orchestra produces beautiful music because everyone performs to one beat. Imagine a performance in which musicians are told to choose any beat they like, with the objective being to hit as many notes as possible, as fast as possible. It would be pure chaos! However, this is exactly the way we tend to run a traditional batch manufacturing operation. We tell employees to work as fast as possible, disregarding whether a particular operation is in tune with the next process in the loop and, most important, in tune with customer requirements.

In TPS, everything is driven by takt time. As I have said, I do not consider it a driving principle, but it is an excellent tool that has its place as you move the process of WFM forward. Takt time is nothing more than customer requirements divided into the total amount of time available to produce those requirements. This is generally expressed in terms of time per shift or per day, and serves to identify a time per unit, typically reflected as seconds, minutes, or hours. What it really pertains to is deciding how long the "store is going to open each day," and at what frequency during those store hours a finished product should be fully completed, ready to be shipped to the customer.

As an example, if a customer established a requirement for 120 products (units) per day and the plant was operating on one 8-hour, shift (which included two 15-minute paid breaks for the operators), the prescribed takt time would be 3.75 minutes/unit:

```
8 hours × 60 minutes/hour            = 480 minutes
480 minutes – 30 minute (breaks)     = 450 minutes
450 minutes/120 units                = 3.75 minutes/unit
```

This would mean every 3.75 minutes a finished product should be moving onto the shipping dock, and each supporting process should be producing only enough parts and/or components to meet this prescribed "beat." It sounds simple enough, but not so when one is striving to shift an operation from a system of producing to a schedule, which is derived from projected orders. With this approach, the production of parts and components usually has to start days, if not weeks, ahead of the time they are scheduled to be consumed in final assembly. The challenge is to move an operation away from this to one where parts are produced only as needed, and then pulled by the operation that has a need for them. Takt time becomes the tool to achieving this end.

Toyota supports takt time production by using visual management controls such as kanban. Kanban is a replenishment system used for the production of specified parts and subassemblies. It is the operating method that manages and ensures JIT production. With kanban you establish prescribed lot sizes for equipment and processes that cannot, due to capacity constraints, produce on a one-for-one basis (one part as needed to supply the next process up the stream). Additionally, sight management tools ("andons") are used to visually inform employees, supervisors, and others how they are performing against this prescribed beat.

What all these tools simply boil down to is using a common sense management approach to the entire production process, a system of production that relates customer requirements in terms the work force can better understand, and which synchronizes all facets of the plant operation toward one common objective.

Where, When, and How to Use Takt Time

I am discussing "producing to the beat" at the beginning of the WFM journey because, though I contend takt time is not a principle, but rather a tool, there is a place for it in almost every operation—at some point. It clearly is one of the more difficult tools to implement at the start of your journey. Yet most consultants in the field, and particularly the Japanese consultants, insist that it is the start or foundation for everything that follows.

Takt time is, in reality, a very simple tool to use. But I assure you that the first time you introduce it (and kanban) into a batch manufacturing environment, it will get passive acceptance, if not downright hard resistance. This is because it goes against the grain of most existing business planning systems, like manufacturing resource planning (MRP). Whereas MRP systems are driven by schedules (using actual and projected orders), efficiency (using volume and throughput considerations based on past performance), and utilization (using people and equipment uptime and performance factors), kanban's philosophy (which uses takt time) has no room for these basic planning assumptions, because its focus is only on current customer requirements.

Simply put, MRP is a *push* system where production and purchase orders are initiated by projected demand (master production schedule), whereas kanban is a *pull* system where replenishment is initiated by customer orders (consumption). With a push system, MRP will continue to demand that all items be procured or manufactured regardless of whether customer orders (consumption) are taking place or not. The push system supports batch manufacturing. Kanban supports JIT.

I mention these two systems because this is a very important crossroad for mass manufacturers on their journey to becoming waste free. In fact, I contend that using the push system for materials replenishment is one of the major reasons why U.S. manufacturers cannot and otherwise will not make the kind of change needed in their method of production. So what happens when management starts off by trying to use takt time in a system of production (push) that is designed to do the exact opposite, in terms of approach, is that management's credibility is seriously challenged by employees. This is because management is prescribing that the work force adhere to a method of production that the present push system simply cannot accommodate. To the worker, it then appears as if management isn't truly serious about the matter or that management isn't wise enough to know that the true problem is the system under which the plant is designed to operate.

In making effective change, what it will usually boil down to is two basic options: completely pitching the existing MRP and production planning systems and starting all over (which most often is totally unrealistic), or working toward achieving the end result desired through the existing planning systems already in place. Considering that the latter is usually going to be the only truly acceptable option, it then becomes a question as to when, where, and how the application of takt time is utilized. (There are some new software programs on the market that are attempting to merge and use the best attributes of MRP and kanban.)

This is one of the few times anyone will hear me suggest a rather slow path to using any of the prescribed tools, for I strongly recommend that you only implement takt time through the training and subsequent events conducted by the WFM promotion office. You will find this in step three, in the 10-step road map, outlined later in this chapter. Otherwise, what you will find is a factory full of employees trying to produce music to one beat, but because of the location of equipment and facilities (and things in the way that are not needed) simply will not be able to see the conductor. You can imagine the resulting harmony!

When you first introduce takt time to the work force in one of the prescribed WFM promotion office exercises, it is best to pick a final assembly process. The reason is, that even without point-of-use manufacturing and other scheduling system changes being fully in place, normally a final assembly line can break down its requirements in terms of precise customer orders and can then focus on a production schedule that highlights takt time performance. What I am suggesting is that an operation can grow into effectively using takt time, over a period of time. At some point a production unit will have equipment, facilities, and other things in place to make it a workable tool, but, again, not at the outset of the process of change.

TEN-STEP ROAD MAP FOR THE RAPID DEPLOYMENT OF WFM

In Chapter 5, we covered a new set of manufacturing drivers (principles) for WFM. Thus far we have been laying the groundwork and conditioning ourselves for starting the journey. Now it's time to get on our way by using a 10-step road map for rapid deployment of WFM (see Table 6-2). These 10 distinct, yet interconnecting steps in the map each have a particular emphasis (type of action) and impact (where it applies) when deploying WFM. Examining this road map in more depth you will find a suggested path of concentration.

It is important to point out that if you follow this road map and successfully implement each step, in the exact order, this will not necessarily

Table 6-2. Ten-Step Road Map to the Rapid Deployment of WFM

Step	Emphasis	Impact	Path of Concentration
One	Educate	Management staff	Provide training for the plant management staff in the principles of WFM. Then, and only then, train all others.
Two	Organize	Shopfloor processes	Apply workplace organization throughout the factory. Determine what is and is not needed. Establish a right place for everything and keep everything in its place.
Three	Promote	Change process	Create your WFM promotion office. Staff it with your best people and begin an aggressive training program for all those in the plant's professional and key hourly ranks.
Four	Decide	Core processes	Decide what the factory's core processes are. Then determine how to organize resources for and flow those processes to clearly assume a competitive advantage.
Five	Manage	Operating principles	Manage according to the fundamental principles of WFM, rather than pure economic justification.
Six	Move	Equipment/Facilities	Move as many pieces of equipment and processes as close to point of use as possible, and as fast as possible.
Seven	Transfer	Inventory	Also transfer inventory produced by equipment relocated from out of stores areas to point of use, and over time, eliminate all centralized stores.
Eight	Limit	Production quantities	Establish a kanban system to limit parts produced on equipment or to processing that cannot accommodate one-piece flow or which serve multiple product families.
Nine	Institute	Product cell management	Begin to aggressively implement product cell management.
Ten	Link	Principles (Drivers)/ Work habits	Work to link the four WFM drivers and thus promote change in general work habits.

make a plant globally competitive, nor totally waste free. This map will help you position a factory so you can effectively implement the more advanced aspects of WFM. In context to WFM, it establishes a firm foundation on which the plant can build to make WFM a lasting reality. Now we will address each of the steps in more detail.

Step One: Educating the Management Staff

First and foremost, the plant manager and his or her direct staff must learn all they can about waste-free manufacturing concepts and techniques and then play an active and continuing role in driving the process down through the rank and file. As you know by now, the basic goal of WFM is to move one's operation from conventional mass (batch) manufacturing to a customer-focused pull system of production, and do this as fast as possible. It is important that the management team understands what this implies and fully buys into the process.

In conjunction with this step, emphasis must be placed on understanding common manufacturing wastes and involving the production work force in seeking out and eliminating these on a continuing basis. Far too many programs in the past have been decided upon by management and then, more or less, pitched over the fence for the troops to implement. But here you are changing your system of production, not passing on a "program of the month." This is a situation where the magnitude of change simply cannot be transferred to the work force to champion. The champion must be management.

Management must take an extremely active role in both educating themselves and in leading day-to-day change. Because of this, management typically needs the training (certainly the recognition of the need to change) as much and perhaps even more than employees. Making the type of change required to implement the fundamentals of WFM must be a top-down-driven process. Otherwise, without exception, it will be doomed for failure.

Step Two: Implementing Workplace Organization

A very important aspect of leading a WFM effort is clearly demonstrating change for the better. There is no clearer way of doing this than working on the thorough organization of each and every manufacturing process for maximum efficiency. Here, I am going to make a very important statement that is perhaps the major difference between what I am proposing and all the other JIT initiatives currently taking place. It concerns an approach that allows a plant to make a start that becomes the catalyst for very strong support from the union and the employees working on the shop floor.

> Even if a factory has no intention of changing from batch manufacturing to waste free, simply applying good workplace organization will significantly improve productivity, reduce quality defect rates, lower scrap and rework costs, and improve employee morale.

In most conventional manufacturing operations, at least 25 percent of all the equipment, stock, tools, fixtures, equipment, tables, benches, storage cabinets, and other things that take up valuable floor space simply is not needed. Think about this. What I am saying is, on average, a great deal of the modern manufacturing shop is consumed by things that are *taking up space and just getting in the way*. Now think about how the factory might look if you removed the items that were not needed. Think about how the employees might feel if the factory was organized and "spanking" clean.

I can assure the reader that in my travels and consulting activities with factories I never witnessed a work force that didn't appreciate the benefits of workplace organization. What most employees will say is that they never understood why the shop floor was so cluttered with unneeded things in the first place. However, as discussed in Chapter 5, workplace organization is more than simply straightening things, cleaning aisles, and so on. Best put, it is an effort to identify everything within the four walls of a factory and to make a conscious quantifiable assessment as to its intended purpose. If something is not needed, disposition is quickly made. If it is needed, it is given its proper place and care.

I believe most manufacturing plants would be well served by shutting down their factory for a few days to engage their entire work force (hourly and salaried alike) in good workplace organization. The objective should be for employees to see floor space as precious—like gold! Thus they would quickly remove anything sitting on the production floor that was not supporting or adding immediate value and was taking up valuable space. Of course, before they do this they should understand what workplace organization really is, and, in most cases, this cannot happen without some extensive training and communications.

Step Three: Establishing the Promotion Office

Before anything else, it is essential to select the right people for the job. Remember, that this office will be the principal ambassador for the substantial change about to occur in the factory. In essence, the office becomes the conscience of the process. Therefore, the people involved in leading the change and more specifically educating the work force must not only be qualified to train others, but must come to express a genuine belief in both the need for the tools and techniques utilized and the benefits (outcome) of the process itself. In short, they must be "true believers" in the principles of lean manufacturing.

Put another way, if those involved with promoting, auditing, and following up on the process are not true believers, but are holding on to aspects of the old mind-set of mass production, they simply will not be effective in the work they are assigned to perform. In fact, they may be a serious obstacle. Your promotion office people must be your best trained people in the principles, drivers, and techniques of WFM. They need to understand how the four WFM drivers link, have the coaching skills to bring others aboard the process, and possess a solid background in manufacturing. I guarantee you, having the "right stuff" in your promotion office will make it much easier for you to *rapidly deploy* WFM. The promotion office carries two specific responsibilities.

1. To conduct ongoing training sessions to provide the knowledge and skills required for the entire work force to become engaged in the WFM journey.
2. To monitor the entire process and to measure and report on how the plant is progressing with implementation.

This office should carry no other duty or responsibility. By dedicating a full-time staff to this initiative it shows the work force the seriousness of management's support and commitment to a successful process. Besides, to train the whole work force and convince them that indeed you are moving into the lean revolution, is unquestionably a full-time job.

Step Four: Deciding on Your Core Processes

This step calls for management to clearly determine the processes in the factory that establish the plant's unique manufacturing expertise; in other words, the process or processes that serve to establish the special expertise that makes the factory unique. Usually you decide this by determining the heart of the product being produced.

As an example, the heart of an air-conditioning unit is the compressor. The secondary core component is the coil. Everything else is material or components (sheet metal, tubing, wiring, etc.) produced by a variety of others who tend to make this their core expertise. While the truth is anyone could decide to purchase compressors, coils, and other components and get into the air-conditioning business, the fact is they would be at the mercy of those businesses that specialize in the design and manufacture of compressors and coils. There would be no way they could take advantage of any first in product design, and it is highly unlikely they could take any significant advantage in overall manufacturability.

The central question for any manufacturer has to be how many core processes they are willing to undertake and then to provide the talent, resources, capital, and management required to stay abreast of the best in the industry. This may well be the most serious strategic issue any firm has to undertake in this new age of globally competitive manufacturing. In reality, many manufacturing operations simply do not know what they need to be. Over time they tend to become a hodgepodge of processing that drains resources and takes time and energy away from the thing that could set them apart from the competition.

I am certain you have probably heard the old adage that manufacturing is just "one damn thing after another." In all probability, the simple truth of this statement usually resides in those manufacturers who strive to be an expert in far too many fields of endeavor. Regardless, every manufacturing plant must have at least one core process, and must work to make it the very best in the industry if it hopes to achieve and maintain any degree of advantage over its competition.

Once this is decided, management must determine if they should place the core processes at point-of-use or centralized under substantially improved flow (staffed with some of the best talent and expertise). In most cases the latter will apply, which can go against the grain of most conventional thinking about JIT manufacturing. However, the key is understanding your business and applying some common logic to the process, because most operations simply cannot afford the resources required to split their core processes and distribute them all over the factory floor.

Step Five: Making Decisions Based on WFM Principles

It is an absolutely crucial step in the journey to WFM to make operating decisions based on principles, rather than economics. In most manufacturing facilities, this can be the one thing that kills any attempt to move forward in a reasonably aggressive manner. If senior management does not believe strongly enough to allow decisions based on WFM principles, and the four drivers in particular, it will not be able to move forward at the speed required to maintain momentum. Over time, the effort will become so unbalanced it will assuredly fail.

For example, under most standard financial logic you cannot economically justify the expenses associated with moving equipment to point-of-use. You must make the decision based on the knowledge that this is where the equipment *must* be located in order to effectively serve (satisfy) the customer. Plant management must work to avoid the consensus barrier that always tends to creep into the decision-making process. It is probably beneficial to point out here that a gross misconception exists regarding the issue of consensus management. In the U.S. there has been a tendency by those who have attempted to implement Japanese management practices to overuse the team consensus theory.

Although it is true that Japanese companies tend to utilize consensus management much better in analyzing various strategies, be it for new products or new equipment, there are operating principles within manufacturing that are top-down-driven, and that offer absolutely *no* consensus when it comes to day-to-day practice. Most notable of these are the principles associated with JIT manufacturing. These are considered to be *policy,* and employees at all levels are expected to follow these principles as a condition of employment—period! We must accept nothing less from our employees if we hope to be solid competitors in a swiftly changing global marketplace.

Step Six: Moving Equipment to Point-of-Use

Critical to this step is empowering select people with the right to move equipment when and where they choose, without formal approval. The objective is to get as much equipment to point-of-use as fast as possible, in order to be in a position to produce to true customer requirements (takt time application). As a result, you may have to move some equipment a number of times. Often, this can be the source of frustration to maintenance employees, engineers, and others who are taught to believe you should locate equipment in some permanent position in the factory.

These are the same people who think nothing of rearranging their own furniture at home on a regular basis. Again, we are taught in U.S. industry to strive to get things right the first time. However, we seldom do. So it is important to point out that there is *no ultimate point-of-use application for equipment and plant facilities*. What I am driving at is that equipment (and sometimes other facilities) in a manufacturing operation should be continuously moving—sometimes only small distances—in order to make the operation just a little more efficient than was previously the case. The truth is, if I were a plant manager and did not see equipment moving in the factory for quite some time, I would start asking why.

Step Seven: Transferring Inventory to Point-of-Use

In keeping with step six, it is also important to transfer all previously produced work-in-progress inventory, including all supporting raw materials, along with the equipment being relocated. When enough equipment has been repositioned to point-of-use and the associated inventory transferred accordingly, it will usually be very evident that inventory is far too high.

Step Eight: Limiting Parts Production

Now you are ready to begin using kanban's visual system of production control to limit the production of parts and components. There will be instances where you have already put this in place on a small scale, as you go through steps one through seven. However, it is now time to ensure that all production is pulled through the shop and kanban is the tool that you should use to do this. The rules for kanban were established by Toyota and were enhanced over the years as a means of ensuring the system worked within well-defined parameters.

In his book *Toyota Production System*, Taiichi Ohno describes the Toyota Production System as "The Production Method" and kanban as "The way it is managed." Mr. Ohno went on to say:

> Under its first and second rules, kanban serves as a withdrawal order, an order of conveyance or delivery, and as a work order. Rule three of kanban prohibits picking up or producing goods without a kanban. Rule four requires kanban to be attached to the goods. Rule five requires 100 percent defect-free products. Rule six urges us to reduce the number of kanbans. (p. 40–41)

I will not get into the details of implementing kanban here. They can be readily acquired by any organization interested in knowing the how and why. An excellent book on the subject is from Productivity Press: *Kanban: Just-In-Time at Toyota*, which was edited by the Japanese Management Association and translated by David J. Lu. I highly recommend this book to anyone seeking to implement kanban in their factory.

Step Nine: Instituting Product Cell Management

This is one of the more critical steps in the WFM journey. It requires a firm commitment to organize (or reorganize, as is usually the case) into a cross-functional management team approach. This team serves as group owners of the products produced in each manufacturing cell in the factory. It is usually important to pilot this approach before striving to completely reorganize the entire professional ranks. A good place for this pilot is in conjunction with steps six and seven (moving equipment and inventory to point-of-use). Doing this allows a great learning experience to occur, and sets the stage for what the future organizational structure is going to look like in the factory.

The key in conducting the pilot is to select some of your best people from each established function and provide them with both training and a vision for where the factory is headed. They then become the core professionals in leading this effort, when a plant is ready to take step nine, in an aggressive and expedient fashion.

Step Ten: Linking the Four WFM Drivers

When a factory has taken steps one through nine, it is time to begin an advanced application of linking the four WFM drivers and measuring levels of achievement in waste-free manufacturing, as pointed out in Chapter 5. It will become important as one proceeds to educate the work force in the linkage of the drivers and for them to understand the levels of WFM as well as establishing targets for achievement of the various levels throughout the plant as a whole.

YOUR GREATEST WARRIORS AGAINST WASTE— INDUSTRIAL ENGINEERS

Everything mentioned thus far evolves around a war against waste in manufacturing. The 10-step road map is key to winning that war and industrial engineering is a professional function that is instrumental in assuring a lasting victory. I believe the best trained and most highly committed people in the process of WFM should be the plant's industrial engineers (IE). If a plant makes an effort at doing this, they can establish a group of "warriors against waste" that can make remarkable strides. Without it, a plant faces considerable problems in keeping proper disciplines and appropriate focus in place on the shop floor. Unfortunately, what we are seeing in modern industry is a steady transition away from industrial engineering. In the process, IEs have taken on the role of pencil pushers, data gathers, and other such grossly wasteful duties.

I mentioned standard work earlier, and the Japanese manufacturing approach to it. The truth is, I am not absolutely certain that Toyota and other Japanese manufacturers practice what some of their past employees (who are now serving as consultants in TPS) are teaching around the world. What these consultants are proposing is that anyone can learn how to perform work measurement in just a few hours and, therefore, trained and qualified work measurement analysts (normally IEs) are not needed. It is to this philosophy that I say again: *while it may be an admirable objective, it just doesn't make a lot of sense.*

In my trips to Japan and the various industries I visited while there, I saw exactly the opposite. In most of the factories, a relatively large, very active industrial engineering function existed, and to the best of what I could gather, IEs were responsible for leading, if not personally performing standard work. Regardless, there is no doubt in my mind that delegating the responsibility of work measurement to those who are woefully inadequate to perform it is simply poor business logic. Remember, standard work is the tool from which you establish critical labor levels, product labor costs, shopfloor work methods, and manufacturing cycle times. Therefore, it is not something to be taken lightly.

Industrial engineers are qualified for this task and you should fully utilize their skills. When I was plant manager, I strived to assign the best industrial engineering talent I could find throughout the manufacturing cells we established, and I must say they served as the unsung heroes for the progress we were able to make. I believe the factory that fully and effectively utilizes its industrial engineering talent will make enormous strides over those who do not, because they are indeed the greatest potential warriors against waste.

SIMULATING THE ROAD MAP TO DEPLOY WFM

Let's use the road map and take an imaginary trip and visualize what should happen. First the leader, normally the plant manager, communicates to all concerned that the plant is about to enter into a never-ending journey that will change the entire course of the way the factory conducts business. This is followed by the plant manager and the entire management staff going through some very extensive training in WFM principles, concepts, and techniques. Here, it matters little who is hired to conduct the basics in JIT manufacturing for the plant manager and his staff, as long as they are qualified and experienced in both teaching and implementing such techniques. The key is for the staff to come to appreciate the benefits of the concept, to understand how to use the techniques and, most important, to come to know and appreciate what to expect in terms of results. Concurrent with this initial training and education is the selection of those "true believers" who are to manage the promotion office.

Following this training and selection, the promotion office is put in place and officially established. Also, training of the work force begins, with special emphasis on WFM's first driver, workplace organization. Every area of the factory is trained in the basics of JIT and applies workplace organization to a minimum level II throughout the entire plant. Once you accomplish this the factory will take on a remarkable new look and become dramatically more efficient. And you'll achieve all of this with no real disruptions associated with changing the existing system of production.

At this point, the promotion office begins an earnest training initiative in the more advanced aspects of WFM, thus starting to seriously promote the change process. This advanced training is, again, given to all employees, hourly and salaried alike, and it becomes continuous. In time the events or sessions conducted will become more implementation oriented than training, but the training and education aspects of the process are truly never-ending. Your true believers also begin to place a strong emphasis on the other three WFM drivers, insignificant changeover, error-free processing, and uninterrupted flow.

Then work begins on clearly identifying all core processing and in some cases it is decided to outsource some work currently performed internally. In addition, management has begun to demonstrate that it will operate on the basis of the guiding principles (drivers) rather than pure economic justification for any and every expenditure needed to drive the process of continuous improvement forward, at a rapid pace.

You then begin to move equipment on a regular basis throughout the plant to support and enhance point-of-use manufacturing techniques. Old centralized stores areas begin to dwindle in size, and in some cases, completely disappear as you move inventory along with equipment to point-of-use. As well, production quantities normally produced begin to shrink in size as you introduce takt time, one-piece flow, and kanban.

Reorganization begins to take place to accommodate a product cell management approach and more and more the teams guide and direct the day-to-day management of production activities within the cells. Lastly you and your true believers place a strong focus on linking the drivers and tracking specific progress in this area. As you use your IE warriors to mount your successes you'll be converting more and more true believers to your cause, and your revolution, moving from a conventional mass manufacturer to a lean manufacturer, will become the new business process. But it will never become business as usual because the WFM journey is a never-ending process.

As a result, your plant has seen remarkable improvements in product quality, customer orders are being met as never before, operating costs have shrunk dramatically, and, overall, the place has the look of an efficient and productive operation. Because at this point in your journey you have laid a solid foundation for continuous and lasting improvement. You've had the will to make substantial changes, and go past your initial threshold of pain. Now your conditioning will begin to get easier and easier as you begin to transform your factory and move into the lean manufacturing era.

Month Fourteen—The Power of Why

I wasn't satisfied in the least with the progress we were making in decentralizing the press shop to point-of-use and I decided to meet with Jim about it. It was getting late in the afternoon when he finally dropped by.

"Hey, Jim," I said, "have a seat. You look a little bushed."

"I am. It's been a long day . . . and you?"

"Fine," I replied and then decided to get right into it. "I just wanted to chat with you a little about your progress on decentralizing the press shop. How's it going?"

"Okay," he replied. After I made no immediate reply he continued, "Well, not to your satisfaction, I'm guessing."

"You're right," I said, with a half smile, but being sure to maintain somewhat of an air of seriousness.

Jim wasn't one to dwell on the particulars. Although he was a loyal trooper and someone I had utmost confidence in, I felt that I was going to have to probe if the whole story was going to surface. Since it was late and obviously both of us were a little worn, I decided my office wasn't the place to continue the conversation. I felt we needed just a bit more relaxed atmosphere.

"Tell you what, Jim. It's late but I would like to discuss this with you before the day is out. How about us getting out of here and meeting somewhere for a cold one?"

"Sounds good to me," he replied. "Where?"

"Well, there's a nice little place on our way home. O'Bryon's. You know where it is?"

"Yeah," he said. "I know where it is. What time?"

"I'm ready when you are."

"Okay," he replied. "I'll see you there shortly."

(continued)

I left almost immediately, trying to avoid some unforeseen situation that would keep me at the plant. As a result, I arrived before Jim and ordered a beer. The waitress, a young lady named Julie, was a cheerful sort and assured me that she would watch for my company.

"You from around here?" she asked.

"Down south," I replied.

"I knew it," she replied laughingly. "I could tell from your accent."

I noticed her staring over my shoulder and turned to find Jim waiting patiently behind me. I extended my hand, gave him a firm handshake, and asked him to sit down. He ordered a beer and we spent some time making small talk before I got back to the conversation we had started at the office.

"Tell me more about the press shop situation," I said.

"Well, it's proceeding, but we have a problem that I've been trying to resolve."

"A problem? Why haven't you told me?"

"You have enough to worry about, and I don't like to bring every little issue to you."

"Jim," I said, "there's no problem too small if it's going to get in the way of us getting the press shop decentralized. It's the single most important thing."

"I know," he interrupted. "But it's not a show stopper."

"It may be if we don't get on with it. You've got to understand. I have union support at the present time. This won't last forever, and especially if we don't show some positive results. What I'm saying is we have to make sure this is done as fast as possible."

"We will," he snapped, obviously somewhat annoyed.

"When?" I probed.

He looked at me intently but didn't speak for a moment. Then he leaned back and took a deep breath.

"You have to allow me to get the job done. You didn't give me a deadline, but I am working on it."

"Come on, Jim. You've said there's a problem and you won't even share it with me, then you tell me to trust you. Did you ever see the movie *The Agony and the Ecstasy* about Michelangelo?"

"I don't recall. It's an old one isn't it?"

"Yes, it is. It starred Charlton Heston and Rex Harrison. Anyway, Michelangelo was commissioned to paint the ceiling of the Sistine Chapel, which, as you know, took him years to finish. Well, the Pope grew very impatient and kept asking him, 'When will you have an end?', and Michelangelo kept replying, 'When I'm finished.' Jim, I need to know when you are going to have an end to this project, and please don't tell me 'when I'm finished.'"

He chuckled briefly before relating what he felt we were dealing with: "Joe says we have a big problem moving some of the larger presses. They're located over pits in the flooring, and he says the press manufacturers tell him we're gong to have to dig new pits if we want to relocate them."

"Did you try the *five why's* Art taught us? You know, keep asking why, until you get to the root cause."

"Not really. Not yet, at least."

"Try it. I'll bet the press manufacturers are being very conservative. I've seen large presses without pits and I'm going to ask you to be totally convinced before you're willing to accept what you've been given thus far."

"Joe's usually right," he replied. Joe was Jim's chief manufacturing engineer.

"Joe thinks he's right, I'll grant you that, but we have to get the press shop decentralized to point-of-use and we can't be digging new pits all over the place. I'm from the old school that says, where there's a will, there's a way."

The next day after lunch Jim dropped by to let me know that he had used the "why" technique and was pleasantly surprised. He said he was happy to inform me that he was moving forward immediately with press decentralization and felt he would be through with it before the end of the month.

He went on to relate that he had discovered the only reason for the pits was to ensure the bed height of the presses was at a proper work height for operators. He said, smiling, "Heck, as I told Joe, we can put the operator on a platform if that's the only issue."

One morning a few weeks later Jim asked me to go out in the plant with him. He wanted to show me first-hand that the press shop no longer existed. As you might imagine, I was absolutely delighted and couldn't wait to bring Bill up to speed. Later that afternoon Jim and I took Bill on a tour, and he was almost floored when he turned the corner off the main aisle leading to the press shop and was greeted by nothing but a clean, shining floor, devoid of any equipment whatsoever.

The Why Technique

Later in my career when I spent much time teaching the principles and concepts of WFM, I always made a point of saying to my pupils that why was "the most powerful, influential word in manufacturing." Actually, that probably is true for any business. It is *powerful* because, used in a repeated fashion, it allows the true root cause of a problem to be established or at least provides a means for everyone to come to the realization that no one really knows the root cause. In the latter case, it simply means more work is required in order to clearly identify it. It is *influential* because stepping through a series of "why's" to any issue or problem tends to clearly address and rule out what isn't root cause. As a result, it is much easier to come to a consensus on what the true root cause is as well as provide data and indicate countermeasures needed to prevent a recurrence of the problem. Some readers may be familiar with what is referred to as the 5-why technique. It's a very popular tool that has been around for awhile and there are plenty of books that provide various examples and customized adaptations.

Revolutionary Pointers

- With the barrage of new organizational structures and operating philosophies the average U.S. manufacturing employee has become complacent. To change this leaders must (1) understand and be dedicated to the process, (2) project a clear, concise vision to the work force, and (3) be constantly engaged in the process.

- Before starting the WFM journey you must explain to the work force that the journey is not a program, *but a never-ending process that simply will not allow business as usual.* By putting appropriate communications in place at the very beginning, your journey will be far smoother.

- When you examine the fundamental differences between TPS and conventional mass (batch) manufacturing you will understand why the rapid deployment of WFM is both necessary and revolutionary.

- When beginning your WFM journey (your revolution) you must have the will to recondition yourself (and the factory) to deal with all the changes and resulting pain threshold.

- Changing your conventional mass production thinking is a serious part of your initial conditioning, but the farther you move along, the easier the change to WFM becomes.

- Be prepared for a lot of resistance the first time you introduce takt time (and kanban) into a batch manufacturing environment. Takt time is a very difficult tool to implement at the start of your journey and it goes against the grain of most existing materials replenishment systems.

- By fully utilizing your industrial engineering talent you will not only make enormous strides in your war against waste, you will assure a lasting victory. These "warriors against waste" are your secret weapon.

- By following the 10 distinct, interconnecting steps in the road map, you will interlink the four WFM drivers and immediately see improvements in quality, customer orders, operating costs, and operating efficiency as well as lay the foundation for continuous and lasting improvement.

- Using the powerful and influential 5-Why analysis will give you amazing results in uncovering root causes and coming up with countermeasures.

7

Changing the Culture

VERY FEW PEOPLE would argue that making the revolutionary transition from conventional mass manufacturing to lean manufacturing doesn't require a significant change in the culture of an organization. This chapter will address the matter of cultural change but there is no way we can possibly cover every issue for there are distinct differences with each factory that, at least in part, determines its particular culture. However, this chapter will address such key issues as working with your union, finding opportunities within the professional ranks, and helping a work force understand the "center of value-added."

The basic culture of most organizations is usually a reflection of the vision local factory management portrays. If local management does not project a clear vision, the culture will tend to become what people who are in a position to influence think management envisions. This is both dangerous and deceptive. It is dangerous in terms of the possibility of the established vision not being representative of the true expectations of a firm's customers. It is deceptive in terms of placing a work force in a position of working hard on doing what local management portrays as right, even when it is all wrong. If it is indeed wrong, it will usually end up putting a plant on a collision course that is today commonly referred to as a reengineering or restructuring.

To further clarify the point, consider what occurred in the '50s and '60s. Back then the Big Three were convinced the only thing important to consumers was bigger and brighter automobiles. It was not important how much gas the cars guzzled or the fact that they simply were not put together very well. A squeak here or there really wasn't all that bad.

After all, no consumer would be brazen enough to expect anyone to manufacture and assemble that much sheet metal without at least a few fit-up problems. None of the Big Three wrote and posted this on factory walls, but even unspoken, this "vision" was portrayed to the general work force and a culture was established in accordance with it. In turn, this was reflected in the workmanship and quality of the automobiles produced. And all during this time, the vision and culture were totally out of sync with what the average customer really wanted and expected. Then in the late '60s and '70s, Japanese manufacturers began to produce cars that met customer expectations and in the '80s they even exceeded those expectations. The rest is history.

THE PRODUCTION WORKER IS THE CENTER OF VALUE-ADDED

In deploying the four drivers of waste-free manufacturing it is important to understand what I refer to as the *center of value-added*. This concept will make the task much easier to get the work force to fully focus on the benefits of WFM. Not only will this concept provide the leader with a way to lead change—get the message through to the work force—but it will affect the culture of the organization because lean thinking will start becoming preeminent throughout the rank and file.

To do this, the leader must first recognize where the true center of value-added rests within manufacturing. This will require a substantial change in your conventional thinking. In probing the common perception of where value-added resides in an organization there is an appropriate example that says it all—any typical manufacturing organization chart. Where do these charts lead one to believe the center of value-added resides? The answer, of course, is with the senior manager and his or her staff. Such charts send a strong, silent message. It says that management believes that the only people within the organization who add true value are those within the management (professional) ranks. Otherwise, why don't organization charts include hourly production associates?

There are, of course, those who would see this example as taking a simple, straightforward document like a company's organization chart and turning it into something that implies management doesn't think very much of its production work force. I can only respond—if the shoe fits, wear it. I further contend that if organization charts are necessary at all (I think not), they should have the names of the operators on the shop floor, who are performing value-added work, at the top of the chart and everyone else below—in a clear support role. Because this is where the center of value-added resides. This is an important change in thinking, a change that must occur if one hopes to become a waste-free manufacturer. You can define the center of value-added under the umbrella of the following criteria:

- The true center of value-added is the people who perform work the customer *is willing to pay for.* Therefore, this only pertains to the production associates who perform work that transforms material and components into a finished product.
- Everyone else operates in a clear support position, with their principal goal being to do all within their power to help and assist the production associates be as efficient as possible in meeting customer expectations.

Is this seriously different thinking than what exists in most U.S. manufacturing firms today? You bet it is. In fact, it is so different that some manufacturing managers, supervisors, engineers, and others can never fully bring themselves to accept it—even though there are many in organizational change management and total employee involvement (TEI) proclaiming that we should flip the traditional corporate structure and put employees on top. However, this "old guard" mentality is fast becoming an obsolete breed as the world moves toward a globally competitive environment and those manufacturers who recognize and work at strongly supporting the correct center of value-added will have long and successful futures in manufacturing. Those who do not will eventually see a demise of their outdated thinking and, potentially, the business they represent.

The Rules of the Game Have Changed for the Professional Ranks

To further emphasize how far we have to go and the need for change, take a look around and count the number of U.S. manufacturing firms that are truly using WFM's principle of center of value-added in their operations. Very few indeed. What we see instead are people in the professional ranks who view production operators as fellow employees, yes, but employees who are inferior (intellectually or otherwise) because of the nature of their position. The professionals would never admit this, of course, but the truth is not easy to hide when one probes beneath the surface of well-defined and established values. As a result of this perception, professionals take on roles (depending on personality, ambition, and/or what they perceive to be the best path to success) that will either place them in a position of absolute authority over the production worker, or that will allow them to contribute in a fashion where they do not have to deal with production associates on a regular basis. In either case, they certainly do not view the production worker as the center of value-added.

Unfortunately, what follows is not going to sit well with some, and I would point out that my intention is not to criticize any particular function or role in a company. But it is important that we in manufacturing wake up and realize that as today's professionals in a global market, there is a universal trend to concentrate on values that are virtually obsolete. Professionals within manufacturing must accept much of the blame for our current woes—for much of it stems from their inability to foresee the change needed. For too long they diligently (stubbornly) clung to the practices of the past that were established in a more localized competitive market—where all business practices were essentially the same. Certainly manufacturing, until very recently, was running mass (batch) production operations. Today the playing field and the rules of the game have dramatically changed and U.S. business professionals must learn and also adapt ... quickly. This is why it is important to examine some common perceptions within various manufacturing-related fields of endeavor and then to look at the kind of change in work habits that is needed.

Obsolete Best Business Practices of the Past

Both manufacturing engineers (MEs) and industrial engineers (IEs) are notorious for coming out of school with a perception that they must decide on almost everything operators do, if those operators are to be effective in their jobs. In the industrial engineering ranks (where I worked for many years), IEs were taught that their role was to develop the best method (standards) for the work production associates perform.

As a result, I have witnessed some myopic, bizarre, and just plain wrong behavior. The following are some specific examples.

- Industrial engineering departments audited operations to ensure that associates were doing exactly what was prescribed in the written standard, even if it wasn't the best or most efficient way of doing the job.
- In more extreme cases, I have seen IEs hide behind machinery and equipment, or on mezzanines to check if operators were indeed performing work in a manner not prescribed as standard.
- Within the manufacturing engineering ranks, I have repeatedly witnessed engineers purchase and install equipment that was grossly in excess of the basic requirements for the job and usually far too expensive—without so much as even asking production associates their opinion about what they felt was needed in order to do an adequate job.
- I have seen quality engineers justify, purchase, and install outrageously expensive test equipment without ever involving production associates in discussing the need or in establishing other potential options.
- In addition, I have seen them spend countless hours processing data that detailed what was *wrong* with the people and equipment doing the job, and then act insulted when someone asked what they were doing to make things *right*. This is because many of them see themselves as "cops of quality," rather than as professionals who hold a responsibility to engineer continuous improvements to it.
- I have seen accounting professionals spend weeks in preparing a report and drawing conclusions dealing with some facet of the manufacturing operation, without ever speaking with the operators involved, or the foreman, or the production manager, or others who might be familiar with the situation.

If one honestly comes to believe that the center of all value-added is the worker on the shop floor, then it becomes easy to begin to see the opportunities associated with making the professional ranks a true competitive weapon. For example:

- Imagine IEs performing full-time on the shop floor, working hand in hand with the operators on things that would make the job easier, safer, and more efficient.

- Imagine MEs working closely with production associates and discussing equipment and facilities to see what changes are needed to make the operation more effective overall (from the standpoint of things like increased uptime on equipment, devices that help eliminate errors, maintenance procedures that start at the operator level, etc.).
- Imagine accounting professionals working directly with the operators in helping them to understand the financial measurements of the company, and in reviewing financial progress and potential problem areas. Imagine them working on data that indicate how the competition is doing and holding meetings, not to tell manufacturing what it is doing wrong, but to solicit the input of the production associates in what might be done to make the operation more cost competitive.
- Imagine quality engineers working full-time on the shop floor, side by side with the operators, getting direct input from production associates as to quality problems within the process and analyzing what might be done to attack those problems at the source.

Although these are just a few examples, it is the production facility that can manage a true change in thinking, who can help flip the organizational chart (and thinking), and can take the business to new heights of accomplishment. How does one go about making this kind of partnership thinking universal throughout the organization? It starts with a plant manager who believes strongly in the WFM drivers, and who is willing to demonstrate that belief in everything he or she says and does every day, day in and day out. I seriously doubt you can make change of any real value without this kind of commitment from top leadership.

MAKING THE UNION A PARTNER IN CHANGE

A manufacturing culture is much like a piece of production equipment. One has to live with it to really get to know it, and to be able to sense what sort of "stroking" it needs to make it work more effectively. The culture in a manufacturing plant is greatly influenced by the track record a company has in working with its union officials. Good working relationships are difficult at best and can be extremely complex when you're trying to maintain an effective relationship under a scenario of change. However, I have never worked with a union where you could not accomplish this if management had a sincere desire to make it work. The task is about building trust—lasting trust.

There are two "always" and three "nevers" that I believe a plant manager must solidly adhere to if he or she hopes to make the union a true partner in change. These are:

- Always show union officials unquestionable respect.
- Always tell them the absolute truth—even when it hurts.
- Never hide important information from them.
- Never tell them anything you do not intend to do.
- Never surprise them—*ever*!

This may look like a relatively easy format to follow; however, given that management and the union typically start at two very different levels makes staunch rules like these difficult to follow. For example, marketing may provide a plant manager with information that sales are starting to deteriorate in a certain region of the country. Typically the company would not want to hand this information out to others until the timing was appropriate—if ever. There are those who would adamantly adhere to limiting what should and should not be shared with union officials and production associates. Again, beware of old conventional mass-production thinking. The changes that must occur are not limited to production processes on the shop floor. They include revising conventional thinking as to what role the union (if one exists) plays in a successful manufacturing organization and in doing so, what level of awareness they should maintain regarding business conditions. To make WFM work (or any lean manufacturing effort), it is crucial that plant management build the kind of relationship with the union where they can readily share and discuss information, such as marketing's forecast above, without fear of the information leaking out and potentially compromising the company's position.

On the flip side, most union officials are trained not to trust management—and through experience in dealing with some of the always and nevers above this mistrust can easily grow into acrimonious relations. In fact, many officials are elected because they have demonstrated a willingness, if not a downright desire, to "take on the company" regarding almost any issue. Bringing this sort of union leadership around to the point of becoming a true partner in the WFM process is not simple, nor easy to accomplish.

Serious change often creates a great amount of stress within the work force. This is because change can be truly threatening if people fail to understand the purpose is to attack and eliminate wastes that are making the company less than totally competitive—not the elimination of jobs. Even when they are told this, they sometimes perceive it as just another management ploy that will, over time, dissipate into empty promises until another "improvement" ploy pops up its head. Changing the union leaders' and work force's perception of the purpose of the change process—the long-term benefits and that WFM is a never-ending journey—is something you must constantly be reinforcing until they buy into the change process. Otherwise they will view your efforts as suspect.

No two plants are alike when it comes to the matter of culture, and certainly when it comes to management-union relations. However, there are common cultural threads surrounding what I have repeatedly referred to in this book as conventional mass manufacturing. Most union officials can clearly see the inaccuracies, and are usually willing to work with management in trying to change them.

I believe it is important to review these cultural threads, because they set the stage for the kind of interface between union and management that can collectively work to the advantage of both. A good starting point is for the company to openly lay it on the line to the union that the way the company is currently running the business of production (batch manufacturing) is totally wrong—and then expand on those common cultural threads that all batch manufacturers believe in. This opens the door for a discussion about the shortcomings of conventional mass manufacturing thinking and the benefits of WFM. For despite the negative perceptions that most union officials have of management's intentions, they are usually willing to work with management in trying to make genuine improvements. Table 7-1 provides some of the more common cultural misconceptions between management and unions.

In principle, *no* union leader under the sun could agree with these. It would be an admission that the people they serve are little less than brainless robots (which certainly is not the case). If, then, management and the union can agree that the above perceptions are indeed false and there is a need to work together in changing them, this sets the

Table 7-1. The Management/Union Checklist

The "Do You Believe" Checklist of Common Cultural Misconceptions
• Do you believe operators are going to produce bad parts, thus we need inspectors (police) to check the work of others?
• Do you believe the company must incur the expense of training people, but only in the most basic skills required to gain very narrow, specific job knowledge?
• Do you believe the company should only measure what it can report with great accuracy, even if the information is of little value in making effective day-to-day business decisions?
• Do you believe the only way to set up a production operation properly is to have a group of engineers study the process and determine the best method?
• Do you believe the company must have a paper trail for everything?
• Do you believe that machines and equipment are simply going to break down, thus the need for large and expensive maintenance functions?
• Do you believe the production process must be driven by some system of computerized production control (specifically MRP) because operators would not know what to do otherwise?
• Do you believe operators should always check their brains at the door and stay busy producing parts?

stage perfectly for the kind of working relationship required in order to deploy waste-free manufacturing. Although there is no cookbook to follow in making the union a partner in change, good common sense judgment generally provides the best route, given one understands the areas where concentration should be applied.

One thing I am certain of, however, is that if a union exists, the leadership of that union must play an active, supportive role, if change from conventional manufacturing is to take place. It is not a matter of *if* the union will become a true partner, it is only a matter of *when*. The key, again, is creating an atmosphere of understanding, trust, and teamwork. Concerning this challenge, I once spoke with an operation manager who informed me:

> You can forget it here. There has been such a history of poor relationships with the union, nothing is going to repair the damage. They see us as the enemy and any attempt on our part to have them take an active role in change would be seen as a political ploy on our part.

My response was:

> If that's the case and I were you, I would get my resume updated as quickly as possible because it's only going to be a matter of time before this place goes entirely out of business, or until you are replaced by someone who believes they *can* find a way to make it happen.

Slightly less than 18 months later, manufacturing operations ceased in the plant and production was transferred to Mexico. More than 600 people lost their jobs and, as a result, the local community was forced to absorb added unemployment and a reduction of valuable revenue. The questions by many were: Was this the only answer? Was a transfer of the business the only way out? My guess is probably not, had plant management done the job it should have in partnering appropriately with the union.

Building an Interface with the Union—Some Words of Advice

Regardless of how much experience, knowledge, and expertise a plant manager may have in the H.R. manager and supporting staff, he or she simply cannot become divorced from direct and consistent contact with the union president and other elected union officials. A plant manager's chances of substantially changing the factory's operation are slim, at best, if he or she allows the H.R. office to conduct all communications with the union. I assure you that the union (and in all probability, the work force as a whole) will view such an approach by a plant manager as totally unconcerned for their general welfare.

The truth is that any plant manager who desires to move a plant forward with "revolutionary" change must be closely involved with the union. This means establishing a regular and consistent interface with the union as well as demonstrating a genuine interest, not only in their concerns, but their opinions about how things should be done. In my various dealings with union officials I practiced a number of things I believe are beneficial in building a solid working relationship. These are the important guidelines:

- As plant manager, hold regularly scheduled weekly meetings with the president of the union. Pick a day of the week both you and the union president can agree to and then meet religiously at that time. Keep the meeting informal in nature and practice *listening* more than talking during the meetings. If there is no business that either of you have to discuss, then just strive to enjoy the time together over a cup of coffee. Find out what his or her hobbies or interests are and simply chat for a time about those, if nothing else. Generally, however, issues will surface during these meetings and it is an opportunity for the plant manager to share information in an off-the-record manner about the business and then, in turn, get the union president's perspective about how things are going.

- At the offset, you could find that the president of the union is uncomfortable with a one-on-one setting, and would prefer to have some of their elected officers in attendance. If so, allow the union president to bring along those he or she suggests as long as the size of the group doesn't get out of hand. In any case, strive to convince the president of the need for both of you to meet one on one, if at all possible. Often, what might start out as a group will progress to a one-on-one meeting as more confidence is built in what the agenda is all about.

- As the opportunity arises express repeatedly to the union president why the change is required and what the eventual impact can be if it is successfully carried out. *And do not be afraid to provide your views of the result if it isn't.*

- If you have plans to hold communication sessions with the work force pertaining to the state of the business or other such matters, sit down with the union president and, preferably, his or her executive committee beforehand and share with them what you intend to say. In the best case, actually hold a dry run of what you intend to present with them at least a day or so in advance of the meeting.

- If you plan on writing and posting an announcement or a memo pertaining to a business-related issue (such things as organizational announcements, etc.) allow the union president to review the document before it is posted. This provides him or her with knowledge beforehand to prepare for any questions, comments, and such that might come from the general membership.

- Remember to do everything possible to show a genuine interest in keeping the union leadership informed and, most important, *avoid surprising them.*

Working closely with the union requires an understanding of the rocks and boulders that will surface in the midst of great change, boulders that can have a fatal impact on the relationship, if care is not taken. For example, conducting an employee satisfaction survey when you are squarely in the middle of this kind of change is something you don't want to do. However, that is exactly what happened to me. It was the first plant where I was plant manager implementing this kind of change. It was a corporate-driven initiative, so we had little say regarding when it was to be conducted, but as a result, we received one of the lowest employee satisfaction ratings in the company. To make matters worse, they posted the ratings for the work force (and union leadership) to review.

Two years later, shortly after I had left my post to take on another assignment, the company conducted another employee survey and the plant had one of the highest employee satisfaction ratings. Upon learning of this, you can probably guess my first reaction. It was that it probably got better because I left. But, regardless if that actually had any influence or not (hopefully not), a more ominous driver was in motion at the time of the first survey. At the time, the plant was in the middle of laying off a substantial number of employees, destroying long-standing traditions, changing work habits, and basically upsetting a manufacturing lifestyle that came to affect almost every employee, in one manner or another, throughout the factory. The union (and, yes, even some in the management ranks) essentially took this as a strong message that the magnitude and level of change was far too aggressive and I would be remiss if I did not say I was tempted more than once to pull back somewhat, under the considerable pressure that arose as a result of the survey. Thankfully, I did not.

When the second survey was conducted, the plant had taken on a new product line from another factory, which was forced to close its doors. Employment was back up to its previous high, the plant was running efficiently and it was getting accolades for being a showcase facility for the corporation. Why wouldn't employees be more satisfied? Perhaps an interesting side note to this story is that the plant that ended up closing its doors received one of the higher employee satisfaction ratings in the initial survey.

Month Fifteen—Storm Clouds Brewing

I arrived at work to find six production employees sitting in my office. I had an open-door policy, but my first reaction was, this is taking it a little too far. However, I tried to maintain an air of calm, so I entered and set my briefcase down before turning back to them.

"Well . . . how have you been?" I finally asked.

"Not so good," one of them replied.

"Is there a problem?"

"We're here to give you something," a woman named Ruth said as she proceeded to walk to my desk carrying a rather large cardboard box. With that she tilted it over and what appeared to be thousands of pennies gushed forth onto the desktop. Some of them spilled over and hit the floor, but by the time they had finally settled, a pyramid of coins lay squarely on the center of my desk.

"We want to give this back to you. You obviously need it more than we do," she proclaimed before staunchly marching back and taking a seat.

I'm certain my mouth dropped open as I stared at the display covering the desktop, but I tried to stay composed. I was thinking, "What's this all about and how do I handle it?" I stood for a moment more, then walked over to my desk and sat down. I was wondering to myself where Joyce, my secretary was and why she would let something like this develop. It wasn't like her. Then the telephone rang. I asked them to keep their seats, but excused myself long enough to walk outside and pick up my secretary's phone. It was Joyce.

"Hi," she said. "Sorry I'm late but I had to take my daughter by to see the doctor. She's had a cold and—"

"No problem," I interrupted. "Look, Joyce, I've got some people in my office so I'm going to have to cut this short. Sorry."

"That's okay," she said, "I'll see you when I get in." I hung up the phone and walked back into my office, taking a seat before speaking.

"Well . . . please don't keep me in suspense. What's this all about?"

What I was about to discover was that it related to the company's wage compensation program. The program provided the opportunity for production employees to earn a weekly bonus, based on a prescribed standard for various levels of production output. An employee who exceeded the quantity specified as standard earned a 1 percent bonus for every 1 percent they produced over the prescribed rate.

The employees in my office that morning were all power press operators and before we had decentralized the press shop to point-of-use, it was not uncommon for them to earn a 30 percent to 40 percent bonus every week.

(continued)

As a result of moving the presses to point-of-use, they became part of production cell 012, which was on group rate and which could only earn a
bonus based on the output of the entire group, as opposed to the old press
shop setup, where everyone was on individual incentive.

Ruth spoke again. "We went along with you on moving the presses to the
assembly lines, but we can't live with this. We depend on our bonus to help
pay the bills. If all we're going to get as a result of following your lead is
pennies, then we think you obviously need the money more than us."

"Come on, Ruth," I started.

"No, you come on," interrupted Ben, a man known for being very outspoken and certainly unafraid to challenge anyone. I could see anger steadily
rising in his expression. "This is your fault and you're going to have to do
something about it!"

I paused a moment to let the atmosphere cool a bit before continuing,
ignoring Ben's outburst and trying to focus on what I could do to move
things to a point where we could reach an effective resolution. "Look, folks,
it's early. I just got to work and I don't know about you but I need a cup of
coffee. How about this? Give me some time to look into the matter and get
the facts, then I'll schedule a time for all of us to get back together this
afternoon. Okay?"

They looked at each other, finally nodding their consent, and with that
got up to leave.

"Just a moment," I interjected. They stopped and turned back. "Does the
union know that you dropped by to see me this morning?"

"No, but why do you ask?" Ruth replied.

"I just think they need to be aware."

"Fine with us," said Ben, "but we thought you had an open-door policy.
Guess you're trying to tell us not to bother you."

"Ben, please stop trying to put words in my mouth," I stated firmly. I
could see that he was terribly irritated, and was going to take anything I said
in a negative manner. And the truth was that my patience was also starting
to run a little thin at that point. But I managed to contain myself. "I'm simply suggesting that they should know of your concern."

"Well, then we suggest you tell them," Ruth replied and without further
ado they turned and departed.

An hour later Carl, Joe, Paul, and Ron listened patiently as I explained
what had occurred. Carl was the president of the union. Joe and Paul were
two other elected union officials and it was generally among the three of
them that all decisions regarding local union issues were made. Ron was the
plant's H.R. manager.

"What did you tell them?" asked Carl.

"I asked them to give me a little time to get the facts, and that I would get back to them before the day is out."

"You know the reason why earnings were so low last week in 012, don't you?" Paul quizzed.

"No, not really," I responded. "But I assume it was because we just started a new level of production."

"Exactly," he replied.

"Well, I know one thing," said Ron, "we're going to have to write all of them up for walking off the job without permission."

Since I had summoned them all together at the same time, Ron was obviously trying to figure out where I wanted to go on the issue, and had decided it was time to don his H.R. hat. I was thinking that in all fairness, I probably should have called him in to discuss the matter before we met with the union, but at the time I wasn't thinking about politics. I was just seeking a workable resolution to the matter, and I felt the union had to be involved on the front end of the dialogue.

"Ron, I'm going to suggest that in this particular case we don't do that," I replied, trying to offer a diplomatic challenge rather than a disagreement, considering the circumstances. "Believe me, I agree we can't have everyone running to my office every time they may feel there's been some sort of injustice done. But given that our friends here," I said, waving a hand toward the union representatives, "have gone along with us on making the change we recently made in moving all the presses to the assembly lines, and knowing some of the operators who visited me this morning as being something other than troublemakers, I would just prefer we not exaggerate the problem by writing someone up."

Ron quickly saw where I was trying to go and was fast to agree with me, as did Carl.

"Yeah. One thing we don't need is to be writing someone up," he announced.

"Let's get back to what Paul was saying," I suggested. "You were trying to make a point, were you not, Paul?"

Paul went on to say that he felt we might defuse the situation by helping to identify the reason for the low bonus and, more important, by showing everyone involved that it was just a short term earnings problem. This was because the assembly department of which they were now members, was going through a new line balance (for a new level of output). At the outset of such change earnings are normally low, but generally rebound quickly. In turn, he said, we had the chance to show that over the long haul,

(continued)

the earning potential in a group rate scenario versus individual piecework was actually better. This was because while the bonus percentage was not as high as they had been used to earning on individual piecework, there was more time on bonus work (less downtime). Thus, their overall pay for a given week could be as good and sometimes even better than they had been used to in the past.

We went on to agree that the union would meet with the operators to explain the situation and that I would not bring them back together unless Carl gave me the word there was a need to do so. As it turned out I heard no more about it from the operators, and Carl let me know later they had been satisfied with what the union had to tell them—at least for the time being.

I know I could have just as easily chosen to bypass union involvement since it was not a formal employee grievance, but, by being conciliatory and getting the union directly involved on the front end I accomplished a couple of important things: (1) I avoided surprising the union by immediately getting them involved after the incident occurred, and (2) by doing so I was able to get them to work with management on both an answer and a resolution. Thus the incident did not turn into a management versus labor affair, which of course can bring everything to a standstill.

Work with Rather Than Deal with the Union

Working with a labor union is much different from *dealing* with them. In successfully working with the union, the plant manager must be a catalyst in establishing and maintaining an adequate relationship. This can't be willed to others in the organization. The plant manager has to personally carry this out and must recognize it as one of the more important responsibilities of the job. Regretfully, however, I must say that this is an area where I have seen a serious shortcoming by many plant managers. The tendency is often to give the not-so-easy task of involving and interfacing with the union to the plant's H.R. representatives. In other words, the plant manager divorces him or herself from establishing and carrying out any serious day-to-day working relationship. This is not only a terrible mistake; it is an injustice to the operation as a whole because change for the better cannot effectively occur without the union becoming a partner in the change. And this simply will not happen if the plant manager does not personally make the union feel both wanted and needed.

I can assure any plant managers who view the union as an enemy to be dealt with, rather than a potential ally in bringing about change, that they are in all likelihood doomed for failure! True enough, one may be able to strong arm change without the help and support of the union, but in almost every case this simply does not tend to be lasting and, more important, it negates the establishment of a relationship in which employees truly believe they are a vital partner in the change process.

The key, again, is to help the union clearly understand the need for substantial change in the manufacturing process and the long-term potential benefits if it does take place or the dire consequences if it does not. Once you accomplish this you'll find that they can be most helpful. On the other hand, if you don't follow through on this (due to the fault of the plant manager in the performance of this task or because there is union leadership who simply will not, under any circumstances, allow such a relationship to develop) then your change effort is probably going to be most difficult, if not totally impossible.

INSTITUTIONALIZING OWNER-OPERATORS

An important part of waste-free manufacturing is institutionalizing an owner-operator philosophy. Though it's not necessary to make every production associate in the plant an owner-operator, *it is a must for all key processes and equipment.*

There are different ways you can approach this, but most important is to clearly identify what is expected of those employees. Table 7-2 can be helpful in establishing the depth of training the company will be obligated to provide. (Check owner-operator responsibilities.) Under the most positive and constructive circumstances, the company will need to train the employee to perform these eight functions before he or she can truly become an owner-operator.

If you examine this eight-point list carefully, it is very obvious that you must provide extensive communications (as to purpose) and intensive training (as to how) before a production associate can qualify as a full-fledged owner-operator. This is one of the bigger challenges for those plants making the move from conventional mass manufacturing to WFM, and one of the more time consuming. To make the concept

Table 7-2. The Owner/Operator Responsibilities Checklist

How Much Training Will Be Needed?		
Yes	No	
☐	☐	1. Is your owner-operator keeping up and maintaining the equipment so that no support personnel for basic maintenance is required?
☐	☐	2. Is your owner-operator producing total quality parts on the equipment so that no inspectors are required to verify quality?
☐	☐	3. Is your owner-operator performing all setup and changeover on the equipment so that there is no need for specialized setup and changeover personnel?
☐	☐	4. Is your owner-operator maintaining housekeeping on and around the equipment so that there is no need for janitorial support for the process?
☐	☐	5. Is your owner-operator maintaining general tool control and maintenance so that there is no need to carry a supply stock in a centralized crib or for maintenance personnel to change tools on the equipment?
☐	☐	6. Is your owner-operator keeping his or her own time so that there is no need for time-keeping personnel.
☐	☐	7. Is your owner-operator continuously "kaizening" the process so that there is no need for a team of people to visit the process occasionally to make continuous improvement?
☐	☐	8. Is your owner-operator maintaining, updating, and changing kanbans, thus eliminating the need for a production control system to define quantities to be produced?

work as intended, you need to view the owner-operators as the *most valuable* of all employees in the plant and compensate them accordingly.

In relation to this, personally I am biased that a pay-for-skills-earned program is the best method of compensation. What may surprise some, once you start such a program, is the extreme pride that owner-operators tend to take in their equipment. This, at least in part, is because most of them do come to see it as *their equipment* and as a result, the care and upkeep on the equipment is enhanced.

Championing a Cause for the People

It is difficult enough in itself to lead change and almost impossible to achieve success in doing so, if both the union and employees do not believe the leader has a genuine interest in them and that he or she is willing to take a stand on their behalf. Thus, the plant manager seeking to accomplish substantial change has to first show the work force that he or she is willing to champion something of benefit to them. In every manufacturing firm, the largest resource base is the plant's production employees. While they may or may not be represented by a collective bargaining unit, they will always look hard at the actions of the plant manager and decide for themselves if that person is indeed a champion for the people.

I firmly believe that it is critical for the leader to examine the most basic needs of this particular group of employees and ensure he or she has done all within their power to champion a cause for them, *before venturing into waste-free manufacturing.* This can be something as simple as implementing an open-door policy that really works or as complicated as justifying a multimillion-dollar air-conditioning system for the factory. Of course, being a champion for the people should not be misconstrued as a reason to step outside the boundary of good judgment or as some effort to buy employees' support. Whatever you do has to make sense for the business, as well. If a cause tends to serve both purposes, then the leader should work diligently at making it happen. If it doesn't, forget it and proceed to find something appropriate to champion. The key is to seek out things that are meaningful and important to employees and then to take aggressive action in demonstrating your willingness to step at least slightly over the line, if needed.

Month Eighteen—A Heated Issue

It was July and hot. The entire Midwest was in the grip of a drought that was to last two full years, unbeknownst to those who were suffering through this particularly dry summer. Surprisingly, although the plant produced air-conditioning equipment, the factory itself was not air conditioned. This was not unusual for a plant in the Midwest. In fact, air-conditioning was probably the exception rather than the rule. On the other hand, it had always been the source of great complaint by employees, because they felt since the plant produced air-conditioning equipment, they were *entitled* to work in an environment that was air-conditioned.

From my point of view, I had always found it a bit embarrassing when dealers and distributors toured the factory. I saw it somewhat like proclaiming:

(continued)

"As our customers we want you to purchase our equipment, but we don't see the need for it ourselves." So, in one of my meetings with the union, I mentioned that I intended to get air-conditioning justified for the plant. They looked at each other, smiled, and then fought an apparent need to laugh. It was obvious I had either said something very funny, or I had proceeded to make a fool of myself. Finally, the president of the union spoke.

"Better men than you have tried, John, "he said apologetically. He then told me this had been a source of much debate over the years, even to the point of becoming a contractual issue at one point. The problem, he said, was it was far too expensive and additionally, the factory roof was in question because it apparently would not support the weight of the required air handlers. He then topped it off by coyly noting that every plant manager had said they were going to get the plant air-conditioned, but none had been successful.

"I suggest you don't tell the folks on the floor you are going to get air-conditioning for them. They might throw something at you," he jokingly advised.

"Well," I replied, "maybe they didn't try hard enough." I was determined to give it my very best effort because there was a deep-seated reason for my interest in seeing this to a successful conclusion. I was convinced if I was going to be successful in leading the kind of change the plant needed, I had to show employees, especially production associates, that it was not going to be business as usual. This included delivering on some things from my end that had long been viewed as "impossible."

I saw getting air-conditioning for the plant as something that would project my desire and interest in making the work environment better for employees. Additionally, it was something that would be beneficial for business, considering the emphasis that was being placed on bringing more and more customers to the factory. Certainly, if nothing else, it would serve as a visual monument, indicating change for the better.

Deciding there was not a lot of time to waste, that afternoon I called a meeting with Jack to discuss the matter further. He was a long-standing friend of mine and we had spent much time on the road together when we were both serving supporting roles in strategic planning. Most important, he was a person I could count on to tell the truth, even if it hurt.

The truth did hurt. The issue of air-conditioning in the factory had been "evaluated" a number of times and he informed me the cost would approach $1 million. And no one had been able to come up with a solution to the structural problem involving the additional load the roof of the factory would be forced to carry.

"Jack, if there's someone who can find a solution to this, it's you. I'd like you to work on it, and come back to me with a recommendation. What I'd really like is an appropriation we can pass on to the powers above."

"Okay," he replied, "but you're going to be opening up some old wounds, believe me. What do you want to use as justification?"

"Customer satisfaction," I said, pausing and waiting for some approving response from him.

"How so?"

"Well, something like this. During the summer months, operator efficiency is negatively affected due to the heat index in the factory." I paused, studying his expression.

"Go on," he encouraged me.

"As a result, the attention span on quality is shortened and ..." I stopped. He had started to fidget in his chair and the expression he usually had when I was completely out of line was starting to form on his face.

"Oh, to hell with that, " I said, standing and walking from behind my desk to take a seat next to him. I turned to him and leaned in close, for effect.

"Jack, the justification is that we *need* it. Marketing is planning on having more and more dealers and distributors visit the factory and I'm all for that; but, frankly, it's embarrassing to have customers leaving the plant after a tour soaked with perspiration. On top of this, you know my feelings about making this place look better, and from a housekeeping perspective, air-conditioning would only serve to enhance what we've been striving to achieve." I was starting to feel a little better, because he was nodding his head approvingly.

"John, I agree that since we're having more customers visit the plant, it becomes more of a business issue than it may have been in the past. But I've got to tell you that it isn't going to be easy and you know the rumor starting to float around that the company has intentions of closing some plants in the future. It will just make an investment like this all the harder to sell."

"All the more reason to strike now, Jack," I replied. "I firmly believe the plants that are going to survive are going to be the ones that free space the quickest. I have plans for that, but I need this for other reasons. All I'm asking is that you follow up on this for me."

And he did. I set up a plant tour with the vice president and general manager of the division, and was relieved the morning of the scheduled tour when his secretary called to inform me he would not be able to make the 10:00 a.m. appointment we had arranged. She went on to say he could make it that afternoon. What luck, I thought, an afternoon tour of the plant ... perfect!

(continued)

We spent an hour and thirteen minutes in the factory. I remember the time precisely because I was counting the minutes and trying everything within my power to keep him on the factory floor as long as possible. When we finally concluded the tour, his shirt was soaked in sweat and his tie had long since been loosened. The temperature in the factory had to be at least 110 degrees, if not more.

Nearing the conclusion of the tour, I mentioned my feelings about taking customers out into the plant during the hot summer months. He had not responded at that time, but as he was shaking my hand to bid me farewell, he remarked: "I've been thinking about what you said regarding our customers."

"Yes?"

"What do you think it would cost to air condition the plant? Any idea?"

"As a matter of fact, I have an appropriation prepared for your review, but I haven't had the chance to run it by you."

"How much?" he interrupted.

"One point two million," I sheepishly replied, "but there are some reasons—"

He cut me off again with a polite wave of his hand. "Bring it to me. I'll have my financial advisor look it over. If it's in order, I'll sign it."

It was. He did. And exactly eight months later, in the spring of the following year, I was honored to throw a switch, which was answered with a responsive surge of cool, soothing air circulating through the factory.

USING THE COMPRESSED PRODUCTION SYSTEM TO RAPIDLY DEPLOY WFM

There has been much discussion in this text regarding WFM drivers and the need to change both the *culture* of the factory and the *system* of production. It poses the question as to the difference between WFM and the *compressed production system*. In context, the WFM drivers center on clearly defining production wastes and establishing the tools and techniques you need to use to provide continuous improvement. The compressed production system becomes the forum, or fast track, for effectively implementing the WFM drivers. In the compressed production system strong management attention is placed on:

- Compressing the time required to do repetitive production work.
- Compressing the time required for response by support functions.

- Compressing the time required to introduce new products and implement ongoing product enhancements.
- Compressing the time required to respond to special customer needs and/or requirements.
- Compressing the amount of inventory required to run the operation.
- Compressing the time required to set up and change over equipment.
- Compressing the time required to change and/or amend layout of equipment and facilities.
- Compressing the time required to eliminate errors commonly made in the production of products.
- Compressing the time required to implement employee suggestions.
- Compressing the amount of travel required to produce parts and components.

Setting forth an effective action plan to accomplish this will, in turn, result in:

- Compressing the cost of manufacturing.
- Compressing common manufacturing lead-times and cycle-times.

Of course, in order to do this, a manufacturing operation must go through a good deal of training and reorganization that has the full support of senior management. Most important, however, inside the manufacturing plant itself, individual operating units will have to be established that can essentially support themselves from *every* aspect of the business (material procurement to finished product). The basic organizational structure required for this approach has often been called *unit management*, but the problem has been that most plants have not taken the concept far enough, because they are unwilling to make the needed investment in the basic resources required to make it work effectively. So it is often viewed as a good idea, but far too costly.

Let me assure those responsible for running manufacturing operations in today's globally competitive environment, and especially those who are interested in leading the type of change required to become truly globally competitive, there is *no economic justification for any decision against fully incorporating a cell management concept in your factory*. Economic justification, for or against, has absolutely nothing to do with the reality of the need for it. Management must clearly do it, and the management team responsible for its implementation must do it with some applied diligence.

In the process of diligently moving forward with a cell management approach, mistakes will happen. Do not let that deter you. Most often the mistakes will have to do with making the appropriate appointment of individuals and/or the number of people assigned to the cell. Let employees know on the front end that you are charting new territory and the staff assigned to the cell, as well as their individual roles, will be subject to change until it is operating as intended.

The Foundation of the Compressed Production System

It is my feeling that having a clear set of steps to follow allows manufac-turing managers the opportunity to do this in an effective manner; for it is one thing to know change is needed and to be impatient for something to happen, and quite another to know what should happen (first, second, third, and so on) and then practice deliberate impatience in seeing the steps implemented. Part of my struggle as a plant manager trying to implement significant change was my inability to portray a vision of where I wanted the plant to be and, therefore, having to make it happen by sometimes blindly pushing forward. As the old adage goes: "Had I known yesterday what I know today, I would have done things differently." This is why I created the 10-step road map discussed in Chapter 6. The road map is also the foundation of the compressed production system and the rea-sons why some of the steps are aligned in the format that they are.

For example, it may be surprising to some that training employees is not the first step outlined. It is not called for until step three, when you establish the promotion office. This does not mean that some training is not necessary in the early stages of the process. Training must be given to key personnel. What is different, however, is that in the effort to drive the process of change, JIT consultants usually recommend that you pro-vide training for the general population as the very first fundamental step in the change process. The theory is that training allows people to understand the need, benefits, and tools to be utilized, and it is then a matter of providing them the opportunity to make it happen. Usually following this is monitoring the program and occasionally providing direction to those who have been empowered accordingly. But have they really been empowered? Could this be why so many programs start, live short lives, then die, in American business? I believe so.

Lasting change has to start at the very top of an organization and has to continue with strong involvement from the top. The most knowledgeable and best trained of all employees in WFM should be the plant manager and his or her direct staff. Responsibility cannot be willed ("empowered") to others in the early stages of the process. The best management commitment will be worthless if there is no forum that drives the process forward, thereby *forcing* needed change to be thoroughly addressed. This is accomplished in the compressed production system by following the 10-step road map. Step six, for example, calls for moving all supporting equipment to point-of-use. Step seven specifies that all inventory associated with the equipment be removed from stores and taken with the equipment being relocated. This forces major operating decisions, which affect such things as pay points, scheduling, and the like.

The compressed production system, in practice, forces management to address and resolve the issues associated with how it will run the business under a new and different set of operating rules for manufacturing. If management follows the 10-step road map it cannot vacillate on the decisions that need to be made to move WFM forward. It is truly obligated, by the sheer nature of the changes required, to manage the process because no other choice exists.

As you implement each step in the road map, you should be making plans to move quickly to the next step, then the next. Again, communications are essential. Employees must see conventional batch manufacturing as a cancer that is slowly killing the operation, and that the only cure is to quickly cut it out, destroy it, and replace it with a customer-driven pull system of production. Every minute wasted in vacillating about the need to change only allows the cancer to spread further and only makes the cure more lengthy and difficult.

But what is really different about the compressed production system is that it eliminates the tendency to procrastinate through a series of straightforward actions (steps), sequenced to build off each preceding action. This allows a manufacturing operation to systematically implement the four WFM drivers and make waste-free manufacturing a reality in a reasonably short period of time. I cannot emphasize strongly enough that unlike Japan the United States does not have decades to switch to waste-free manufacturing. Over the years Toyota has already proven the basic JIT concepts, but we do not have to follow their specific path of implementation, although that is precisely what many consultants are prescribing. If U.S. manufacturers are to copy anything from TPS (and Japanese manufacturers in general) it is to take the best of what they have already wisely accomplished and do it better and much faster.

But you cannot do this, or use WFM's compressed production system, without first adopting a cell management approach throughout the entire factory. And in association with this you must put in place well-qualified and fully empowered cross-functional teams who are dedicated to the process. Without this in place, even with the implementation of waste-free manufacturing techniques, you won't get much more out of it than if you had an elaborate kaizen activity. The purpose of the compressed production system is to go beyond just another kaizen activity to develop a system of production that can accommodate the maximum potential of the lean process.

Month Nineteen—Revitalizing the Morning Meeting

We were now at a point where the entire management staff, members of the union, and a number of key hourly associates had been exposed to world class manufacturing techniques. With the help of Art, we had done some in-house training in the more advanced tools and had made some meaningful changes on the shop floor which were serving as a good example of the benefits of JIT manufacturing.

The press shop operation had been entirely transferred to point-of-use, and we had begun to train and establish some of our employees who worked in key processes as owner-operators. The plant had been cleaned up and workplace organization had been applied in most areas of the factory. In essence, it was beginning to take on the appearance of being a "lean and mean" manufacturing operation.

In fact, shortly after implementing an owner-operator approach, Jim, my production manager, approached me about visiting a certain area of the plant to examine a piece of equipment. I was very busy preparing a special presentation for an upcoming staff meeting and said so, but he pleaded that I take the time.

"You have got to see this, John," he insisted.

"Now?" I asked.

"Now," he reiterated with a broad smile. It was clear from his expression that there was something he just couldn't wait for me to see and that it wasn't one of those occasions where there was a need to hustle out to the factory floor for some bad news.

Jim was a man I was beginning to highly respect and while I like to feel that I provided the basic vision and direction for the success of our "lean and mean" look, the truth is, Jim was unquestionably the "mover and shaker." What I liked most about him was his drive and energy in getting things done in a fast and effective manner. He was not a man who saw things others would typically view as an impossible roadblock and he wasn't quick to take no for an answer. Jim would definitely be at the top of any plant manager's "10 most effective managers" list.

So at Jim's insistence, we proceeded to the shop floor and once we got where we were going, he asked the owner-operator to show me what he was doing to keep "his machine" in good working order. I ended up being totally astonished. The equipment was a specialized and rather large and sophisticated process, which had a carousel feeder where four separate components were stored for automatic injection into assembly fixtures. One of the problems with the equipment was that it had to be shut down rather frequently for maintenance to clear the feeder chutes, where dirt and grime tended to build up. When this happened, parts simply would not feed in a proper manner. Therefore, frequent downtime had been a problem that seemed to plague the equipment and, to some degree, we had to accept this as just an inherent part of this particular process with little we could do other than have maintenance be as responsive as possible when shutdowns did occur.

As I mentioned, I was astounded. First, the operator had cleaned and painted the outside of the machine, but what was really amazing was that when he lifted the lid to the carousel to show me how he was keeping the inside, it was spotless! I am sure my mouth dropped open. The operator went on to tell me he cleaned the inside of the carousel at the end of each shift, which is no simple task. No one had ordered him to do it. He did it because he knew dirt and grime caused the machine to shut down. But he also did it because he viewed it as his piece of equipment and he took pride in the way it looked and operated. (In the end, downtime became almost nonexistent on the equipment and it ended up being a showcase, where we often took visitors and certainly other employees who were being trained in owner-operator concepts and techniques.)

(continued)

But at this point we had new issues to deal with. Although we were beginning to see the fruits of our efforts in improved customer satisfaction through improved product quality and an increasing responsiveness to customer demands, I decided it was time to go further—much further. It was time to move forward at a much more rapid pace. In order to do this it was clear that I had to change the format of the morning business meeting so we could better focus on doing those things we needed to do.

I was convinced we needed something that would motivate us toward more concentration on the things that still were making us less than totally competitive. I felt the cause of any problems we were experiencing in this area was due to old, obsolete manufacturing practices, and I was certain our measurements tended to drive us in the wrong direction. I was determined to do something about it.

I started by meeting with my accounting manager and insisting that he attend some seminars to learn all he could about world class measurements. However, I had decided I was not going to wait for this to change our morning meeting format.

I followed my meeting with him with a series of discussions with various members of my staff, who served as my brain trust. We spent a considerable amount of time debating how we should go about changing the format of the meeting and came to agree on three things that were pertinent to the issue:

1. That the present structure of the meeting instigated conflicts, which often ended up being a contest as to who could outwit the other. It was a show of sorts, where the participants were driven to act out clearly defined roles in a staged performance.
2. That the meeting served no real purpose in addressing and resolving the root cause of many problems that were keeping the factory from better serving the customer and the corporation.
3. That the meetings were often extremely stressful, especially for those in functions that received a great deal of attention.

I suggested that we commit the unpardonable sin in a production meeting and that was not to discuss schedule reliability (i.e., how we were performing to the prescribed production schedule in terms of units produced). Instead, I supported concentrating on things like the number of total quality defects and what caused those defects. I was certain that if we began to focus on the right things the schedule would take care of itself.

Additionally, I suggested we begin to measure and report, on a daily basis, how we were doing with efforts pertaining to decentralizing stores areas to point-of-use. Further, I said that I would like to look at inventory in terms of pieces rather than dollars, and begin to track if we were indeed working our inventory levels down. Most important, I wanted to review, each and every day, field failure rate reports, in other words, what the customer was telling us about our products.

I was finally able to get a consensus out of the group and we scheduled the first revised meeting format for the following Monday morning. It was awkward, to say the least, because we were experimenting with something that was completely foreign to everyone involved. But after the first few meetings the flow of information and data started to become a natural thing and there were some pleasant surprises.

First, there was a great deal less finger pointing. Next, I began to see an immediate improvement in advancing the efforts of decentralization. Lastly, concentrating on quality set up an entirely different frame of mind regarding the topics of discussion that arose during the meeting.

As we came to learn, revising the business meeting format was one of the more important initiatives we undertook and later many other changes and new measurements were implemented that were key to helping us in our transition to waste-free manufacturing.

THE ONE-LEVEL ORGANIZATION

In conjunction with the compressed production system, it is imperative that a manufacturing organization limit the number of management levels and be as close as possible to a one-level management approach. Ideally, cell managers would report directly to the plant manager. In addition, the company should make an effort to keep management positions between the cell manager and production associates to an absolute minimum. The closer the plant manager can remain (from an established organizational and reporting standpoint) to the people on the shop floor, the better the plant is going to operate. Also, the fewer levels cell managers have to work through, up and down, the better the flow of information and the faster you'll be able to address and resolve problems. It has been my experience that a one-level organization is never as hard to put in place as it is to keep in place. What will inevitably occur are issues, problems, and such where the easiest and fastest solution is to add resources and, subsequently, more levels within the organization.

In truth, an absolutely pure one-level organization may be totally impossible either to achieve or to sustain over the long haul. But the key is to keep a sharp focus on the matter and to adamantly oppose anything that might add unneeded levels within the organization. A "lean and mean" attitude should prevail pertaining to this issue. Otherwise, the best of initial efforts will divert back to building unneeded levels within the organization, with the subsequent result being an organization that becomes fat in resources and with levels that dramatically slow down an effective decision-making process.

Revolutionary Pointers

- Local management needs to project a clear vision, otherwise the basic culture of the plant will tend to become what people who are in a position of influence think management envisions. This is both dangerous and deceptive.

- The culture in a manufacturing plant is greatly influenced by the track record it has in working with its union officials. Good working relationships with the union are difficult at best, and can be extremely complex under a scenario of change.

- To change from a conventional mass manufacturer to a waste-free manufacturer, the leader must recognize that the true center of value are those production associates who actually transform material and components into a finished product. Everyone else operates in a clear support position.

- Rather than assuming their role is to develop, prescribe, audit, and police what they think are the best methods for the production associates, it's time for manufacturing engineers (both IEs and MEs) to adapt to the lean manufacturing paradigm and work full-time on the shop floor with operators to solve problems.

- There are two always and three nevers that a plant manager can use to make the union a true partner in change (see page 167).

- A good place to get the union leadership to play an active, supportive role in changing to WFM is to tell them that the way the company is currently running the business of production (batch manufacturing) is totally wrong and then work from here to find common cultural threads and clarify misunderstandings.

- Regardless of how much confidence a plant manager may have in the H.R. manager, he or she simply cannot divorce him or herself from direct and consistent contact with the union president and the other union officials. The plant manager must be a catalyst in establishing and maintaining an adequate working relationship with the union.

- You should view owner-operators as the most valuable of all employees in the factory and compensate them accordingly. The most effective method of compensation is through a pay-for-skills-earned approach.

- Before starting a venture into WFM a leader should examine the most basic needs of the employees and then aggressively champion a cause that is meaningful and important to them.

- The compressed production system is the forum, or fast track, for implementing the WFM drivers and the 10-step road map is its foundation for effectively accomplishing this.

- The compressed production system eliminates procrastination through a series of straightforward actions, sequenced to build off each other, that free the manufacturing operation to systematically and rapidly deploy WFM.

- The compressed production system *cannot* function without the adoption of a cell management throughout the entire plant as well as qualified and fully empowered cross-functional teams that are dedicated to the lean process.

- For the compressed production system to work, it is imperative that a manufacturing organization limit the number of management levels and strive to become a one-level organization.

8

Measuring Progress—
What to Measure and How

I RECALL A TRIP TO JAPAN, which provided me the opportunity to visit a number of leading manufacturers in that country, where I visited a facility that was touted as being world class. The plant manager served as our tour guide and although he spoke relatively good English, we had an interpreter accompany us. For the most part, the plant manager allowed the interpreter to do most of the talking; however, there were numerous times over the course of the tour that he openly remarked "no good," as we passed various processes in the factory. Occasionally, he would leave our group to go into a production process and speak with an operator or group of operators. I would see polite nods displayed among all those concerned, but it was evident he had not stopped by to exchange pleasantries and that he wasn't necessarily a happy trooper.

At one location the interpreter asked a production supervisor to tell me about the process. During the overview the supervisor stopped to apologize about a tool that was poorly positioned in a shadow box, where tools for the job were intended to be kept in a neat, orderly fashion. I tried to be polite: "At least you can find all your tools and they're in the right box. We can't even do that most of the time." The plant manager quickly intervened, waving a finger in the air for effect as he very sternly corrected me. "No ... no good!" I apologized, a little surprised at his evident frustration with my comment. Then I imagined what he must be thinking: "Stupid American. Why would you say something like that in front of one of my employees?" I realized that what I had done was no different than having him tell an employee of mine, after witnessing the employee producing parts with very poor workmanship, "It's okay, looks fine to me." I'm certain I would have been a little offended by such a remark.

Later in the conference room with a number of his key associates, I quizzed them about their annual product costing practices, capital expenditures, and such. They seemed quite befuddled with my questions, but tried to answer them as best they could. I had noticed a number of engineers on the shop floor during the tour working very diligently with the production associates. When I got around to asking about formal objectives for their support functions like their production engineers, the plant manager responded: "We have no such ... as you call it ... formal objectives for our engineers. Why would we have them write down what they know is to be done?" I remember thinking it was a good point.

Since I have not researched the matter, I honestly do not know the depth of measurements used in Japanese plants, but my guess is that it is considerably less than most conventional manufacturing operations in the United States and Europe. In the United States, however, there is a standing need to measure performance for it has been said: "We are what we measure." This obviously was meant to imply that measurement is a critical factor in motivating employees to act and/or to react in certain ways.

While manufacturing is usually not in a position to arbitrarily change long-standing financial measurements, they are fully in charge of how they measure their own effectiveness. Most conventional accounting methods concentrate on weekly or more often monthly measurements. The general feeling is that daily measurements are far too erratic and fail to show appropriate or realistic performance trends.

Again, I must caution ... beware of conventional thinking.

Manufacturing is the only segment of a business that must produce on a real-time basis. To a large extent, tomorrow, next week, next month, and next year are unimportant; certainly secondary to today. Every day that a manufacturing plant operates, it operates to meet a prescribed customer demand. This serves as the end result of all the other planning taking place within the company or corporation. Accounting and other such functions have more freedom for forward planning, and thus the need for longer term measurements. Manufacturing is where "the rubber meets the road" (in the eyes of the customer), and it is here that not only every day, but almost every minute, a plant must know how it is performing. This does not mean that manufacturing performs blindly without consideration of anything past the immediate, but it does imply that, on a scale of importance, today is the number one priority. Additionally, manufacturing measurements should be structured to focus on *process* rather than economics; the theory being that if process is taken care of, the economics of the business will automatically improve.

What we should be targeting for in today's globally competitive market are plants that are exceptionally good at making small, yet steady and consistent improvement in *all* key areas of the business. To do this, we must approach the business of manufacturing with a new and totally different mind-set regarding the task at hand.

TEN KEY AREAS OF MEASUREMENT

Table 8-1 outlines 10 key areas of measurement that are essential for achieving and maintaining consistent improvement throughout the entire manufacturing arena. Something that should be apparent about these measurements is that all but one are process oriented, and the one associated with economics is focused on eliminating the cost of applied capital for purposes of increasing capacity. Table 8-2 further defines

Table 8-1. Measuring for Improvement

Ten Key Areas of Measurement
1. Measure for completeness of production processing.
2. Measure yield that is defect and error free.
3. Measure for zero setup and/or changeover.
4. Measure total skills of the work force.
5. Measure operations for mistake proofing.
6. Measure mixed-model capability.
7. Measure waste elimination activities.
8. Measure elimination of capital expenditures.
9. Measure parts travel distance.
10. Measure speed to market for product enhancements.

Table 8-2. Measurement Definitions and Objectives

Key Measurements	Primary Objective
1. *Completeness of production processes.* Measure the number of orders that are completed without stoppages and/or the intermediate storage of parts, components, or assemblies.	To produce in a manner that has absolutely no interruptions in the flow.
2. *Yield that is defect and error free.* Measure output that has to be repaired, reworked, or scrapped at any point in the production process, for the plant as a whole.	To produce in a manner that is entirely mistake free.
3. *Time spent on set up and changeover.* Measure the total time spent to set up equipment against the total time available.	To produce in such a manner that the waste associated with equipment and people waiting for setup is significantly reduced, if not entirely eliminated.
4. *Skillfulness in the work force.* Measure to find if the plant is becoming more flexible in training, transfers, new hires, terminations, retirements, etc., and at what pace skills are being improved throughout the plant.	To increase the skills of the work force and become an even more skillful and flexible manufacturer.
5. *Mistake-proof processes.* Measure to find how many processes in the plant have had complete and intensive mistake-proofing applied.	To steadily work at perfecting each manufacturing process so inherent errors are entirely eliminated.
6. *Mixed-model capability.* Measure the capability to produce in a mixed-model fashion on each key product process.	To steadily increase the capability of the plant to produce any product, at any time, in a totally efficient manner.
7. *Waste elimination activities.* Measure the amount of formal and informal continuous improvement activity in the plant.	Establish an environment in which continuous improvement becomes an important task of every employee.
8. *Elimination of capital expenditures.* Measure planned capital expenditures for capacity increases that have been eliminated as a result of continuous improvement activities.	To reduce the number and amount of capital expenditures required to meet customer requirements.

(continued)

Table 8-2. Measurement Definitions and Objectives *(continued)*

Key Measurements	Primary Objective
9. *Part travel distance.* Measure the distance parts, components, and assemblies travel throughout the plant, from raw material to finished product.	To encourage the placement of equipment at point of use and steadily eliminate the waste of transportation and work-in-process (WIP) inventory.
10. *Speed to market for product enhancements.* Measure the time to implement engineering changes that serve to enhance the quality, safety, serviceability, reliability, function, or durability of the products produced.	To continuously enhance the overall value of the product(s) in the eyes of the customer.

these measurements and states their primary objective for WFM. We will now examine these measures in terms of scope and primary result (purpose) for waste-free manufacturing.

Measurement One: Completeness of Production Processes

A manufacturing firm working toward becoming globally competitive should be establishing a flow throughout its entire operation. You don't want your parts or components having to stop and wait, with the consequence usually being their intermediate storage at various points in the production process. What happens when flow is interrupted in a typical manufacturing operation? The answer is waste is created and unnecessary costs are added. The following example will emphasize this point.

Let's assume we work for a small manufacturing firm that produces paper clips. The process requires purchasing wire, which is cut to length, plated, and then packaged for delivery to the customer. There are different models, different shapes, different sizes, as well as different diameter wires. The wire is cut and formed on a single piece of equipment, which requires 20 minutes of setup between each different model. The other two major processes are a centralized plating area and a final assembly line.

First, visualize the wire being cut and formed in rather large batches, to maximize the efficiency of each setup. The batches (parts) are taken to a storage area where they remain until they are called for by the plating area where they are coated, again in batches, and then stored until they are called for by final assembly for insertion into boxes and shipping crates.

Now visualize the operation as follows: The wire cutting and forming processes have been engineered to require only the push of a button to change from one model to another. The paper clips are made to the exact quantities ordered by the customer and go directly from cutting and forming into plating (in much smaller batches than before) and are then immediately assembled into containers as they come out of plating for delivery to the consumer.

Which process has less waste? Which process can deliver to the customer faster? Which process would have the least potential scrap? The least potential rework? Most assuredly the last! To be precise, the first process had a not so impressive 33 percent performance ratio for completeness of production processing. (Two intermediate storages for the completion of one or more finished products, thus two storages for the three operations performed. The calculation of performance would be: $3 - 2 \div 3 = 33$ percent.)

The second process noted has a 66 percent performance ratio (three operations and one intermediate storage) because parts were only required to be batched for a kanban prior to plating, but in much smaller quantities than the previous process. Obviously, the second process is twice as waste-free as the first, but is it perfect? The answer is no. A waste-free manufacturer would clearly recognize this and try everything possible to make it so by:

- Breaking down the large centralized plating process into smaller plating units that might allow continuous flow.
- Buying (purchasing) the wire preplated.
- Eliminating the plating altogether.

These are only a few examples of the potential solutions available. There could very well be some better ideas. The key is: *Accept the fact that no operation is perfect until something is done to eliminate every break in the flow.* I apologize here to any firm actually making paper clips because what I have used as an example is, in all probability, a gross oversimplification of the actual process. However, the manufacturing firm that can produce in a flow without stoppages or interruptions unquestionably has a much more efficient and less costly operation than the competitor who batches and stores throughout the production process. The goal should be to achieve uninterrupted flow and, as a result, eliminate as many breaks as physically possible.

Measurement Two: Yield That Is Defect and Error Free

A manufacturing operation should be like a fine-tuned machine, efficiently meeting requirements, at a cost the customer sees as true value. You cannot achieve this when the operation is producing wastes in the form of scrap or rework, or when repair stations have become an inseparable part of the production process. You need to always think in terms of eliminating *all* wastes and the only means of doing this is consistently working at perfecting each and every process in the factory—*to the point where scrap is never produced and where rework is never required under any circumstances!* Measuring when and where scrap, rework, or repair takes place in the plant highlights these as unacceptable and places emphasis on actions that serve to eliminate them.

In contrast, what you usually see in conventional manufacturing operations is work on engineering ways to make waste generation more efficient, for example, developing and implementing a better and more efficient method of repairing units for a given production process in the factory. Generally, if you applied the same level of effort in getting to the root cause of the problem for the rework and driving this out of the operation in its entirety, the factory would be much better off in the long run.

Often what it boils down to is engineers and others, with good intentions of course, working on things that have little to do with making a plant more efficient and productive overall. This again is because what a factory measures often points employees in the wrong direction. If, for example, an engineering department is assigned the task by management of building a repair station into a select process, the message that is sent to all employees is that *rework is expected* and that the principal objective is to *salvage as much product as possible.*

If, however, the assigned task is to seek out and eliminate the root cause of the rework, you portray a completely different message.

Measurement Three: Time Spent on Setup and Changeover

Setup is usually the single largest area of waste in conventional mass manufacturing and thus the single greatest opportunity for fast and effective improvement. Totally eliminating all setup or changeover time may not be entirely feasible, although this should be the goal. It is an area where you should place high visibility and very special rewards (possibly financial) on ideas and recommendations that eliminate setup. Tracking the total time spent on setup in a factory against all time available to produce focuses on this waste and sets the stage for appropriate concentration on its steady elimination.

Measurement Four: Skillfulness in the Work Force

Many manufacturing firms measure skills gained by employees. However, these are most often static measurements. Few if any of these measurements actually measure skills considering everything occurring in the operation, such as terminations, retirements, and so on. The key is to establish if current employee skills are on the increase, decrease, or essentially static in nature. You must come to know, at any time, if total skills have increased against your most current base of employees. If, for any reason, they are less today than yesterday, the plant has slipped backward in its quest for global competitiveness. If they are better than anything on record (even if this is through new hires who just happen to possess more skills), then the plant is making progress in the right direction.

Measurement Five: Mistake-Proof Processes

Every manufacturing process should be looked upon as a process that can produce in a totally mistake-free manner. Once, when I made that statement to a business associate, his response was: "That's crazy. Expecting each and every process to be perfect all the time just isn't realistic. Processes are made up of people, materials, and equipment, none of which are perfect. Plus, things happen that just can't be planned for.

You're asking for something that just can't be done." My response was: "If what you're saying is right, then you don't get on an airplane expecting the engines to be reliable, because those engines were built by people and equipment ... and, yes, before you say it, while there have been cases where engines have failed, it is that mind-set of *perfection* that has been the catalyst behind what is today a very safe and reliable airline industry."

As managers, if we truly expect our manufacturing processes to be perfect, then they'll probably be very close to it. More important, if we project the feeling that we can't produce in a mistake-proof manner, then rest assured we are going to have many costly mistakes on the factory floor. But, the truth is, we do not have to rely completely on a mind-set. The science of mistake-proofing, called poka-yoke by Japanese manufacturers, looks at methods and devices that eliminate common mistakes made in the production of parts, components, assemblies, or finished units. There are numerous books, seminars, and so on, available to the manufacturer who needs to learn how to utilize this technique. What you will find, for the most part, is that it's nothing more than a common sense approach to resolving recurring production problems.

Measurement Six: Mixed-Model Capability

Flexibility is the key to becoming truly globally competitive and the ultimate in flexibility is the capability of mixing models in production, so as to be able to produce what the customer wants, when the customer wants it, and to do this in a relatively efficient manner. Measuring for mixed-model capability provides a firm with a focus on achieving something the competition may not be able to offer. If, however, the competition is already pursuing globally competitive manufacturing practices, this becomes something that *must* be put in place, as soon as possible, in order to maintain parity.

Measurement Seven: Waste Elimination Activities

Imagine a factory where all employees came to work each day feeling they had an obligation to make improvements to some portion of the manufacturing process before they left for home. Would this not be a powerful competitive weapon? Once you establish a WFM promotion office you should track the results of this activity on a regular basis and highly publicize the results. It is also very important to develop the means to track the informal continuous improvement activities of employees and give some appropriate recognition to these as well. Actually, you should place just as much emphasis on informal activities as formal, structured, continuous improvement events, because it is through the encouragement of informal activity that roots of WFM will begin to take hold. This will help make continuous improvement a way of life throughout your organization.

Measurement Eight: Elimination of Capital Expenditures

Interestingly, many manufacturing plants feel a downright obligation to spend every penny of capital that has been tentatively planned for their operation. Unfortunately, many of these same firms view capital as money outside of their official operating budgets—the "corporation's money," so to speak, and they feel if they do not spend what they have been allotted, they will be provided less capital next year. So the unpardonable sin becomes submitting a capital budget and not fully depleting all the funds that were initially outlined.

You might be surprised at the number of highly regarded managers in charge of important functions within manufacturing who really do not understand how capital is applied and paid for (typically, it is depreciated over a course of time and applied as a direct overhead cost against every product produced in the factory). As a result they fail to understand that capital expenditures, especially those that are intended to increase production capacity, add costs to the products produced, and, in turn, make the plant less cost competitive.

It has been my experience that the vast majority of capital expenditures for capacity increases can be totally eliminated through the application of waste-free manufacturing principles, and it therefore should be a measurement of progress when you eliminate some, if not many, of the capital expenditures as a result of continuous improvement.

Measurement Nine: Part Travel Distance

This measurement centers on highlighting how much waste the factory is experiencing with transportation and associated WIP inventory, and how much work is being done to eliminate it. The ultimate goal should be zero part travel distance within the factory. While this may never be fully achieved, the work force should view travel distance as a substantial waste, and they should apply serious effort to continuously shorten the distance.

Measurement Ten: Speed to Market for Product Enhancements

Any manufacturer that is best in the industry in time compression possesses a very noteworthy competitive weapon. The manufacturer that can deliver its products faster than its competitors, especially those that can deliver product enhancements faster, will always have the competitive edge. Time compression is a key benefit of WFM's compressed production system, and you can use this to pay close attention to how well your plant performs in this area. Just as a result of measuring this process, improvements in speed to market for new product designs and revised product enhancements should start to take place.

OTHER IMPORTANT MEASUREMENTS

Table 8-3 shows a number of other measurements that you can adopt to track your factory's operation for global competitiveness.

Performance to Takt Time

Understanding how a factory is performing to takt time is very important. If a manufacturing cell is consistently performing faster than the established takt time (takt time is customer requirements expressed in time per unit), this could, among other things, indicate the distribution of work and/or labor power is incorrect or that something prescribed is not taking place. It is an extremely serious situation when a cell is consistently running behind its prescribed takt time, because customer requirements simply are not being met. This is usually an indication that work is not balanced properly, that something has been added to the operation which was not called out in the standard for the job, and/or that someone may be doing something that isn't necessary.

Measuring performance to takt time, in areas (cells) that are using it is important for firms who wish to establish and maintain a globally

Table 8-3. Additional Measurements

More Measurements for Global Competitiveness
• Performance to takt time (+ or –).
• WIP and finished goods inventory (in pieces rather than dollars).
• Number of suppliers certified to deliver to point of use.
• Number of value-added suggestions per employee and percent implemented.
• Non-value-added (essential versus nonessential).
• Number of repeat visits to equipment or processing.
• Degree (extent) of management team located on the shop floor.
• Value-added to non-value-added floor space utilization.
• Total square foot manufacturing space for each product family.
• Total manufacturing lead time (receipt of order to finished product).
• Total manufacturing lead time (including supplier's lead time).
• Total cycle time to total hours worked.
• Total cycle time to total lead time.
• Number of employees trained in waste-free manufacturing.

competitive position in their markets. I said earlier that I do not view takt time as a principle and that it can or cannot be applied, depending on the circumstances. While I do think it definitely should be used in all manufacturing cells to establish the required beat for customer requirements, there are factories that have had the principle of takt time beaten into them so diligently that they have tried to establish a time for every piece of supporting equipment and/or processing in the factory. I think this is absolutely ludicrous. In addition to being extremely time consuming to calculate and communicate, it serves no logical purpose. If you cannot fully dedicate a supporting piece of equipment to a process (for example, a machine that makes parts for a number of cells or units), simply kanban the quantities required off the equipment and forget about establishing takt time.

Inventory Expressed in Pieces Rather Than Dollars

Most work-in-process and finished goods inventory measurements are expressed in dollar value. In many cases, people have a hard time visualizing the actual level of inventory, because it is not always easy to associate the cost of inventory with its true volume and mass. This is why I suggest you measure inventory in pieces rather than dollars. As an oversimplified example, if a plant running 500 products per day, which uses only three purchased components (one costing $1, another costing $5, and a third costing $1,000), and has a standing objective to maintain (hold) two days of working inventory, regardless of the piece-part price per component, the on-hand inventory level required would be simply 3,000 pieces.

Looking at this same example in terms of dollars, this would mean on-hand inventory should not exceed 500 times the dollar amount expressed for each individual part $\times$ two days of on-hand inventory, or a total of $1.006 million. However, assuming the plant actually was carrying $4.0 million in inventory, where do you think it would look first to reduce it? In the high dollar purchased component, of course (the $1,000 component). This is fine as long as the reduction does not go beyond the daily requirements needed to meet customer demand. But this is not always taken into proper consideration when a company is looking for ways to quickly slash inventory levels.

Measurements that help a plant track and maintain correct inventory levels, based on pieces rather than dollars, will help establish much better control of inventory, and as a result, keep inventory costs to a minimum. It will also provide total assurance of meeting customer needs on a consistent basis.

Suppliers Certified for Delivery to Point-of-Use

Many manufacturing firms have supplier certification programs. However, few take it to a level that gives them a real competitive edge. Using measurements that support supplier delivery to point-of-use provides this thrust. Ideally, the best working relationship is for a plant's supplier to be certified to deliver the parts directly to the place of use, bypassing receiving/inspection and any typical paperwork trails. Billings would be made by the suppliers based only on actual usage and the plant would gain the competitive advantage of having to carry no on-hand inventory for those particular materials or components.

Number of Value-Added-Suggestions and Percent Implemented

Employee suggestion programs are nothing new to manufacturing. In fact, most factories have some type of suggestion program. Nonetheless, as a production associate once mentioned to me: "Everybody's got ideas, but it's only the good ones that are fully put in place that make any real difference." This is so true. Often, employee suggestion programs become a forum for petty complaints and special interests, and this does defeat the purpose. To have an employee suggestion committee waste even one minute of time considering an idea to paint the women's restroom pink is downright wasteful, if not totally stupid. But it does happen. The answer lies in constructing a suggestion process that has very clear specifications, with very clear boundaries that concentrate only on the issue of value-added.

On the other hand, such an effort would be of no avail if employees did not understand what constitutes a value-added idea. Therefore, employee training in value-added principles is of utmost importance before you begin such a suggestion program. Just as important is the amount of attention you pay to implementing these good ideas. You must have in place a process that can quickly apply any and all value-added ideas or, over time, the suggestion program will undoubtedly fail.

Non-Value-Added—Essential Versus Nonessential

It is totally impossible to eliminate every non-value-added activity in a manufacturing firm. There has to be some activities that are often referred to as *essential non-value-added*. No customer is going to argue that a business does not need some management, some sales, some marketing and the like. Conversely, there are very few manufacturing firms who have actually evaluated value-added versus non-value-added and even fewer who know what portion of their total non-value is truly essential. How can a business hope to know it's competitive, unless it knows what is and is not value added in its operation, and what portion of its non-value-added is absolutely critical (essential) to the business? In truth, it can't.

This is an area of measurement where I do not have a magic formula. Each and every business will have to make its own evaluation and determine for itself what is and is not essential. One way to start is by understanding your competition. For example, if your sales force is somewhat larger than your toughest competitor, then the question should be, *why*! If you are indeed experiencing greater sales and you can attribute this to the size of the sales force, then it might be appropriate to keep it intact. If, however, your sales are not proportionally more, then you might need to ask what real benefit you are deriving from having a larger sales force.

When a company begins to measure and place emphasis on value-added, and begins to try to understand what portion of its non-value-added is, without question, essential to its business, it will begin to better understand what the customer is really willing to pay for. It will also begin to see the potential for lower costs and, therefore, more profitability through the steady elimination of non-value-added resources.

Number of Repeat Visits to Equipment or Processing

This is an important area of measurement because it clearly identifies a great opportunity for improvement and for gaining a competitive edge. Any production in the factory that requires parts to visit an operation more than once represents a grand opportunity to reduce part travel distance and speed up overall processing time. There are a series of questions you need to ask when you discover parts, components, or assemblies making repeat visits:

1. Is there a way through redesign of the product to eliminate the need for the repeat visit?
2. Is there a way to change the sequence of processing so one trip would do the job?
3. Is there a means of changing the equipment so the work could be accomplished in one visit?
4. Is the repeat visit (operation) really needed?
5. Is there simply another way to do the job?

Extent of Management Team Located on the Shop Floor

The globally competitive company recognizes the need for the management team to be on the shop floor where the action is. One of the best ways of achieving this is by having a large percentage of the support team housed on the production floor. Yes, you read it right–*physically* located on the shop floor. A manufacturing firm with anything less than 50 percent of its salaried work force located on the shop floor probably represents a company where management has no real idea what is happening, and where production associates receive a clear, unspoken message that management is not really interested in the work they do.

For a start, you should, without question, locate your support functions such as industrial and manufacturing engineering on the shop floor. Over time, you can add many other management team functions to the shop. One of the more powerful decisions I made as a plant manager was to relocate my office from the nice, spit-polished executive quarters to a mezzanine located in the center of the factory. Over the course of time, 80 percent of the entire management team reporting to me gradually relocated from the front offices to various locations in the shop. It made a tremendous difference in overall response time to floor problems, and in creating a more positive perception of the management team in general.

Value-Added versus Non-Valued-Added Floor Space Utilization

It is critical that you understand what portion of total available floor space your plant uses to add value and what is used for other purposes. On average, most manufacturing plants use a very small percentage of their available space for true value-added activities. The best way to explain this is to consider the space that production equipment and processing physically consume as the only true value-added space consumption. Anything else is considered as non-value-added space. This would include things like aisles, storage areas, inventory, and so on.

Total Square Footage of Manufacturing Space per Product Family

You should also know how much floor space each major product family consumes. If, for example, a plant has two product families and one, with far less impact on profitability than the other, takes up more floor space, it could be time to take a good look at the processing required. Letting this go unchecked would be like providing the largest portion of your own kitchen storage cabinets to something your family seldom uses. It just doesn't make a lot of sense.

KNOWING WHAT AND WHEN TO MEASURE

Understanding what to measure and why is very critical to the process of turning a conventional mass manufacturing operation into one that is making steady progress toward becoming waste free. Knowing when to measure is also important. I think you would agree it wouldn't make a lot of sense for the crew of a sinking ship to take the time to measure the flow rate of the water pouring through a gaping hole in the vessel. At such a time, every ounce of energy must be expended by the crew in trying to keep the ship afloat. To consider new or different manufacturing measurements at a time when the "ship is sinking" would be wasted effort. However, when shifting from conventional batch manufacturing to waste-free manufacturing a facility must at some point begin measuring itself in very different terms.

Employee Reactions to Implementing New Measures

Many employees are often frustrated when a manufacturing operation starts to measure itself differently. Additionally, when manufacturing takes it upon itself to install new and vastly different performance indices, some of the company's support functions, who consider measurement to be their forte, will tend to fight the effort in a very energetic fashion. It is interesting that this happens. However, this is another example of how change is not easily accepted.

When it comes to the matter of measurement, the greatest resistance will always be from within the professional ranks. There is a reason for this. Professionals are generally well-educated employees. As a result, they have learned there are, within limited variations, conventional performance measurement practices that apply for almost every type of generic business condition. Being human, their first reaction is to resist any effort that would imply there is something lacking in these. After all, these measures have been tried and tested over the years and have proven to serve U.S. industry well (at least from their perspective). Every business, regardless of the sophistication of their system (or lack of it), has standard, accepted financial measurements that it will not be interested in changing to accommodate the manufacturing arena. Therefore, any attempt to entirely discard the accepted performance measurements of a company or a corporation will be futile, and it really is not necessary.

As I have said repeatedly, communication is the key. Employees, professionals, and associates alike, must come to understand why performance measurements must change, and how the new measurements are going to be more effective for the business. Additionally, communication must take place with support functions that tend to drive the measurement process within the company (generally the accounting function). They must understand your intent is not to challenge or eliminate their measurements, but to try some new ones which you feel will be more practical in driving the process of continuous improvement forward.

These functions must be given the opportunity to see the effectiveness of the measurements you are proposing and be allowed, over time, to convince themselves they should eliminate some of their old measurements and adopt some of the new. I am sure there are manufacturing managers who are probably asking at this point: "Is the author so bold as to suggest that we pitch the measurements we have used for years in manufacturing and begin to measure ourselves solely as he is suggesting?" That is a very good question and my response would be: It depends. Allow me to explain.

To begin, please remember what was mentioned earlier about knowing when to measure. I would repeat again, if the ship is sinking, forget about instituting new measurements and work on the basics—getting equipment to point-of-use, reducing setup and changeover, improving general flow, improving productivity, reducing lead time, and the like. However, once the process of waste-free manufacturing is actively started, it indeed is time to look at measuring progress very differently.

Most of the manufacturing measurements used throughout our nation have led us to put concentration in the wrong areas. Common efficiency measurements place strong emphasis on overproduction, thus the growth of excessive and costly inventory levels. When these levels become too high, the company then moves to a short-term inventory reduction program. When the inventory is reduced to some level that is seen as reasonably acceptable, the measurements in place drive the operation to overproduce once again. It is, indeed, a vicious cycle.

Measurements within the professional ranks (usually called MBOs, management by objectives) often drive engineers and others to work on projects that add little value to the task of making the manufacturing operation waste-free. The result is most often an entire lack of a proper focus within U.S. manufacturing. An appropriate change in thinking has to evolve as a result of changing the interests, concerns, desires and motives of all workers. No employee empowerment programs or other such ventures will do the job when a plant's measurements essentially drive it in the wrong direction and tend to motivate employees to do absolutely the wrong things.

Month Twenty—Making Both Steady Progress and Strong Enemies

It was March and the first signs of spring were beginning to peek through in the form of a little added sunshine in the afternoons, a few flowering sprigs here and there; and moisture that now came in the form of rain rather than ice or snow. As sure as spring follows winter, it is just as certain that a person at the helm of a manufacturing operation in the process of towering change will develop both strong supporters and hard enemies. It was no less true of me.

At the turn of the new year we had paved the way for an overhead reduction in the cost of the products the factory produced, which was a factor in bringing back some lost share of market. Product quality had steadily improved and relationships with the union and hourly associates had gotten substantially better. Customers were beginning to visit the plant on a regular basis to see for themselves what had transpired to make the factory a much more reliable supplier.

General operating costs had been slashed. The factory was clean, much cleaner than it had ever been in the past. By opening up considerable space in the factory, warehousing and distribution had been brought on-site (allowing us to close an off-site distribution center), and WIP and finished goods inventory levels were at an all-time low.

One might think that a person responsible for leading such change would be looked upon very favorably by a vast majority of all employees. This simply wasn't the case. I was still seen as an outsider by some in the salaried ranks, who really weren't welcome to make the kind of change I was imparting. Others viewed me as little more than a "slash and burn artist," there to bring about some carefully crafted plan of demise. Many were convinced the operation was doomed to close, in keeping with the company's promise that five manufacturing sites were going to be shut down in North America over a two-year period.

But leading the kind of change the plant was undergoing required a sharp focus on the task at hand, and I worked hard at not getting sidetracked in the mission. However, I would be remiss if I said it was all pleasant. Certainly having to lay off employees who had been with the company for a number of years was the hardest task by far. Another was trying not to get too wrapped up in the day-to-day problems associated with batch manufacturing. I realized that doing so would mean all my energy would be directed at addressing the problems inherent to the old system of production and that over time the change required to put a new one in place would become a secondary objective. It was a very difficult balancing act.

However if I had anything, I indeed had focus and the results of that focus were beginning to pay off in terms of improved operating costs, faster response to customers, improved product quality, and the like. But the change was so dramatic, so swift, and so different that some saw my approach as being downright uncaring for the feelings of others. Nothing could have been further from the truth, but that perception can become a serious enemy to the leader making significant change.

In one salaried communication meeting, a rather outspoken employee stood and said: "Sure, there are some good things going on but at what price?"

When I quizzed him as to what he meant, he replied: "I'm referring to the price people have to pay. About the extreme pressure that is placed on everyone. About the long hours that never seem to stop ... that's the price I'm talking about."

I decided that I was not about to challenge him in front of others, but made a few comments about the change we were experiencing requiring extra work and effort by all. Because we were indeed fighting for survival. But, just looking out through the audience, I could see the rather curt explanation didn't sit well with some.

Nonetheless, it is no easy task convincing some employees (who for years enjoyed working for a company who was a clear leader in its field) that there is good reason for changing a system of production that has sustained the operation for many years. In my particular case, the opposition decided to play hardball and I got my first real taste of the battle late one

Friday afternoon. I was on the shop floor when I got a call to drop by Bill's office right away.

I arrived to find him with Jason, the head human resources officer for our division. Bill informed me that I had been the subject of a number of written complaints. Jason went over some of the complaints that had been lodged against me, such as, I was an absolute dictator who was unwilling to listen to anyone else's point of view. In addition, I was temperamental, unfeeling, and uncaring and said to be a workaholic who expected everyone else to be. And the list went on.

Jason said he normally wouldn't take such general and somewhat vague accusations that seriously but his concern was the fact that there wasn't just one, but a number of them, all with the same theme. It was clear to me that what he was trying to say was: Where there's smoke, there's probably some fire and where there's fire I hold a responsibility to put it out!

I wasn't about to ask who lodged the complaints because I fully understood that Bill and Jason held a responsibility to keep them confidential. I, myself, had addressed a number of those lodged against people who reported to me and I understood the importance of the confidentiality associated with such a process.

"Look," I said, "Both of you know I'm intense. I'll admit that. But it has to be apparent that someone is just trying to make me look like the bad guy."

"Well, what do you suppose prompted this?" Jason asked.

"Your guess is a good as mine but, as Bill and I have discussed before, there is definitely a group here who still view me as an outsider and they've had no reservations in complaining about the changes we've been making. That's about all I can think of."

Bill spoke up. "John, some of these complaints are saying that maybe the pressure is starting to get to you. You've taken on some very tough challenges and this may have perhaps caused you to act out of character on occasion." Jason was nodding his head in agreement.

I was perplexed. It was obvious there was more they had to tell me and I decided to probe. "Bill, I'm at my best under pressure. You know that. But, if there's something you need to tell me, please feel free to come right out with it."

"Well," Bill continued, "a plant manager gets a lot of visibility and I know you don't mind getting in someone's face when you feel the need to. The question becomes, have you perhaps gone a little too far in an instance or two."

"Excuse me," I interrupted. "I don't know what you're looking for me to say. As I see it, I've done what I've had to do to keep this place going and I've treated people as fair as possible in the process. That's it, bottom line."

(continued)

"John," interjected Jason, "to get down to brass tacks, my concern, which I should inform you that Bill shares, is that this goes further than just a number of written complaints. We and others have started to hear it in the halls, in the bathroom, in the cafeteria. It seems to be coming from all over the place and certainly from more than one or two people."

"I'm not suggesting we ignore the situation," I replied, "I'm just saying that given the circumstances this probably couldn't be avoided."

"Well, I certainly don't see any need to belabor this further at this point," he continued. "We've let you know the situation we're dealing with here and while I wouldn't classify it as grave in nature, it is something that could continue to grow and get completely out of hand if it isn't adequately addressed. But I think that any work on that is going to have to come from your court, not ours. However, I do want you to know that I understand what you're trying to say. So, where we'll go from here is that I'll give a written response, which as you know I'm obligated to do, and then we'll see how it goes. Fair enough?"

I looked at Bill to see if I could read anything in his expression as desire to continue, but it was apparent he was ready to put the matter to rest, if at all possible.

"Fair enough," I replied.

There is an old saying , "live and learn." In my case, that was exactly what happened. Although this particular incident largely came and went without further ado, it certainly made me start to think in terms of considering how people feel about change. To some degree, the accusations were true. I had done far more pushing change rather than working on achieving it through solidly encouraging everyone to pull together, but I had not adequately strived to consider how the change we were imparting would negatively affect both the attitudes and perceptions of some.

Give No Quarter and Take No Prisoners but Defuse Negative Perceptions

Something that I later came to fully acknowledge is that the leader of high-level change must consider the potential feelings of various groups of employees and must develop a means of defusing negative perceptions, when and where possible. This is far from easy and in most cases one will still have those strongly opposed to almost any change that begins to affect old operating traditions. The key is to keep the degree of such opposition to an absolute minimum.

What I have discovered is that establishing a forum where people are encouraged to get things off their chest seems to help the most. It is when employees feel there is no means for them to surface concerns or frustrations that they will begin to seek other channels of expression. This can often be through the rumor mill that most every business seems to have, in one form or another, or through gossip sessions that are certain to occur when people feel locked out of expressing their true feelings to management. And it matters not whether those feelings are precisely right or entirely wrong; they have to be taken very seriously and dealt with in an understanding manner by the person who assumes the responsibility of influencing significant change in the way things have always been done.

This is not to say that guiding principles should in any way be sacrificed, but only that employees should have a means of challenging and debating in the presence of their peers and associates. As wise as anyone may be, there is a time and place for every change and sometimes the important issue is not the change itself, but precisely *when* it will be made. Further, there are things you can learn from such sessions, because many times very good thoughts and ideas will indeed surface. The challenge is that such meetings not turn into endless, unproductive gripe sessions. Once a valid complaint or concern is established and recorded, the leader is under no obligation to make any on-the-spot commitment, one way or the other. He or she is, however, committed to come back, in one form or another, with a clear response. And sometimes that response can (and must) be: "We hear you, but in this case we must proceed as planned because..."

In the last chapter of this book I speak to another important tool associated with this matter. It is called the *formula for leading effective change.* I learned to use this quite effectively as I gained more and more experience with managing change. Essentially, the formula deals with a thoughtful consideration of business needs on one hand and the potential of full and active employee support on the other.

Having said all this, I must remind the reader that everything I've had to say thus far has been aimed at rapid deployment of the WFM process. As mentioned early on, you can compare the start of the change process to a surgical procedure. First and foremost, the surgeon must stop the bleeding and this often calls for quick actions where no questions are asked and where little, if any, time is spent on an explanation as to why. So some people will see this emergency procedure being executed by an extremely dictatorial leadership and perhaps they aren't that far from the truth.

On the other hand, most employees tend to go along with almost any type of initial change and will generally give a new approach a reasonable chance to work. However, at some point in the process, the emergency procedure has to come to an end and it is then that communications with the work force and their strong involvement become essential to making change a lasting and effective process. Believe me, I had to learn this the hard way, because it wasn't anywhere close to being obvious to me on the front end of the process.

To sum it up, the leader must see that the process is started and pursued in a relentless manner. At that point he or she gives no quarter and takes no prisoners. But the leader must also be capable of recognizing when the time has come where further improvement is going to heavily rely on a united and determined work force and work diligently to make it happen.

Revolutionary Pointers

- Structure manufacturing measurements so they focus on *process* rather than economics. If the process is taken care of, the economics of the business will automatically improve.

- Employees, professionals, and associates alike must understand why performance measurements must change, and how the new measurements are going to be more effective for rapidly deploying WFM and improving business.

- By measuring your production processing flow throughout your operation you can uncover and eliminate those places where your parts and components stop and wait, creating intermediate storage at various points in the production process.

- You need to measure to eliminate defects and errors so what the customer is paying for is true value. To do this you need to eliminate *all* wastes by consistently working at perfecting each and every process in the factory—to the point where *scrap is never produced and where rework is never required under any circumstances!*

- By measuring and improving your setup and changeover you can quickly and effectively improve one of the single largest area of waste.

- In measuring the skillfulness of your work force you need to establish if current skills are on the increase, decrease, or essentially static.

- Your measures for mistake-proof processes should help you create a mindset of perfection. By expecting your manufacturing processes to be perfect, you'll probably end up being very close to achieving it.

- The ultimate in being flexible and globally competitive is the capability of mixing models in production. Measuring for mixed-model capability provides a firm with that focus.

- To help make continuous improvement a way of life throughout the organization, you should measure the formal and informal continuous improvement activities of employees and provide recognition of these.

- One way to measure the progress of your continuous improvement activities is to measure the number of capital expenditures that you eliminate as a result of applying WFM principles.

- By measuring the distance parts, components, and assemblies travel throughout the factory, the employees will view this as a substantial waste and will apply themselves in the effort to attain the ultimate goal of zero parts travel.

- Measuring speed to market for product enhancements will improve a key benefit of the compressed production system, which is time compression—a formidable competitive weapon for those who are the best in the industry at doing this.

- When you measure value-added and determine what portion of this non-value-added is actually *essential* to your business, you will better understand what the customer is really willing to pay for and/or what non-value resources should be further eliminate.

- For management to really know what is happening, and to let production associates know that management is really serious about the work they perform, at least 50 percent of the salaried work force should be relocated onto the shop floor.

- The leader of high-level change must fully consider the feelings (and natural resistance) of various groups of employees and must develop an effective means of defusing negative perceptions, when and where possible.

9

Organizational and Operational
Issues to Support WFM

ESSENTIAL TO THE TASK and a rewarding challenge of deploying WFM is understanding what changes you need to make to the organization that supports launching the compressed production system. Unfortunately, this cannot happen without some discomfort to some people in the organization. The motives and intent of the plant manager will be seriously questioned, if not actively challenged, by those who lack an understanding of the kind of radical change that must occur. And as the process evolves, communication will be critical to your success. But even then there is no guarantee that buy-in is going to come close to a level of universal acceptance.

LAUNCHING THE COMPRESSED PRODUCTION SYSTEM

Launching the compressed production system may well be the toughest job for the plant manager leading such change and one I wish I had all the answers for. Unfortunately, I do not, but I can share some personal experiences and certainly point out a number of key considerations for this extremely delicate task. It starts by understanding that a number of traditional manufacturing functions (departments) have no place in the compressed production system. Two of the more common functions in traditional manufacturing organizations, which do not fit into a long-term WFM strategy, are the production control functions and the quality control functions.

The Traditional Production Control Department

Production control is typically a department that holds the responsibility for developing a master scheduling plan for the production floor and maintaining control of parts that are produced. This is normally managed through a centralized storage function which usually controls and expedites parts through the shop, as required. It most often uses some form of MRP (material requirements planning) to establish production run quantities, lead time requirements, and so on. In a compressed production system, once the factory moves its operation to uninterrupted flow (U-flow) the production control function becomes obsolete (or closely approximating this). This control function simply is not needed.

In its place, visual management controls become the tool that "controls" production. Through tools and techniques such as point-of-use manufacturing and kanban, production quantities are predetermined and then produced and pulled through the shop in an almost automatic fashion that is in tune with the takt time established by direct customer orders. This is not to say that some kind of customer and production coordination activities and associated resources are not needed, only that the production control function as it exists today in most manufacturing operations is simply not needed under WFM.

Eliminating the Traditional Quality Control Department

The need for quality assurance is of utmost importance in any manufacturing operation. However, WFM does not need a quality control department to oversee the work performed by production associates, which is typically done through some sort of factory policing (inspection) function. While most manufacturing organizations have dropped the term *quality control* and have begun to use *quality assurance*, many have only changed the name of the function and still rely heavily on inspection techniques. Over the long haul, the WFM objective is to fully eliminate inspection, unless clearly specified by the customer, as is the case in certain segments of the automotive industry.

Analyzing Other Support Functions Under WFM

There may be other existing support functions that you will need to analyze to determine the role they play in your waste-free manufacturing scheme. The key issue is to ensure that you take appropriate actions to eliminate functions that no longer fit and to redirect the people associated with those departments, as the opportunity arises. Concurrent with analyzing functions that do not fit, it is also critical that you begin installing a product-oriented cell organization as soon as possible. (This matter has been previously discussed, and is step nine in the 10-step road map for the rapid deployment of WFM—see Chapter 6.) The list of questions in Table 9-1 will help you refocus on this important task.

You can also view these questions and your analysis of the relevancy of your support functions as part of the preparation work required to effectively deploy the four WFM drivers.

Table 9-1. The Product-Oriented Cell Organization Checklist

Questions to Help You Focus on Installation
Yes No
☐ ☐ 1. Have you formed cross-functional product cell teams? If so, what do they see as their principal roles/responsibilities?
☐ ☐ 2. Have you staffed the teams with the plant's very best talent? If not, what would it take to do so?
☐ ☐ 3. Have the teams been trained in world class principles, concepts, and techniques? If not, when will this be done and what level of ongoing, long-term training is the plant committed to support?

(continued)

Table 9-1. The Product-Oriented Cell Organization Checklist *(continued)*

Questions to Help You Focus on Installation

Yes	No	
☐	☐	4. Have the teams been fully empowered?
		If so, what does this mean to them in terms of any absolute (decision-making) authority?
☐	☐	5. Have you installed any new measurements to support and guide your WFM effort?
		If not, when will it be done? If there is no plan to do so, why?
☐	☐	6. In the new organization, what has been done to effectively achieve one-level management?
		If nothing, are there plans to address this? If not, why?
☐	☐	7. Are the teams compensated in accordance with their roles and responsibilities?
		If not, when will this be done? If never, why?

Month Twenty-One—Selecting a Champion for the Process

I called Don and ask that he drop by my office at 2:00 P.M. I had just finished running an errand and as I strolled back into my office, I found that he had already arrived and had taken a seat in the chair directly facing my desk.

"Thanks for coming, Don," I said as I set aside some parts I was carrying with me. There had been a quality problem and I had gathered up some of the suspect parts before returning to my office from the shop floor, to have them with me for a meeting I was planning with the quality manager a little later in the afternoon.

Don nodded a salutation but said nothing more, as I finally took a seat and peered at him for a moment across the desktop that separated us by a few feet. I was reflecting briefly on what had occurred a few months earlier after I had sent Don along with another one of my staff managers to a JIT seminar. Both had returned with praise for the concept but Don in particular had shown great interest and, in fact, had become an outspoken disciple of the process. Understanding a "train-the-trainer" session was being offered, I felt it was time to try to put a formal, aggressive training program in place. Don was about to become the *key* player in this initiative and embark on a venture that would change both the course of the plant and his career.

"Don," I began, "I want to start a full-time promotion office and really begin to drive home the tools and techniques we need to use."

"We need that, no doubt," he replied.

Getting right to the point, as was usual with me, I asked: "How would you like to have the job of heading up the promotion office?" His look was one of almost total astonishment and I could tell I had hit a nerve. As I continued, I watched his reaction closely.

"What I would like to do is send you to the train-the-trainer session you mentioned when you first returned from the training you took in Denver. When you get back we could then go to work on setting up an on-site training program."

He smiled, trying to remain professional. However, I could tell he was, if anything, offended by my proposal.

"If you're looking for an immediate response," he said, "I have to tell you that I don't think I'm interested in giving up a job as a department manager to become a teacher."

I could see I had my work cut out for me. It was obvious that I had seriously misjudged Don's enthusiasm for the process and willingness to become an active participant. What was even more obvious was that while he had been encouraging me and others to buy in and start the process, he in no way visualized himself as the *key* player. And it was also clear Don had no desire to give up a manager role to become an individual contributor, so to speak.

"Well, Don, at least sleep on it and let's discuss it further tomorrow, okay?" I suggested. He agreed and after we had confirmed a meeting time for the following day, he departed.

(continued)

I had discussed my plan and choice of people with my boss, Bill. He thought it was great that I was considering a concept like a promotion office, but he had wanted to know more about what the office would be responsible for before he could even think of buying into the idea. He went on say that regardless he certainly didn't think Don was the right person for the job.

I didn't just think Don was the right person, *I was convinced he was*, and I was determined to assign him the job. I had seen him in action a few times and he was a natural working with people and expressing thoughts and ideas. He was especially good in working with production employees and his rather broad background in manufacturing gave him the knowledge, if not the respect, needed for such a role.

He had served for a period as a production manager and currently held the role of manager over the production control function and, overall, I was convinced he was absolutely perfect for what I had in mind. However, I now had a number of problems to deal with in seeing this to a successful conclusion.

First, while Bill apparently liked the thought of a promotion office for continuous improvement activities, he had made it clear he wanted a lot more from me, in terms of what the function would specifically be charged with accomplishing. Secondly, he hadn't agreed on my choice of the individual who would head it. Last, but far from least, Don hadn't jumped at the chance himself.

The rest of the day and into the evening I struggled with myself regarding what I could say to make Don more enthusiastic about the position, but I kept coming up empty handed. For every reason I could give that would show it was a positive move, I could give five counterarguments why it didn't make sense for him to accept the position.

Finally it hit me. If we were going to do the type of things Don himself was prescribing, something we certainly would not need, at least at some point in the future, would be a production control function. Thus, the best reason was clearly evident. His current position was going to disappear!

The following afternoon we met again, as planned. I took some time on the front end setting the stage and getting to the point of passing on my belief that I did not see a long-term future for the production control function. I told him I felt it was a chance for him to move on to something that could help advance his career much faster (and further) than he would ever be able to achieve as a production control manager.

Even with this new sales pitch, Don was less than excited about my proposal. He expressed concerns regarding what would happen to "his people" when all this finally occurred. I, in turn, assured him they would be trained for other roles, but I made no bones about the fact that some just might not buy in and, if so, they could unfortunately become obsolete and end up being "casualties of progress." Having gotten past that particular concern, it seemed, Don proceeded to ask about how many people he would have on his staff as the promotion office manager. He was very surprised when I said none.

"Don, this is an individual contributor role, at least to begin with. You would still be on my staff, reporting to me, but you would not have people reporting directly to you. On the other hand, I can assure you of my support and when you have a project going on the shop floor everyone, including the managers in the area would, in essence, be reporting to you."

He gave a shrug and a slightly sarcastic chuckle before replying, "Sure, but anyway, say I do trust you, what about when you're not around any more? When you move on?"

"There are never any absolute guarantees in this business, Don. You know that. There simply is a risk, in one form or another, associated with any position in manufacturing."

"Well, John," he said, "I have to tell you that while I understand what you're trying to say, I'm really wrestling with the fact that I would have to give up my position as a department manager. Isn't there perhaps some way for me to do this on temporary assignment and at some point down the road go back into production control as—"

"I'm afraid that would be out of the question. If we don't make a serious commitment to the process, it won't be taken seriously. Just trust me and believe that I have your best interests in mind." He opened his mouth to reply but I raised my hand to stop him before continuing.

"Don, it's Friday. Take the weekend to think about it and discuss it with your wife and family as needed, then get back to me Monday. If at that time you're dead set against it, I'll pursue another avenue. But, keep this in mind. You have the chance to step forward into a new, exciting, and what I think can be an extremely rewarding career or to simply shrug it off and stay where you are because I definitely am not going to force you to take the position. However, I have faith that you're a forward thinker and this is your chance to get in on the front end of a wave that I believe is going to flow through all modern manufacturers. So, if you do end up turning this job down I think you're going to be doing both yourself and our plant a great injustice. But I can assure you if that is your decision there won't be any hard feelings on my part. Fair enough?"

"Fair enough," he replied.

(continued)

> The following Monday, Don accepted the post and exactly two months later we conducted our first in-house training session. Neither of us realized at that time just how significant this effort was going to be as a driver in turning the factory around or the special influence it was going to have on both our careers.
>
> With regard to Bill, well, as always, he did not stand in the way and proved to be most supportive, even though I realized I could not give him the depth of justification he wanted at setting up the promotion office. Later he came to admit that I had definitely made the right choice in Don.

ESTABLISHING NEW FUNCTIONS IN THE COMPRESSED PRODUCTION SYSTEM

I have discussed the need to eliminate some functions, but on a more positive note there is a need for the insertion of others, including a waste-free manufacturing promotion office. The extent of new functions will, of course, vary from company to company, but a promotion office, staffed with some of the better people in the organization, is an absolute must. The role of the WFM promotion office is basically twofold:

1. It serves as the *key* training function in the factory and holds the responsibility to formulate a process that will teach the tools of WFM and allow participants to practice them in an event that should become a part of the training curriculum.
2. It is responsible for auditing the operation and insuring that the disciplines of WFM are maintained on the shop floor.

Outside of new functions such as the promotion office, there is a need to reorganize the salaried work force so that each production cell becomes as self-sufficient as possible. This means manufacturing and industrial engineers should be assigned to the cells full time, reporting to the cell manager. This also means accountants, buyers, maintenance personnel, and others should become full-time members of the team or what might best be viewed as a "plant within the plant." Each cell should look organizationally as much like an independent factory as feasible, and the further a plant progresses along this path, the more effective it will become in making WFM a reality. A couple of other new functions to consider are:

- *Sustaining engineering.* This is a department or special function that rather than spending time on the more traditional duties of industrial, manufacturing, or mechanical engineering instead focuses a full-time effort on the more advanced aspects of WFM, such things as advanced applications in SMED, kanban, mistake proofing, and the like.

    For this task you should select some of the better engineers in the factory. In fact, it can be used as a career stepping-stone. While traditional engineering work must go on for upkeep of prints and process sheets, measurement of direct and indirect labor, new machine and equipment justification, capacity planning and the like, this function provides a means for those engineers who have "paid their dues" to be rewarded with a chance to step out of the day-to-day grind and get into what is usually perceived to be much more rewarding work.

- *IRPC (Inventory reduction planning and control).* This function is dedicated full time to managing inventory to ever lower levels. The basic objective of the group should be to get a plant's raw material and WIP inventory levels down to *hours* rather than days, weeks, or months. This is an excellent opportunity to use employees who have been displaced from the elimination of the traditional production control department. Here, a substantial amount of work must be performed in the supplier arena and in many cases, this function will be called on to train suppliers. Therefore, these employees should be some of the best educated in WFM and next to specialists in kanban and pull production concepts and techniques.

APPLYING WFM IN THE OFFICE ENVIRONMENT

So far my primary emphasis has been on making change on the manufacturing shop floor. It is also essential that you apply WFM principles and techniques in the office areas. Other than overcoming the old conventional mind-set, there is no reason you can't apply management methods, and WFM principles in particular, to office operations. Eliminating waste in office operations is often a neglected opportunity for developing a globally competitive company. This is especially true for manufacturing companies that have many levels of departments such as order entry, process planning, cost estimating, scheduling, and so on.

A good time to start this process is after your in-house promotion office has been in place for a period of time (which is primarily structured toward enhancing production processes). Select an office process and apply the same basic WFM principles and techniques. You may have to revise the WFM training material somewhat to make it more adaptable to an office environment. In the process you will find just as much, if not more, wastes in the office as on the shop floor and tremendous opportunities for improvement will clearly surface. In fact there is a good chance that this will be the first time that you actually see the steps and processing procedures involved in completing orders, transactions, and so on.

Considering that office policies account for a good percentage of your cost of goods sold (COGS) for a product (though office costs are usually allocated into overhead as part of a fixed multiplier on direct labor), office operations play an important role in your ability to expedite orders. Improving your office operations is no secondary or afterthought activity. In fact, it is essential if you are to become a true lean manufacturer. Some of the obvious potential benefits of applying WFM to the office are:

1. A substantial reduction in paperwork.
2. A substantial reduction in redundant activities.
3. A substantial reduction in the steps required for most activities.
4. A huge increase in the number and quality of ideas from the work force for improvements in the operation.
5. A clear reading on underutilized and/or overburdened employees.
6. A much better work flow throughout the entire department.
7. A reduction of lead times.
8. A much better customer-oriented work team.

These are just a few of the many enhancements that you will reap by extending the training and improvement process into the office area. A word of caution, however. Do not apply the change process into the office area until much improvement has first been achieved on the manufacturing shop floor. We must not forget that the shop floor is where real value is added and this should always remain the first priority. But do not ignore the office when you are at a point in the overall improvement process to extend it there. The same basic WFM principles, techniques, and measurements that are used to bring dramatic improvement to production processes can, with very little adjustment, be used for the office arena.

HOW TO USE DISPLACED PRODUCTION EMPLOYEES

One of the most difficult tasks in moving from a conventional mass manufacturer to a lean manufacturer is deciding how to use displaced personnel. Certainly one option is to simply plead the need for a reduction in the work force in order to remain competitive, and then lay off displaced employees. This, however, could be the worst decision that could be made.

Companies seeking to implement waste-free manufacturing must stop to consider that the key to a successful transition rests with getting the entire work force participating in continuous improvement. Given that the work force sees the end result of WFM being a reduction of employees, it will not be long before they will cease to willingly participate and, in turn, begin to energetically fight the process.

On the other hand, productivity improvements are a must in conventional batch manufacturing operations, so at some period *there has to be a reduction in the existing work force or much greater output with the same number of employees.* It is this latter situation that provides you the best opportunity to positively move the process of waste-free manufacturing forward. As a seasoned industrial engineer, it has never ceased to amaze me how short-sighted many manufacturing firms are when it comes to simple arithmetic. But there is a traditional reason for this. Manufacturers have for decades been in the process of saving money. If this effort truly worked, most U.S. manufacturing operations would have (by now) learned how to save their way into glowing profitability. And head count reductions, be it production associates or salaried professionals, are always the first thing many companies attack when there is a need to cut expenses (save money). Little, if any, thought is given to redirecting the work force toward a concerted effort to *make money.*

The resulting expense reductions always provide some short-term relief, but usually have a negative impact on long-term profitability. The simple truth is: A work force where a reasonably large percentage of all those employed have an ongoing concern about job security is a work force that will have one consistent worry in mind—staying employed! It is very important to realize that companies with employees who feel they have reasonable job security are companies that usually have a work force directing energy to its business. The key is to ensure their energy is in tune with work that provides a competitive edge.

The poorest option a company could choose when there is a decline in profitability is to lay off people who can help to make the business profitable in the future. When layoffs occur frequently enough, it is only a matter of time before the operation begins to run on cruise control, and needed creativeness becomes extremely lacking, throughout the organization as a whole. This is not to say that many batch manufacturing firms are not presently top-heavy when it comes to people resources, and in this particular case there is little choice but to reduce the work force accordingly.

My strong position regarding the negative aspects of layoffs concerns manufacturing operations where there is not a substantial top-heavy condition in the ranks and where any short-term decline in business is almost always answered with a corresponding reduction in the work force. These operations will have difficulty surviving over the long haul, because they cannot possibly have a work force collectively dedicated to improving the business and who are aggressive in their efforts to continually pursue an improved competitive position.

I feel I should extend this discussion to address the issue of using the concepts and techniques of any world-class manufacturing process, such as waste-free manufacturing, as a catalyst for reducing labor in a factory. I am seriously opposed to this approach, for it goes against the grain of employee involvement and their active and lasting participation in the process. Using WFM as a primary means of reducing direct and indirect labor head count is like telling employees: "I'll buy you a new rope if you will then proceed to hang yourself." Such an approach simply won't work. While there are few, if any, manufacturing operations that can guarantee employment, there are none who cannot say to the work force:

> If you help us make this initiative a success, we will do everything within our power to retrain, reassign, and fully utilize any employees who are displaced, and we will not lay off employees as a direct result of utilizing the tools and techniques incorporated in our process of

continuous improvement. If and when layoffs occur they will be directly tied to downturns in business conditions only.

Believe me, there are many manufacturing managers who will have extreme difficulty buying into and living up to this simple commitment. This is because they still carry old-line thinking when it comes to the hourly work force and believe one of their primary obligations to the company is in making reductions in this area, whenever possible. This is the old mass production paradigm that workers are interchangeable and easily trained. If you haven't already gathered, let me remind you, the world of manufacturing has changed. The new lean manufacturing world is about listening to your customer (which includes your employees), eliminating waste, and enhancing value-added work (improved quality at lower prices). It is never about eliminating those who add real value to your product to "save" money.

What the manager needs to remember is that your principal obligation to the company is to do everything within your power to remain competitive and to help the company make money—even while it's operating under the old mass manufacturing paradigm. Those managers who look upon saving money (cost cutting) as a primary mission tend to thrive on examining how much paper and ink is being utilized and how many people the operation can afford to get rid of and still limp along. I personally see this as a "penny wise, pound foolish" attitude toward the business, because I can assure you that no firm, whether it is a manufacturing operation or a popcorn stand, has ever saved its way into profitability.

The key is to focus on making money and this is done by doing the right kinds of things—right! Critical to this is having a work force that is both trained and united in the effort and that does not fear at every turn they will be the subject of some head count reduction effort—especially as a result of their waste-cutting efforts. When production employees are displaced as a result of continuous improvement (kaizen) efforts, there are a number of options a plant can consider, outside of layoffs:

1. Removing senior rather than junior people from the process affected by kaizen activity and putting those senior people through special training, so they can then return to their process (or other processes) and lead further improvement efforts. Their knowledge,

as a result of years of experience, usually makes them well qualified for such a role.

2. Using displaced employees to kit parts and components in the
   exact order of usage for the production associates performing
   value-added work, and delivering the parts and components to a
   special staging area in the process (called supermarkets), so the
   operators can pull the parts they need in the exact quantity needed
   and thus make their work easier and faster.

3. Using displaced employees as relief operators so on-line production associates can be freed to take special training or hold needed
   communication meetings.

4. Using displaced employees who show the talent and ability as full-
   time members of the promotion office.

5. Using displaced employees as supermarket or pull zone managers.

6. Training and using displaced employees on special setup and
   changeover teams designed to attack this considerable waste and
   where possible reduce or completely eliminate it.

7. Training and using displaced employees in clerical activities associated with production record keeping and other like tasks currently performed by salaried personnel.

Remember, your experienced employees are irreplaceable. They possess the collective knowledge—the memory and wisdom—of your company. As I've mentioned, in the salaried (professional) ranks there are
many potential options for displaced employees. One of the greatest
benefits comes from expanding the in-house promotion office which
requires more instructors. These instructors can come from your displaced professional ranks. It is one means of effectively utilizing and
holding onto this important resource. There are many other options, but
I would strongly recommend if professionals are displaced as a result of
an improvement process they be used wherever possible to strengthen
the continuous improvement process. The benefits are long term, also.
When the company begins to hit high gear in their WFM deployment
and are expanding production, they won't be suddenly short of experienced personnel because of the brain drain resulting from the standard
cost-cutting (saving money) policies of mass manufacturing.

Developing the best manufacturing flexibility in the business is the
key objective and whatever that takes, in terms of reorganizing the professional ranks, should be done. Without a doubt, people love stability

and this includes people who are in the support ranks within manufacturing. On the other hand, they must come to accept that making no changes to the people in the support organization is no different from making no changes to the manufacturing process.

Hopefully, I have more than convinced the reader that continuous change (improvement) to the production process is a must if one hopes to become globally competitive. This absolutely holds true for the professional and technical functions supporting manufacturing as well. It's important to note that organizing for the compressed production system is not an end unto itself, but rather a continuing process—on the shop floor, in the office, working with the union and your work force.

While there is no cookbook that I can provide that has all the answers to utilizing displaced employees, I hope some of these ideas will be helpful. Most important is to keep a focus on using your employee resource to strengthen your improvement process. As you progress with deploying WFM many exciting opportunities, new roles, and subsequent levels of responsibility will open up for employees as they face the complex tasks of helping firms become globally competitive.

Revolutionary Pointers

- The objective of WFM over the long haul is to fully and completely eliminate inspection unless it is clearly specified by the customer.

- The key issue in organizing to support WFM is to ensure that appropriate actions are taken to eliminate functions that no longer fit and to redirect the resources associated with those departments to new functions as the opportunity arises.

- Concurrently with addressing functions that do not fit, it is also critical to put a product-oriented cell organization in place that is as self-sufficient as possible and gives the appearance of an independent factory within a factory.

- The role of the promotion office is to serve as the key training function in the factory. It holds the responsibility of formulating a process that will teach the tools of WFM to participants so they can put them into effect. Additionally, it is responsible for auditing the operation and ensuring that the disciplines of WFM are maintained at all times on the shop floor.

- As you eliminate the departments and techniques of the old mass manufacturing system you need to be establishing new functions to support WFM. Two of these are sustaining engineering and the IRPC function.

- With very little adjustment you can use the same WFM principles for the office arena to eliminate waste. Don't start the office process until after your in-house promotion office has been in place for a period of time.

- In moving to a WFM environment a company has many options to reassign, retrain, and productively use workers as they're displaced during the journey from mass to lean manufacturing.

- It is penny wise, pound foolish for managers to focus on short-sighted policies to save money. It's critical that you have a work force that is both trained and united in your WFM effort and that does not fear they will be axed—*especially as a result of their waste-cutting efforts.* Remember, your experienced employees possess the collective knowledge—the memory and wisdom—of your company.

10

Staying the Course on
Your Never-Ending Journey

As I'VE REPEATEDLY STATED, the process of waste-free manufacturing is never-ending. Thus, there is a danger that the operation will begin to relax once a factory starts to benefit from the initial wins resulting from its deployment. Nothing could be more damaging. In fact, to slip back will often prove to be more harmful than never beginning the process. This is why you must know what to be constantly doing to stay the course once your factory starts to put the WFM drivers in place and begins to show some notable improvements.

To begin with, initial wins are exactly the moment for the management team to begin to express some "deliberate impatience" (as writer and lecturer Tom Peters so aptly puts it) in moving the factory along at *an even more rapid pace*. In fact, at every turn in the process the management team should make efforts to influence both the *speed* and *continuance* of change. An operation that allows itself to become complacent at *any* point in the process will find that things tend to swiftly revert back to that old system of production and the habits everyone was comfortable with at the start of the process.

Staying the course is much more difficult than making initial change of any kind. Change in manufacturing is to a large degree expected by the work force. But usually it is the type that doesn't substantially influence the way things have always been done. New machines and equipment are brought aboard, old products disappear and are replaced by new products, and facilities age and must be refurbished. People move on to new jobs, new positions, and new careers. In reality, manufacturing is always in a state of constant change, even if nothing is ever done to abort an obsolete and ineffective way of conducting the business. But moving your employees beyond the old mental and physical barriers of conventional mass manufacturing and into embracing a completely different paradigm (way of doing business) takes management's continuous thoughtful effort as well as much more time than they've traditionally given to change efforts.

A RACE WITH NO FINISH LINE

Imagine asking a group of athletes to prepare to run a race that had no finish line. They would think you were either joking or had completely lost your mind. However, that is exactly how manufacturers must approach the task of not only achieving but maintaining a globally competitive manufacturing status. In today's world there is no time to rest or to assume you have crossed some imaginary finish line. Getting halfway down the track and then relaxing leaves a factory with a combination of some new (waste-free) and some old (conventional) manufacturing concepts. As pointed out, this can be more damaging than never starting, because *a factory is most vulnerable when it is trying to run a business using aspects of both concepts.* Sadly, this is the state of affairs that afflicts many companies today who have attempted to implement JIT concepts.

We simply must not forget the past. Manufacturing in the United States became complacent in the sixties and seventies, when it assumed it had reached a pinnacle of industrial achievement. Concentration was shifted to everything but continuing to improve the system of manufacturing. Huge sums of money were pumped into showcase facilities that were very highly automated. An extreme amount of energy was expended in creating an atmosphere of satisfied employees and, as a result, programs were institutionalized that concentrated on such things as the quality of work life. The result? Employees became no less dissatisfied and the quality of work life has, if anything, deteriorated—especially with the restructuring strategies that are today permeating almost every major industry in the United States.

Due to a failure to be foresighted enough in our thinking, the unfortunate result is that U.S. industry has spent billions of dollars trying to learn how to implement the manufacturing techniques that were first refined by Toyota. But, bottom-line, we simply haven't learned to do it fast enough or how to apply them properly and where we have learned the techniques, we have not had the will or the know-how to stay the course.

At this point in their journey to lean manufacturing U.S. manufacturing needs some very determined leaders who are almost fanatical about seeing the United States at the helm of manufacturing excellence again. There is no logical reason U.S. manufacturers should place themselves outside this spectrum of achievement, yet there seems to be a growing tendency to willingly take a back seat in this arena—just because we are late joining the lean revolution. But are we?

What is negatively affecting the will of U.S. manufacturing is due in part to a society that has been obsessed with making a better future for each following generation. Although this is an admirable trait, it may have created more of a stumbling block than a blessing, making us focus on the wrong priorities and putting the cart before the horse. For years we developed leaders at a manufacturing level who had a propensity for being the best and for staying abreast of the best techniques in the world of manufacturing. Had our leaders focused our "can do-ism" on the process and not the results (more technology is better), we would have seen the writing on the wall long before the automotive and electronics industries became a victim to the lean manufacturing revolution.

Month Twenty-Two—Gaining National Recognition

The president of the company made an impromptu visit to the factory and was astonished. When he walked out on the shop floor, he saw almost 170,000 square feet of manufacturing space that had been opened. As we toured the plant, he also saw point-of-use manufacturing throughout the shop, along with an extremely clean and very well-organized operation.

He told me he liked it so much that he wanted to extend a special invitation to the president of the corporation, to see if he would be interested in visiting and seeing first-hand the improvements that had been made. My response was that we would be highly honored. What I was really hoping for was that it would lead to a commitment that our plant would not be one of the upcoming casualties.

(continued)

It had been announced that three of five plants remaining in North America were to close in a manufacturing consolidation project. No one plant had officially been cited as a survivor, thus all the remaining factories were up for grabs, so to speak. I strongly felt the first plant that opened up enough space to take on another product would be the first to be officially declared a winner. So I had repeatedly gone out on a limb with the work force by indicating to them if they supported me in this effort we would indeed see our operation survive. I had no real assurance of this, except a firm belief that I was on the right track.

I didn't get such a commitment on this particular day, not that I really expected it, although knowing he felt so good about what he saw that he wanted his boss to visit the plant was in itself reassuring to me. I didn't fail to let the work force know about it in the very next communication meeting. Three weeks later, he called and dropped a bomb.

Not only was the president coming for a visit, he was bringing a highly respected Wall Street analyst with him. I was informed the president wanted me to arrange a two-hour overview for him and the analyst, and to follow this with a plant tour. The purpose, of course, was to demonstrate the highly effective change that was taking place at a manufacturing level within the corporation.

The first thing I did after the call was to get with Don and let him know about the visit. I told him I wanted us to put an overview together, but I would only make a short introduction and allow him to do most of the talking. He was excited, but concerned. We had only two weeks to prepare for the visit, which obviously was going to be a session that received a very high level of attention. His concern was how he could give an overview about our improvement process in such a short period of time (typically his classes lasted three days) and secondly, to what extent he could expect the support of the rest of my staff in preparing for the visit.

I told him not to worry and that I would help him in preparing for the presentation. Further, I assured him that we would have every member of the staff located at various points throughout the factory during the plant tour, to say a few words in support of the improvement effort taking place. The truth was he was probably far less worried about it than I was. I fully realized we could end up being heroes or jerks with such an assignment, and there really wasn't much middle ground between the two that I could rely on.

The visit by the president and the business analyst went extremely well and it was soon followed by another—this time involving 10 analysts. During the plant tour, I stopped with the guests I was escorting and proceeded to speak about a piece of equipment located in back of me that had been the center of a very special effort to reduce setup. The equipment itself was over 20 years old, but after the exercise it looked and operated like a new machine.

I couldn't help but notice the look of utter confusion on their face as I referred to the work that had been done on "the piece of equipment behind me." Finally I paused, because the looks were growing more confused, and turned to see what in the world was creating the problem. To my complete surprise, the equipment was gone!

I thought for a moment as to how to continue, then turned to them and finally said: "As you can see the equipment I was referring to has been moved. That's probably the best example of how fast things are happening in our factory. It's really not unusual for a machine to move a number of times with the type of approach we're using. It's a sign of progress, as we see it." Later, I found out they were more impressed with the fact that people were empowered to move equipment without my express knowledge than with almost any other thing they had witnessed.

The affair went well, overall, and we got some rave reviews as a result. I was beginning to feel exceptionally proud of the job being done. The improvements we were making were being expressed in lower operating costs, added business, and additional jobs for the work force. Nonetheless, we still had hundreds of the original work force on layoff; and I felt until we got another product and brought most of them back, we really had not accomplished what we set out to do.

It happened approximately one year later—our plant was chosen to receive a major portion of the products that were produced in a factory that ended up closing its doors. When the dust settled, our plant was one of only two that remained in the United States.

THE CONTINUOUS IMPROVEMENT PYRAMID

I said in the beginning that, this is a "how to" book, and I want to offer something that can be extremely beneficial in keeping a proper focus on your waste-free journey. It is called the *continuous improvement pyramid* and if you recognize and understand the principles, techniques, and tools outlined for globally competitive manufacturing, this pyramid can be the one thing that can help you establish and maintain a proper focus. This pyramid establishes six areas of concentration that are required to implement and, most important, maintain a waste-free manufacturing environment (see Figure 10-1).

The base or foundation is the first area of attack. Much like building a real pyramid from the ground up, constructing a WFM operation requires starting with a strong foundation. The foundation is *establishing and fully maintaining workplace organization*, followed by *studying and analyzing the current process*. After this follows *planning and laying out the new process*, which is logically supported by *proving the new process*. Finally, you apply *visual controls*, which set the stage for *making continuous improvement* to the process. Armed with both the 10-step roadmap, which positions a plant so it can quickly begin to reap the benefits of the compressed production system, and the continuous improvement pyramid, any manufacturing plant can rapidly deploy the WFM drivers in a series of actions that build on one another.

Another way to look at it is visualizing the road map as a grader clearing ground so you can construct the pyramid. Once constructed, the pyramid becomes the process that fully sustains an ongoing effort

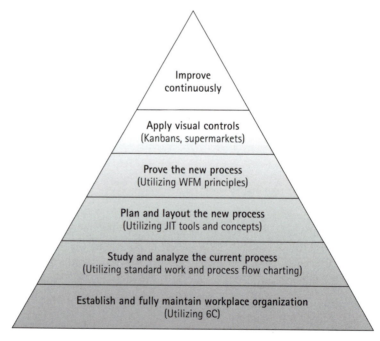

Figure 10-1. The Continuous Improvement Pyramid

for waste-free manufacturing so you can truly become a globally competitive operation. Let's examine this pyramid in more detail.

Layer One—Establish and Fully Maintain WPO

Again, nothing is more fundamental to the improvement process than building a proper and complete foundation. This is a must if one hopes to keep the improvement process intact and operating properly. Do not—and I strongly emphasize this—do not start layering the other elements of the improvement process in place without first completing the foundation. This will only lead to chaos, confusion, and frustration. To clearly understand a *process* (layer two of the pyramid), you have to first be able to see it. As I've mentioned previously, in most cases the true process is hidden from view with items that are not needed. The first WFM driver, workplace organization, then becomes the means of achieving a clear view of the process and thus, the foundation for all continuous improvement.

Layer Two—Study and Analyze the Current Process

At this point there are two basic alternatives to proceeding with the continuous improvement pyramid.

1. *Prioritize all the production processes in the factory in order of importance and take these through all the layers of the pyramid before starting elsewhere.* The benefits of taking this alternative are: (1) it establishes a pilot area for everyone to see, making it complete and ready to make continuous improvement, and (2) the plant starts to reap the full benefits of total process improvement.
2. *Go through the entire plant, pursuing one layer of the pyramid at a time.* However, there is a potential shortcoming with this option. Because production processes are generally selected based on how key they are to the business, selecting the first approach could mean that some production processes would see no real improvement (change) for a substantial period of time. This could seriously damage the enthusiasm of various work groups. On the other hand, you can minimize this risk with adequate communications, and either approach can work. It is something that has to be determined at an individual operating level.

Studying and analyzing the current process involves using tools that were initially designed by Toyota. These, specifically, are the use of standard work and process flowcharting. Toyota did not invent basic scientific time and motion study or process flowcharting. However, they did refine the approach into a simplistic application, which is detailed in many books (see Bibliography).

You must complete the second layer in the continuous improvement pyramid before starting to change the current production process because the data obtained from this effort essentially allow a plant to establish a base from which all future improvement is measured. Additionally, one cannot make effective change unless one fully understands the current process. Completing this layer in the pyramid allows this to happen. Also, you should pay a great deal of attention to detailing the contributing factors for disruptions in flow and what can be done to achieve the second WFM driver, uninterrupted flow.

Layer Three—Plan and Lay out the New Process

After analyzing the current production process, the next step is planning a new approach and then making physical change by re-laying out the entire production process to fully incorporate the principles of waste-free manufacturing. If you complete the steps in the road map as advised, you would have already applied mistake proofing to the equipment, kanbans and pull zones would already be in place, and you would have applied many of the other tools and techniques of WFM (such as setup reduction). At this point, it is time to revisit these to see if you can make further applications to support the continuous improvement process. I can assure you there will be further opportunities.

Whatever layout and production flow pattern you choose, it will not be perfect. As you will find, the process of planning and laying out a new process is continuous in nature. The only true measure of ultimate achievement in process layout is to take the 15-point checklist (covered later in this chapter), make a tour, and ask the questions noted. If the answers are not a definite "yes" to every question, then more work is needed.

The reader might be asking at this point: Do you ever reach a condition of perfection? I think the answer is no. Measuring perfection in production processes is somewhat like measuring perfection in human beings. Just as there is no perfect human—regardless of desire, hard work, effort and the like—there is and can never be an absolutely perfect production process. However, in both cases, some are much better than others. This is why when re-laying out a revised production process you should take great care in the following:

- Getting equipment and facilities as close as possible to the actual point-of-use.
- Reducing inventory and inventory storage areas (staging, pull zones, etc.) to the absolute minimum.
- Shortening production lines as much as possible.
- Doing everything possible to enhance the principle of uninterrupted flow.

Layer Four—Prove the New Process

After you have moved and reinstalled equipment and facilities, it is time to prove the new process to make sure it works as intended. Here revisions to the new layout are likely and work is not complete until the new production process is operating as planned and fully meeting its prescribed takt time. Proving the process, first and foremost, centers on ensuring it can meet its prescribed production requirements. This should not be a problem, given that the equipment and facilities have most likely already shown the capability, prior to the re-layout. But work is not complete by the group involved until they've absolutely confirmed this.

Layer Five—Apply Visual Controls

This layer pertains to implementing appropriate visual controls related to takt time, takt time performance, employee skills, kanbans, and many other areas of the business. The intent is to clearly *see* what is going on in the production cells on the shop floor without having someone *tell* you. *Then, do it again* after most of the production processes in a factory have gone through the layers outlined in the continuous improvement pyramid.

You must apply this technique *a minimum of three times* before any production department or process initially set up under batch manufacturing can begin to truly transform itself into a WFM process. Remember, you should consider any waste in the process to be too much waste and you should apply continuous efforts to make the process completely waste free.

UNDERSTANDING THE ROCKS AND BOULDERS TO DEPLOYMENT

As I mentioned in Chapter 7, conducting an employee satisfaction survey when you are squarely in the middle of this kind of significant change will not show you what you are doing right or wrong. As I said, the plant I was in the middle of changing did conduct a survey and it received one of the lowest employee satisfaction ratings in the corporation. Since I was the plant manager I had to answer why. Naturally my first reaction was: "What did you expect?" The plant is in the middle of tearing down departments, laying off employees, destroying long-standing functions, changing work habits and work rules, and basically upsetting a manufacturing lifestyle that is affecting almost every person in the factory.

When the plant conducted another survey two years later, after I left, it had one of the highest employee satisfaction ratings. They didn't ask me why but naturally my first reaction was: "Why wouldn't the employees be satisfied?" The plant had taken on a new product from another factory, employment was back to its previous high, the plant was running efficiently, and it was profitable. An interesting side note to this story is that the plant originally producing the product we received had one of the higher employee satisfaction ratings in the initial survey. As a result of the product transfer, this plant was eventually forced to close.

So why do you suppose the factory that closed had such a favorable employee satisfaction response, as opposed to the negative one in our factory? Could it have been that if that plant was doing the kinds of things it should have been doing, its ratings would have been lower and it would not have closed? An interesting question, to say the least, but the reason I returned to this experience is because it delineates some important questions regarding leadership:

- Wouldn't it have been much easier and certainly more politically expedient for me to accept the employee satisfaction responses as a clear message that I was definitely on the wrong track? The answer is certainly yes. It would no doubt have been easier.
- Would it, however, have been right to consider this as a reason to make a strong change in direction? To that I think, most assuredly not.

The survey was yet another example that: *leadership, without at least some hard fundamental beliefs and a willingness to stick to the principles that drive those beliefs, is not real leadership at all.* It is rather "follow-ship," based on passive compliance with whatever the most popular theme happens to be at the time. Change in almost any area of business has accepted boundaries, and when one begins to move outside those boundary lines, one may encounter boulders that can make life very difficult. Understanding which issues are rocks (which you can easily remove) and which are boulders (which cannot always be removed) provides you with the knowledge of what you will be faced to deal with. There are three larger boulders that we need to discuss that surround not-so-acceptable change in business.

1. *Changing or entirely eliminating long-standing functions.* It is usually acceptable to amend the various duties of certain long-standing functions within the organization in support of a clearly defined mission. It is usually not so acceptable to propose that such functions make a substantial change in duties and responsibilities and even less acceptable to propose that they need to be entirely eliminated.
2. *Changing or entirely eliminating the existing measurement system.* It is usually acceptable to propose some change to the existing measurement system. It is usually not so acceptable to propose that some measurements (seen as key indices) be changed, and almost totally unacceptable to propose that the old measurement system be scrapped and entirely replaced with a new one.
3. *Changing or entirely eliminating plant's management information system.* It is usually acceptable to propose some revisions to the MIS system the plant uses for purposes of scheduling, order procurement, record keeping, and so on. But it is usually unacceptable to propose substantial change, and totally unacceptable to even think about entirely eliminating the system and replacing it with another means of driving the business of manufacturing.

Management information systems were initially intended to be exactly what the name implied: *information systems*. They were sold to management on the promise of making the flow of information and data faster and much more reliable. What has happened, however, is that they sometimes tend to make the business a slave to the system itself. Regardless of how sophisticated or modern a management information system is, it is only as good as what it collects as data and information (input) and the assumptions that are otherwise programmed into it.

Other Potential Boulders

Some boulders come as a result of desirable change. What one will find is, even when constructive initiatives are undertaken, they can sometimes become barriers to rapid insertion of the process. This is because they often receive so much resistance, that a great deal of time and energy has to be expended in keeping the momentum going. This is not to say they should not be pursued (they most definitely should), only that the change agent should be aware of the depth of leadership and dedication required to see them through—one way or the other. These include:

- Requiring production associates to take on more responsibility in managing the business (sometimes union and/or contractual issues can stand firmly in the way of doing this).
- Taking the responsibility of quality control out of the hands of the quality control department and transferring it to the operators.
- Changing build schedules to be more in tune with direct customer orders, rather than allowing marketing or sales forecasts to exclusively drive the manufacturing build schedule.

What usually happens when the leader of change comes upon a boulder and begins to chip away at it is that strong resistance develops. This can end up being something the leader can overcome with persistence or something that gives the impression that the leader is completely out of line. He or she may be perceived as being dangerous and fanatical, and, as a result, may have a large group of opponents that can forge a strong line of defense against any change required.

A company I worked for many years and which I hold in highest regard set forth its own initiative in world class manufacturing in the early '90s. At great cost and substantial effort, it spread its version of world class manufacturing to all its operations around the world. Part of the training the corporation provided was an exercise in "obstacles to change." The purpose of this exercise was to delve into whether the foreseen obstacles were physical or mental in nature. To begin, course participants were asked to identify all the potential barriers they could possibly think of that could stand in the way of making change from a batch system of manufacturing to pull (or JIT) production. Believe me, there never was any shortage of things that participants felt could (if not would) stand in the way of such change.

After some discussion to be certain that the list of potential barriers was understood, the participants were asked to break into small groups and discuss whether the barriers were, in their judgment, mental or physical in nature. Inevitably, the participants would finally bring themselves to admit that most, if not all of the items listed, were mental barriers. They were items that dealt with how people perceived things *should* or *had* to be.

However, it was interesting that as the training progressed, even though the participants had almost always unanimously agreed there were few if any real physical barriers, they were far less than unanimous about energetically making change. I point this out as an example of how difficult it can be to convince people to react to the need for change. In this example, there was a corporate-driven initiative that had the support of top management. In fact, it had been conceived by top management, with a great deal of communications on the front end as to why. But, regardless, it in no way had the support of some of those who, by their own admission, had come to recognize that the only thing standing in the way were their own mental barriers.

As you may recall I used a mythical story in Chapter 3, the "Legend of the Loaves," to demonstrate five persistent mental barriers that you will confront over and over again. It is important to name them once again: (1) justification, (2) not invented here, (3) done that before, (4) don't rock the boat, and (5) it's not my job. These five mental barriers merely point out what is obvious in human nature. So just know that every single time you make a change you will run into these barriers to some degree, on some level, with someone. Knowing this is half the battle.

Fifteen-Point Checklist to Determine If You Are Globally Competitive

For years in my consulting role, I always took the time on the front end of any initial visit to a factory to walk through the plant and take note of what I saw. Preferably I made this tour with the plant manager and at the conclusion, spent some time with him or her in sharing my observations. Normally, with one pass through a factory I was able to tell them what they knew (or at least, practiced) when it came to globally competitive manufacturing. Some of them marveled at the accuracy of the conclusions I drew and I was often asked: "How can you take such a brief tour of a factory and make such strong judgments?" The answer is that it is not difficult at all. In fact, anyone can do it.

I developed what I call The *WFM Checklist* (see Table 10-1). Armed with this, anyone with any reasonable knowledge of manufacturing can walk through a factory, ask the questions noted, and make a sensible judgment as to whether a plant is on the right track to world class manufacturing or is still operating under old, obsolete manufacturing principles.

If a factory can answer yes to all the questions on the checklist, it has indeed fully laid the foundation for a globally competitive manufacturing operation. If, however, a factory has even one answer that is no, the foundation is incomplete and you should give a sharp focus to making it happen as soon as possible. Additionally, a no answer may establish the need to seriously attack a boulder. To clarify the fifteen points, the following addresses each of the items in the checklist in more detail:

1. *Training your employees.* No manufacturing firm can say it has made a complete shift from a conventional batch operation to a globally competitive pull system of production without having exposed its entire work force to a minimal amount of training and all of its most senior employees to more than one training session. Training is absolutely critical to the process of buy-in and continuous improvement, especially for those manufacturing firms who have for years operated under a batch mode of operation.

2. *Decentralization of stores to point-of-use.* A manufacturing firm that has not entirely eliminated all centralized stores areas to point-of-use still has much work to do before it can say it has

Table 10-1. The WFM Global Competitiveness Checklist

Are You on the Right Track?		
Yes	No	
☐	☐	1. Have all production employees in the plant had at least one full day of exposure to globally competitive manufacturing principles and concepts?
☐	☐	a. Have the more senior employees had more than one training session?
☐	☐	b. Have all salaried employees had at least a week or more of training in the principles, concepts, and techniques?
☐	☐	2. Have all storage areas been fully decentralized to point-of-use?
☐	☐	3. Have forklift trucks and overhead transfer conveyors been entirely eliminated throughout the factory and replaced with point-of-use processing and/or equipment?
☐	☐	4. Have owner-operators been selected, trained, and assigned to all key processes in the factory?
☐	☐	5. Has setup and changeover on all equipment been reduced to no more than nine minutes, maximum?
☐	☐	6. If they exist, have piecework wage incentive plans been fully eliminated?
☐	☐	7. Are there fewer than 10 labor classifications in the factory?
☐	☐	8. Are all processes in the factory down to one-piece flow?
☐	☐	9. Are new measurements in place and being actively utilized?
☐	☐	10. Has enough floor space been opened through continuous improvement activity to bring in another product or process?
☐	☐	11. Are all first-line support personnel located on the shop floor?
☐	☐	12. Are production quantities being fully determined based on pull production procedures and visual controls only?
☐	☐	13. Does the factory look world class? Is it superbly clean? Is there a place for everything and is everything in its proper place?
☐	☐	14. Is there an ongoing, active employee suggestion process in place, and have a minimum of 50 percent of all employees made at least two suggestions that have been fully implemented within the last 90 days?
☐	☐	15. If a union exists, is it actively involved in the improvement process?

laid the appropriate foundation for waste-free manufacturing. This is especially true of stores areas that control parts that are fabricated (produced) in the factory and those that are designed to manage purchased materials and components for the factory as a whole.

3. *Elimination of forklifts/overhead storage conveyors.* A factory that still utilizes forklift trucks and overhead conveyors to store and transport parts to point-of-use has not yet established the proper foundation for waste-free manufacturing. This facet of the improvement process may take some time, due to the need to rethink parts deliveries that are currently being made through the use of often expensive and sophisticated overhead transfer systems. Additionally, eliminating forklift trucks will involve designing a completely new system of delivery for those parts and components that cannot be set at point-of-use. However, fundamentally, a factory must work through this issue before it can truly say it has fully set the stage to be globally competitive.

4. *Insertion of owner-operators.* Until such time that a plant has owner-operators fully trained and in place on a very minimum of all its key processes in the factory, it still has foundation work to do.

5. *Reduction/elimination of setup and changeover.* To aggressively attack setup and changeover in the factory, a factory must have effectively changed the thrust of its engineering and maintenance functions. As I have said, this should be a goal that manufacturing and industrial engineering groups lead. In order for this to occur, some major revisions have to take place within these particular professions regarding group priorities, individual assignments, and the like.

6. *Elimination of piecework wage incentive plans.* If you have not eliminated wage incentive plans that are structured on the basis of purely producing large quantities of parts, then much work is still required in order to become a globally competitive operation. Often, if such plans exist, they are a contractual issue that must be renegotiated. This will usually require considerable effort by the company's human resource department.

7. *Reduction in labor classifications.* The same applies here as noted in item 6. H.R. plays a key role in leading an effort to reduce labor classifications from what typically exists in conventional mass manufacturing. Usually this is at least 50 classifications and

in some cases the number can be hundreds. A manufacturing operation can never be as flexible as required under such conditions, and it is recommended that the number of labor classifications, including the trades (maintenance, tool room, etc.) be less than 10. The ultimate scenario would be one classification for both hourly and salaried employees, called worker, and one department in the plant, called factory!

8. *New measurement systems.* Until a manufacturing firm begins to measure itself differently, odds are it is simply going to revert back to doing the things that make the traditional measurements look good. In a batch manufacturing operation, this will most certainly include the overproduction of parts, components, and assemblies, in order to produce hours for absorption purposes.

9. *One-piece flow in all processes.* Until such time as every process in the factory is rearranged to, at a minimum, accommodate one-piece flow, much foundation work is still required.

10. *Floor space reductions.* Until continuous improvement efforts have occurred that open up enough floor space to bring in another product series or to bring onboard work that is currently being performed outside, the foundation work for becoming globally competitive is still incomplete.

11. *Support personnel on the shop floor.* The premise of WFM is for management to concentrate on the shop floor, where the only true value-added is performed. In order to do this, you must take support personnel out of the front offices and locate them where they can spend a very large percentage of their time concentrating on improving floor operations. If this has not been done, the foundation for continuous improvement is still incomplete.

12. *Production quantities driven by something other than MRP.* If a plant's production scheduling is still controlled through a conventional MRP system, it simply cannot say it has completed the foundation for continuous improvement. You must establish production quantities based on a pull system (kanban) throughout the entire plant, backed with appropriate kanbans and other visual controls. Without this, the plant can only continue to produce in a fashion inherent with conventional batch manufacturing practices.

13. *Appearance of being world class.* If you have not brought the factory to the point that it looks world class, much work is still required on the foundation. As mentioned on numerous occasions,

fully implementing and actively maintaining the disciplines of the workplace organization is the most basic of all the criteria for waste-free manufacturing.

14. *Active employee suggestion process in place.* Unless a plant has established an environment where employees are actively participating, by submitting and helping to implement ideas which improve the business, the plant still has not fully established a foundation for launching a continuous improvement program.

15. *Active and supportive involvement of union in the process.* Until the union (if one exists) is actively involved and supportive of the process, the foundation for continuous improvement is still incomplete.

YOU NEED THE WILL TO JUST DO IT!

I have repeatedly stated the need for U.S. plant managers to renew their focus. However, while this is where it must begin, if the company is to make a successful transition they also need to instill the will for real change into the vast majority of their employees. The work force has to become almost fanatical at making fast, substantial, and effective change or it simply is not going to happen—at least not at the speed needed to salvage many U.S. manufacturing firms.

To some, much of what I have declared as being essential to the future of U.S. manufacturing will be written off as impractical, if not totally impossible. Others will view it as being far too simple (in the context of the things the overall process should serve to concentrate on). There will be those who will see the process outlined as a substantial opportunity for their business and who will proceed accordingly. For those, this section speaks to what it will take to press forward or as a popular theme of many kaizen sessions: "Just do it!" The need for change is growing at an alarming pace and leaders within manufacturing must decide if they are going to be the ark builders or the soothsayers. It is really just that simple. Dan Ciampa very astutely points out in his book *Manufacturing's New Mandate*:

> The fact is that the marketplace has changed and, most of all, the expectations of the customer have changed. The customer wants flawless quality and delivery often and on time. What the last decade has proven is that this is not unreasonable and that if one company

cannot satisfy those requirements, another will, even if it makes its product half a world away. . . . The good news is that the tools and techniques to do the job are available. The first is the discipline of quality as it has developed over the past 50 years. The second direction is from just-in-time. The bad news is that the culture that exists in many companies and, in particular, their organizational climate, does not support total quality and just-in-time. . . . The major reason for this failure is that in these companies people are not working as a team, do not share a compelling vision of what the future can hold, and are not committed to the changes that must take place. (p. 9–10)

If Mr. Ciampa is correct (and I believe he is), how do we make the kind of change that the conventional mass manufacturing culture and its organizational climate simply do not support? The secret may lie in seriously examining the following question: What is it that creates will . . . to do anything? As humans, we know the answer is conviction, faith, and/or desire. However, a more realistic response for the manufacturing arena may be: Creating an environment where change becomes the norm rather than the exception. Assuming this is true, how do the leaders of manufacturing make it happen? It starts with communications *to* the work force, then continuing communications *with* them.

First and foremost, the task of the plant manager seeking to make real change is to communicate to the work force until they realize the need for change. This is probably the most difficult challenge the leader faces in beginning the transition. It requires much more than one or two communication meetings. It requires driving the point home, repeatedly, until it is clearly evident the work force understands the need for change. In doing this, there are three key manufacturing business conditions that the work force must come to understand:

1. The common expectations of the customer have and are continuing to change, and what may have been acceptable only a year ago, in terms of cost, product quality, service, and delivery, in all probability no longer represents an acceptable standard of customer satisfaction.
2. The common technique for all manufacturing, at some point in the future, will be a fully integrated, JIT (lean) manufacturing approach, and those firms who choose not to change will simply fade away.

3. The common expectations for the average employee are that they be much more flexible and they will, in general, continue to be empowered to more effectively run the business and meet both customer and profitability demands.

Leaders must clearly, consistently, and continually communicate this to the work force until they truly believe it. In all probability, it will not suffice for a plant manager to be the only messenger. There are instances where the work force should hear this from sources outside the operation. Most likely you'll need to send some key employees to seminars dealing with world class manufacturing and supply the appropriate reading materials to the work force to reinforce these points.

Even this may not be enough. The truth is, there have been thousands of people, in thousands of books and thousands of seminars (such as Mr. Ciampa and others), who have been preaching these world class manufacturing points for up to a decade. For those who cannot or will not buy into the need for change, for those that actively fight it, the leaders of manufacturing must decide how to deal with them. In the worst case this could require cutting the cord and physically removing them from the operation. However, it is clearly a task and responsibility that management cannot take lightly.

Assuming you have successfully conveyed the proper communications to the work force, your next task is communicating *with* them. This means setting up appropriate forums that allow them to actively participate, and just as important, to have a means to question and understand what needs to be done. Communicating with employees is much different from communicating to them. Most manufacturing managers are reasonably good at making their point and setting an agenda. Most are not so good at belaboring an issue, over and over again, in a patient, professional manner that encourages strong and active participation from all employees, on an ongoing basis.

This is because manufacturing managers are often forced to deal with making fast decisions, and tough choices, on almost a daily basis. This type of working condition sometimes lessens, if not downright hardens, their basic patience. Nonetheless, patience becomes a key ingredient to making a successful transition from conventional to waste-free manufacturing. This is especially true when you're trying to communicate the changes being made in long-standing practices, because, and you should keep this in mind at all times, changing (often eliminating) these practices becomes very confusing to the employee.

Look at it this way. What you are asking your employees to do is to *stop doing* those activities that they used to get a pat on the back for successfully accomplishing. This, obviously, is no easy task and, in fact, it is usually one of the more substantial challenges facing the management team. Think about it. How would you feel if you were told that something you had been trained and/or instructed to do when you took the job (something that over the years you had been rewarded for when it was successfully accomplished and reprimanded when it wasn't) suddenly was the wrong way of doing things? An understatement, in all probability, is that you would feel somewhat confused, right? This is exactly what the person leading change from mass to lean (waste-free) manufacturing will be confronting on a daily basis. And the only way he or she is going to be successful in getting the employee's stake in the change required, and to clarify for them each and every change, is to establish a forum for an ongoing dialog with (and not at) them.

Making physical change to the factory floor is actually not that difficult, given the knowledge as to how and the will and fortitude to carry it through. Making a change to the mind-set of the work force is much more difficult and, if there is a major stumbling block that can stop the process of WFM in its tracks, this is where it will always emanate from. So be patient and take the time to learn more about the employees who will be learning how to implement the changes. They are your team and you are their coach and leader.

THE FORMULA FOR LEADING EFFECTIVE CHANGE

Paradigms sometimes result in people blocking out anything that is unfamiliar, with the result often being an inability on their part to see the positive benefits of change. When a leader begins to press employees seriously to perform in a manner that forces them outside the normal way of doing business, he or she can sometimes place them in an extremely defensive position. Some will simply write this off as just another case of people disliking change of any kind. The truth is people *love* change if it is beneficial to them, and if doubt and uncertainty are removed. I wish I had realized this when I first became a plant manager, for it would have made me approach certain facets of change in a different manner. As I have said before, communication is the key, and I cannot stress strongly enough the extreme importance of not only providing employees with clear and concise communications, but also of doing it on a regular basis.

In support of the importance in clearly communicating the benefits of change to your employees, consider a situation where you are an owner of the business and have just called all your hourly and professional employees together and told them you are making a big change in the company's compensation program. Starting next week, you are going to pay everyone $100 a week more than they earn today. Do you not think this particular change, though significant, would have the overwhelming support of the entire work force? Of course. However, I can assure you it would only be a short period of time before some people would begin to question why the company had decided to be so generous. There would even be those who would begin to plant rumors (perhaps based on honest feelings) that it was done because the company was trying to cover up something with the increase.

Now, let's examine another scenario. Let's say you had instead announced that for the survival of the business you were forced to pay some people a little more and some a little less. How do you suppose that would be received? In this scenario, even though employees were told there was a business condition dictating the change, and even though they were told some of them were going to receive more money than they were currently making, the likely response of the group would probably be extremely negative. Why?

The reason is because the second scenario establishes a condition of *uncertainty*. No one would know for sure who would get more and what more exactly meant. Furthermore, no one would know who would get less and exactly what less would mean. In a situation like this, the group will almost always react as a single unit and usually in defiance of the change proposed.

While these particular examples are an overdramatization of how change is generally received by a work force, there is something in them that rings true regarding any type of change in any organization. Both examples have a *plus* and a *minus* side that ties directly to the issue of paradigms—people are reacting to a preconceived set of notions or habits regarding their present predicament. They are measuring what you are saying according to what they know. And while these paradigms (boundaries) apply to all employees within the work force, it makes significant change within the professional ranks especially difficult to manage. In short, the professionals tend to have more to gain (plus) and lose (minus) when it comes to significant change. We'll elaborate on the professionals' paradigms more in the next section.

First we should examine the pluses and minuses in the examples defined. The plus side of scenario one was the fact that everyone was going to start receiving more money and, not just a little more money, a lot more money! The minus side is even if it happened, as promised, some people would be suspicious as to why it happened. Over time, the potential exists for the change to be viewed, by at least a segment of the general work force, as somewhat of a cover-up on the company's part and, therefore, the potential exists to create a feeling of mistrust on the part of some employees.

In the second scenario, although it apparently was not elaborated on, the plus side was a change in the compensation that would serve to help the company survive. This is not necessarily a pleasant plus in the minds of employees but it is nonetheless a plus. The minus side, of course, was that some employees were going to receive less pay than before.

Using the minuses and pluses of these two scenarios you can establish a formula for making effective change:

$$\frac{\text{Business need}}{\text{Full/Active employee support}} = \text{Success ratio}$$

This formula pertains to the potential success or failure management can expect in moving forward aggressively with a significant change. It deals with a thoughtful consideration of business need on one hand and the potential for full and active employee support on the other. Full support would mean no uncertainty or doubt. The formula is used like this: The business need should always be considered to be 100 percent (expressed as 1.0), in other words, something that must be done in order for the company to remain competitive or in some cases just to survive. If it is not 100 percent, then simply forget it! If, in turn, the full and active support of employees is deemed to be 50 percent at best (expressed as 1.0 – .5 = .5), then the success ratio would probably be no better than 2.0, on a scale of 1 to 10 (1.0/.5 = 2.0), which is obviously a very low potential for success.

With this formula you will find that the ratio both increases and decreases disproportionally with the estimated degree of support. While 50 percent only yields a 2.0 on a scale of 1 to 10, 85 percent still only provides an estimated success ratio that is less than 7 (6.6 to be exact), which still is not the best of odds. Conversely, 25 percent full and active support sets forth a success ratio of 1.3, which is certainly not a lot lower than the 2.0 projected for 50 percent support. What this formula uncovers is that you need full and active support of at least 90 percent or implementation of the need is going to be very difficult, unless, of course, you conduct a great deal of persuasive communicating with the work force on the front end. And, even with that, any absolute assurance of success would still remain highly questionable.

This does not mean if the success ratio ends up being 5 or even 2, that change should not proceed. It would say, however, that a good deal of communication of how this change will affect employees should precede the change and that employees should have a forum that provides the opportunity for both challenge and debate—until they understand the underlying principles of WFM and its benefits. But, the fact is, if a leader is not in a position to accept debate and challenge to any change being proposed, then he or she simply isn't ready to lead it.

SIX COMMON PARADIGMS IN THE PROFESSIONAL RANKS THAT CAN BLOCK CHANGE

With the need for communication in mind, it is important to specifically look at the technical and professional ranks and look at the paradigms that can seriously bog down your WFM effort (see Table 10-2). It is within these ranks that some of the most destructive forces against instituting WFM reside.

These are some of the more common convictions of those within the professional ranks. There are, of course, others, but the thing that becomes clear in dealing with these kinds of convictions, or what could be called professional presumptions, is that the person leading the transition to WFM is going to be facing some potentially hefty professional boulders as significant change progresses through the four WFM drivers. So it is important to understand and weigh the potential reaction of those within the professional ranks as change becomes more aggressive—especially when their professional presumptions are challenged. Through appropriate communications of WFM principles and a clear attempt to create and establish new career paths for those professionals whose careers are affected, you can significantly minimize the size of these potential boulders.

Table 10-2. Paradigms Against WFM

Beliefs in the Professional and Technical Ranks That Bog Down the WFM Process
1. My profession plays a vital role in the success of the business. I hold a responsibility to do the job I am expected (and paid) to do and if I accomplish this, I have done all I can to make the company successful.
2. My responsibility ends at the point where my tasks have been successfully accomplished and passed on to the next function in the chain.
3. My hands are tied with regard to the tasks of other professions (functions) within the organization. I hold no direct responsibility for their success or failure other than to complete my part of the work they need to successfully complete their assigned responsibilities.
4. I was educated in a professional field, then hired and trained by the company to perform a relatively clear set of professional duties and functional responsibilities. I may be asked to expand my duties and responsibilities within my function, given appropriate reasoning and/or remuneration, but I should not be expected to step outside this basic role.
5. There is a need for the various professions to work as separate and independent entities. Even functions that are closely related should never be combined.
6. Change is good, in fact required, as long as the change does not affect the conventional or traditional way I am expected to do things within my profession.

Month Thirty-Four—New and Grand Opportunities

The company, through its corporate manufacturing council, had taken on the challenge of developing a very special, very intense manufacturing training program for all managers and supervisors at or above a certain grade level. This eventually came to involve some 1,500 managers and executives throughout the corporation.

As a result of the progress we had made in our plant and the outstanding publicity we had received from Wall Street and others on the kind of change that was occurring, I was asked to serve as a resource for the business unit I represented. My charge was to help develop the training curriculum, and I ended up spending quite some time on the road, working with others who had been selected to participate in the process. In effect, we were developing a training program that tied directly to the type of fast track and effective change I had been privileged to lead in our factory.

It was exciting work and I found more and more of my time being taken by this activity. I often felt that I was perhaps neglecting my job back at the plant. While I always thought of myself as being reasonably good at delegation, I still felt the time I was taking away from the plant in this effort was somewhat of an injustice to the factory, customers, and employees.

Down deep, I was truly enjoying taking a very active role in helping to put together a training course that would be used throughout the corporation; and it never occurred to me that I might some day be asked to play an active role in actually leading and teaching the process. I knew someone inside the corporation was going to have the responsibility, but I assumed they would be professionals in the training field. How wrong I was.

I got the word from Bill. A final decision had been made regarding plant consolidation and our plant was a winner! We were going to receive a series of products produced in another factory, which was scheduled to be closed. While I truly felt sorry for those losing jobs in the other factory, I could not help but feel ecstatic about our plant being selected. I could hardly keep the news to myself, although Bill swore me to secrecy until the formal announcement was made, which was to include the governor of the state and other local dignitaries.

Right off the bat it was going to mean 250 new jobs for the plant, with the opportunity for employment to grow to 400 or more, especially if we could improve product delivery time and costs. Just prior to the official event, I was given permission to bring the union up to speed. I cannot express, in adequate terms, how thrilled they were to hear the news.

WFM IN THE AUTOMOTIVE INDUSTRY

Having spent a few years as a component supplier in the automotive industry, I learned that there are some definite restrictions in the application of the concepts and techniques of WFM. However, it is not impossible to make strides in the right direction by applying the fundamental principles of WFM. For those who have had no direct association with this industry the restrictions noted come as a result of policy and procedure, driven down by the Big Three, that can make any change to the established and agreed-upon production process difficult, at best. This is not to say you cannot make change happen, only that the process of change has to actively involve the customer.

Further, in the automotive industry, reputation plays an important role in the acceptance and freedom of change. A first-tier supplier to one of the Big Three typically will have more freedom to make change than a second-tier supplier. A second-tier supplier serving a first tier, who has an outstanding quality reputation, would have more freedom than a second-tier supplier serving a first tier who has a history of quality problems. The point is, the ability to make change varies greatly from business to business and, of course, from automaker to automaker. It would perhaps be beneficial to address areas where you can make good progress with waste-free manufacturing, without worrying about such restrictions.

First and foremost, you can fully and aggressively apply the first WFM driver, workplace organization. In addition, you can usually freely apply the third driver, error-free processing, through the application of SMED, TPM, and poka-yoke. You must take care, however, when pursuing uninterrupted flow. The reason is because this second WFM driver often calls for the relocation of equipment and facilities. Typically, in the automotive industry, clear approval is required by the customer before such changes are made.

It is most important to recognize that any change serving to modify production equipment, tools, fixturing, gauges, test facilities and the like, regardless of how logical that change might be perceived, simply *will not* be allowed without the express approval of the customer. This is due to the fact that in the past, there have been cases where such modifications inadvertently created problems in mating automobile systems and/or components and led to the automakers' worst nightmare—a product recall.

The key to implementing the benefits of WFM in this industry is establishing a working relationship with the customer. This typically means involving them in the process of change. In the end, they do want, if not flatly expect, their suppliers to make continuous improvement, leading to enhanced quality, delivery, and price performance. On the other hand, the magnitude of even one error created by a change in the production process is so dynamic that an understandable reluctance does exist.

Bottom line, for anyone in this particular industry, is the need to communicate to the customer, in a clear and forthright manner, any proposals for process change, and then to obtain a documented buy-in before proceeding. Most important is the need to be fully convinced that the change will work without creating the potential for any far-reaching issues or problems down the road.

A CLOSING COMMENT ON YOUR WFM JOURNEY

Any successful journey into waste-free manufacturing will rest largely on two key components. First, that the company clearly accepts the need and fully supports the change effort. Without this, nothing worthwhile will happen. Secondly, to ensure that once the process begins, it is carried forth in a *very swift manner.*

Coupled with these two key components, is the *will* required by the leaders of such change to see it through, even as the winds of ingratitude swirl around them.

The leader should be aware that gratitude will almost certainly not be forthcoming on the front end of such dramatic and swift change. Ingratitude will indeed come from employees and sometimes even from top management as the change proceeds and there will be times when the leader perceives so much of this that the temptation will be to pull back. But, it is good to remember what Dale Carnegie has to say about this in his book *How To Stop Worrying and Start Living.* He points out in part four of this work:

> Rule 3-A: Instead of worrying about ingratitude, let's expect it. Let's remember that Jesus healed ten lepers in one day—and only one thanked him. Why should we expect more gratitude than Jesus got?
> Rule 3-C: Let's remember that gratitude is a "cultivated" trait; so if we want our children to be grateful, we must train them to be grateful.

Last, but certainly not least, is the need for the presence of absolute, unerring dedication to the task at hand. This is the area where I admire the Japanese the most.

Japanese manufacturers, especially, believe that once the answer is clear, breakneck speed must be applied to correct the situation. In what they refer to as pull production, they simply cannot understand how any manufacturing manager could possibly put even one priority before this. This may be why they occasionally refer to some managers as "concrete heads." While this may sound a bit offensive, it is meant to be an analogy, rather than an insult, to point out that when it comes to manufacturing, we Americans sometimes have great difficulty absorbing the obvious.

In truth, however, what may be clear to a business culture that has practiced pull production for decades may not be so obvious to those who were reared under an entirely different approach and, for at least some period of time, were very successful. Regardless, we must face the realization that the old tried and true way of manufacturing for most industry in the United States (good old Mr. Batch) is today fully obsolete and totally ineffective.

Now that we have covered all the revolutionary pointers for rapidly moving from a mass manufacturer to a waste-free manufacturer perhaps they no longer seem so revolutionary. Now that you see the obvious benefits (and necessity) of deploying the "lean paradigm" to become a world class manufacturer, I want to underscore the following important pointers as you continue your WFM journey.

Revolutionary Pointers

- Memorize the principles of the four WFM drivers. They are linked and geared so you can get on a fast track to effectively implement waste-free manufacturing.

- Pick and choose the tools in the tool boxes. Forget any fear regarding selection of the tools in any specific order. Nothing you do relative to the use of these tools will be wrong. Order of insertion is not as important as extent of use.

- Read any related materials necessary to bring you up to speed on JIT (TPS or lean) manufacturing and terminology. Share these materials with those who will be helping you champion the change.

- Put a promotion office in place quickly, staffed with the very best people you can find for the job. This is essential to training and continuous improvement activities. Call it what you like, but make it happen.

- Install a product-oriented cell organization as soon as possible. It requires a firm commitment to organize into a cross-functional management team approach and is one of the more critical steps in the WFM journey.

- Follow the 10-step road map. Keep the 15-point checklist handy at all times to determine if you are WFM-ready. Refer to these often. These two tools will help you to maintain focus on the task at hand and will serve as a measurement of progress throughout the course of the journey.

- Put the appropriate measurements in place as fast as possible. Remember employee performance is, to a large extent, a reflection of the measurement system. Whether you use all or only a few of those specified in Chapter 8, strive to put measurements in place that will encourage and reward the continuous improvement process. The measurements should, at least, focus on doing the right things, rather than gauging progress solely on the basis of past, traditional values, which have done little to make and keep us competitive.

- Keep the continuous improvement pyramid in mind as you make changes to each production process in the factory. This will help ensure a reasonably disciplined, structured approach for change.

- Be a true leader. Renew your focus and commitment and stick to the principles—but with an understanding of employees' feelings and the need to effectively communicate *with* them as you move forward in the change effort.

- Last, but certainly not least, work hard at getting the job done. In relation to this, I would remind the reader of a well-known phrase used frequently by Japanese consultants as words of advice to those companies around the world who are committed to becoming world class. The phrase goes: "Just do it." My advice would be: *Just do it—but with knowledge!*

Bibliography

Carnegie, Dale, *How to Stop Worrying and Start Living*. New York, New York: Simon and Schuster, 1984.

Ciampa, Dan. *Manufacturing's New Mandate*. New York, New York: John Wiley & Sons, 1988.

Japanese Management Association, translated by David J. Lu. *Kanban: Just-in-Time at Toyota*. Portland, Ore.: Productivity Press, 1989.

Liker, Jeffrey K. ed. *Becoming Lean: Inside Stories of U.S. Manufacturers*. Portland, Ore.: Productivity Press, 1997.

Ohno, Taiichi. *The Toyota Production System: Beyond Large-Scale Production*. Portland, Ore.: Productivity Press, 1988.

Schonberger, Richard J. *World Class Manufacturing*. New York: The Free Press, 1986.

Womack, James. *The Machine That Changed the World*. New York, New York: Rawson Associates, 1990.

About the Author

JOHN W. DAVIS describes himself as a "self-made man." After high school and four years in the United States Air Force, a family situation made it impossible for him to attend college on a full-time basis. He therefore began his career on the shop floor with Virco Manufacturing (school and office furniture) while attending tech school at night, and over a period of years worked his way up to the position of time study analyst in the industrial engineering department.

After eight years at Virco, Davis accepted a position as industrial engineer for a sporting goods firm (Shakespeare Manufacturing) where he says he received a "practical education" in both manufacturing and industrial engineering. It was at Shakespeare that he successfully assumed responsibility for a major product transfer of the firm's trolling motor operation from Kalamazoo, Michigan to Fayetteville, Arkansas and, in addition, was responsible for engineering a 100 percent gain in warehouse space, without brick and mortar, working with Towmotor Inc. in a LIFO warehousing approach.

In 1974 Davis joined Carrier Corporation, a subsidiary of United Technologies, and over the years took on increasingly responsible positions, including the successful management of a number of industrial engineering departments within both the residential and commercial sectors of the business. In 1987 he assumed the position of manufacturing strategic planner which eventually led to being appointed plant manager of an operation in Indianapolis, Indiana. After making a most impressive turnaround in the manufacturing sector of this operation, Mr. Davis worked as a corporate consultant and team leader from 1993 to 1995 for a special corporate group that was assigned the task of traveling the world and teaching the principles, concepts, and techniques of world class manufacturing. It was during this period that Mr. Davis successfully developed his philosophy on waste-free manufacturing which he aggressively applied from 1995 until his retirement in 1998, while holding the position of Director of Operations over two manufacturing facilities within the Automotive Group of United Technologies.

Mr. Davis has a degree in mechanical drafting, is a certified applicator in MTM, Work Factor and Univel, and a certified instructor in UTC flexible manufacturing. He was past president of the central Arkansas chapter of NMA (National Management Association), was a board member of Columbus Mississippi, Lowndes County Economic Development Association (CLEDA), and a member of Columbus, Mississippi, Lowndes County Association of Manufacturers (CLAM). Today John resides with his wife, Kathy, in Fairfield Bay, Arkansas and is involved in manufacturing consulting activities.

Index

pull zones as interim measure, 70–72,
    113–14, 129, 132
6Cs, xiv, 67, 68, 69, 99–106
6Cs and visual controls, 102
6Cs scoring, 69–70
6Cs staircasing, 70, 87, 100, 101–3
SMED, 65–66, 67, 68, 81
SMED and insignificant changeover,
    65–66, 81, 126, 128
SMED and uninterrupted flow
    implementation, 115
spaghetti diagrams, 67, 68
takt time, 66, 140–41, 143, 158
takt time in cell organization, 203–4
TPM, 67, 68, 78
visual controls, 67, 68, 95, 240
visual controls and 6Cs, 102
visual controls and waste, 77
WFM vs. TPS/JIT, xiii, xiv–xv, 5–6, 66
    driving principles vs. tools, 66, 74–75, 83,
        87, 94
    expenditure and, 94
    football kicker analogy, 75
    pull zones vs. supermarkets, 70–72
    6Cs vs. 5S, 68–70, 95–96, 131
    sports scoring analogy, 62
    uninterrupted flow vs. one-piece flow,
        63–64, 250, 251
    workplace organization, 146–47
WFM waste
    changeover, 72–74, 77, 126, 131
    cutting-edge technology and, 72–74,
        78–79, 202
    downtime, 72–74
    employee involvement lack, 206
    employee knowledge loss, 200, 230–33
    errors/scrap/rework/obsolescence, 77, 78,
        196, 199–201
    flow stoppage (storage areas), 112–14,
        196, 197–99, 200–201

flow stoppage (storage areas) and repeat
    visits to station, 207
flow stoppage (storage areas) and
    suppliers, 205
hidden (systems), 74–79, 87
hidden wastes checklist, 75, 76, 196,
    200–201
inventory, 76–77, 112–14, 197, 200–201,
    204–5
non-value-added floor use, 208–9
non-value-added work, 165–66, 206–7
    in office work, 228
owner-operators lack, 78
push system, 77–78
TPM lack, 78
unbalanced workload, 78
visual controls lack, 77
Why technique. *See* Root cause analysis
Work ethic, 43
Work-in-process inventory. *See* Inventory
Workplace organization, 14–147
    batch manufacturing and, 96
    continuous improvement and, 106–7,
        240, 241
    disposition zones, 98, 101
    vs. 5Ss, 95–96, 131
    floor use, 204, 208–9, 249, 251
    office processes and, 106, 228
    pull zones, 102, 105
    6Cs, 98–106, 240
    waste elimination and, 76, 228
World class manufacturing, 11–12, 253–54.
    See also TPS/JIT; WFM
    flexibility, 126–27
    global competitiveness, xiii–xiv, xxii, 5,
        8–9, 89
WPO. *See* Workplace organization

Books from Productivity Press

Productivity Press publishes books that empower individuals and companies to achieve excellence in quality, productivity, and the creative involvement of all employees. Through steadfast efforts to support the vision and strategy of continuous improvement, Productivity Press delivers today's leading-edge tools and techniques gathered directly from industry leaders around the world. Call toll-free (800) 394-6868 for our free catalog.

The Shopfloor Series

Put powerful and proven improvement tools in the hands of your entire workforce!

Progressive shopfloor improvement techniques are imperative for manufacturers who want to stay competitive and to achieve world class excellence. And it's the comprehensive education of all shopfloor workers that ensures full participation and success when implementing new programs. The Shopfloor Series books make practical information accessible to everyone by presenting major concepts and tools in simple, clear language and at a reading level that has been adjusted for operators by skilled instructional designers. One main idea is presented every two to four pages so that the book can be picked up and put down easily. Each chapter begins with an overview and ends with a summary section. Helpful illustrations are used throughout.

Books currently in the Shopfloor Series include:

5S for Operators
5 Pillars of the Visual Workplace
The Productivity Press Development Team
ISBN 1-56327-123-0
incl. applic. questions / 133 pages
Order 5SOP-B8010 / $25.00

Quick Changeover for Operators
The SMED System
The Productivity Press Development Team
ISBN 1-56327-125-7
incl. applic. questions / 93 pages
Order QCOOP-B8010 / $25.00

Mistake-Proofing for Operators
The Productivity Press Development Team
ISBN 1-56327-127-3 / 93 pages
Order ZQCOP-B8010 / $25.00

TPM for Supervisors
The Productivity Press Development Team
ISBN 1-56327-161-3 / 96 pages
Order TPMSUP-B8010 / $25.00

Just-In-Time for Operators
The Productivity Press Development Team
ISBN 1-56327-133-8 / 84 pages
Order JITOP-B8010 / $25.00

TPM Team Guide
Kunio Shirose
ISBN 1-56327-079-X / 175 pages
Order TGUIDE-B8010 / $25.00

TPM for Every Operator
Japan Institute of Plant Maintenance
ISBN 1-56327-080-3 / 136 pages
Order TPMEO-B8010 / $25.00

Autonomous Maintenance
Japan Institute of Plant Maintenance
ISBN 1-56327-082-X / 138 pages
Order AUTMOP-B8010 / $25.00

Focused Equipment Improvement for TPM Teams
Japan Institute of Plant Maintenance
ISBN 1-56327-081-1 / 138 pages
Order FEIOP-B8010 / $25.00

Cellular Manufacturing
One-Piece Flow for Workteams
The Productivity Press Development Team
ISBN 1-56327-213-X / 96 pages
Order CELL-B8010 / $25.00

TO ORDER: Write, phone, or fax Productivity Press, Dept. BK, P.O. Box 13390, Portland, OR 97213-0390, phone 1-800-394-6868, fax 1-800-394-6286.

Outside the U.S. phone (503) 235-0600; fax (503) 235-0909

Send check or charge to your credit card (American Express, Visa, MasterCard accepted).

U.S. ORDERS: Add $5 shipping for first book, $2 each additional for UPS surface delivery. Add $5 for each AV program containing 1 or 2 tapes; add $12 for each AV program containing 3 or more tapes. We offer attractive quantity discounts for bulk purchases of individual titles; call for more information.

ORDER BY E-MAIL: Order 24 hours a day from anywhere in the world. Use either address:

To order: service@ppress.com
To view the online catalog and/or order: http://www.ppress.com/

QUANTITY DISCOUNTS: For information on quantity discounts, please contact our sales department.

INTERNATIONAL ORDERS: Write, phone, or fax for quote and indicate shipping method desired. For international callers, telephone number is 503-235-0600 and fax number is 503-235-0909. Prepayment in U.S. dollars must accompany your order (checks must be drawn on U.S. banks). When quote is returned with payment, your order will be shipped promptly by the method requested.

NOTE: Prices are in U.S. dollars and are subject to change without notice.